This be

A Short History of South Africa

by the same author

The Second World War
Stories of Famous Sieges
Thomas Morris (editor)
Stonewall Jackson
The Paper Dragon
The Boer War
The Thin Red Line
The Stonewall Brigade
The Iron Brigade
The United States Cavalry
The United States Marine Corps
Shaka's Heirs
Over the Sea to Skye

A SHORT HISTORY OF
SOUTH AFRICA

John Selby

with a Foreword by
Comdt Jan Ploeger
M.A., M.Ed., D.Phil.

London. George Allen & Unwin Ltd
Ruskin House   Museum Street

Printed in Great Britain
in 11 point Baskerville type
by Cox & Wyman Ltd,
London, Fakenham and Reading

Foreword

by Comdt Jan Ploeger, M.A., M.Ed., D.Phil., Acad.
Translated from the Afrikaans by Brigadier J. G. W. van Wyk, S.M.

Any person standing at or near the Cape of Good Hope on a clear sunny day, watching the pounding of the waves as they attack the solid rock masses in a foam of wrath and thunder of sound, cannot avoid being conscious that two massive oceans meet at this precise point which is close to the age-old half-way station on the shipping route between East and West. If then, at another time and at a point some 1,500 kms distant from the Cape of Good Hope, one watches the sun as it dips behind the trees and hills of the highveld, in all its enchanting and infinite variation of colour, daubed on this enormous screen in the western skies, it is hard to believe that one is still in the same land of South Africa, where, in Johannesburg, Cape Town and elsewhere, the ever increasing height of new buildings gives an impression of concrete monsters stretching ever higher towards the heavens in a continual striving for mastery over the available air and space.

In the Western Province, near Cape Town, the Cape–Dutch gables remind one of the seventeenth and eighteenth centuries and the colonists of that day. On the road between the Transvaal and sub-tropical Natal one sees, as specks in the rolling landscape, the traditional Bantu huts of divergent designs in accordance with the inherent, and often artistic traditions of the various tribes. Stand for a moment near the tremendous open mine in Kimberley and imagine the feverish activity which removed a mountain of soil and rock from the very bowels of the earth, in man's relentless endeavours to wrench from its grip the myriad of diamonds which it held in its charge. Or stop by the mine dumps on the Witwatersrand (i.e. the ridge of clear waters) and attest

7

man's continuing and unquenching thirst for gold. In the plains of the Free State there are dust clouds as the farmer ploughs the fertile soil with his tractor or oxen.

Often the plains of this land are ravaged by merciless droughts; then again, how frequently are they not the centre of that miracle before one's very eyes, of surpluses of food-stuffs to fill the hungry mouths of man and beast, both within and beyond the borders of this land; in short, to ensure that the legatees of this bounteous harvest may survive another day. And after the hustle and bustle of the day, when they are such hives of activity, the cities of this land become seas of light, yellowed by distance, yet oases for travellers, while in the countryside, behind the windows of the lonely farm dwelling, a candle burns, and a group of Bantu sit near the fire, discussing the happenings of the day or simply watching the flicker of the flames from the burning logs, as they dream their dreams. In the far distance, the whistle of a train in the darkness; there, the penetrating headlamps of a vehicle moving along the highway; and in the heavens above, in the direction of the stars, the sound of mighty motors and the flickering navigation lights of an aircraft, as it flirts momentarily with the moonbeams and is gone.

During the heat of a summer's afternoon or early evening, one frequently hears the muffled sounds of thunder a long way off. After a tense silence, as the rumbling comes nearer, there is a sudden and quite unexpected blast of violent wind, which comes as a prelude to the storm and is the agent which invariably sets the doors slamming in the neighbourhood. Look up, and see how the ominous dark clouds jostle one another to the accompaniment of a display of electrical pyrotechnics which have to be seen to be believed. Lightning flashes link earth and clouds in a thunder of mighty explo-sions and cracks which send the dogs cringing under the beds and cause shivers down one's spine as one watches and listens to this combination of blinding flashes and a crescendo of deafening sound that rattles the windows. Then as if the sluice gates of the heavens have been opened, the torrential rain pours down, or, as sometimes happens, an ear-splitting

8

cascade of destructive hail descends from the skies . . . and as suddenly as it began, all is silent once more, with hardly a movement of air. Only the sudden drop in temperature, the fresh smell of rain on dry earth, and just the faintest rumbling in the distance, reminds one that the same concert is being staged somewhere beyond the horizon, for yet another audience.

In the winter on the highveld, a chilly wind, which was given birth in the icy wastes of Antarctica, gently ruffles the dry grasses and sets the shrubs and bushes trembling, while man and beast wait anxiously for the life-bringing spring, which invariably comes like the fulfilment of a promise – like a rainbow after the storm. Overnight, or so it would seem, there is greenery once more and wild flowers bloom in the countryside. There, in the wide open spaces, a new cycle has just begun.

This, in brief, is South Africa, a country of many vivid contrasts, a country so varied that it takes time to become acquainted, a country that its White sons and daughters learn to love so dearly, that none other will be acknowledged in exchange. South Africa has a way of tugging at one's heartstrings and exercising an overpowering attraction on those who get to know her in all her moods. And one of the strongest aspects of her magnetism is, and will remain to be, that certain mystery which is part of her make up. In the first place, she never ceases to be a geographic and ethnological part of the greater Africa. Secondly, she forms an integral segment of the Western World, of Europe, of America, and is impelled ever forward by western techniques and youthful energy, energy which, at times, by virtue of her very youthfulness, reveals a tendency towards rashness and a certain lack of consideration which would redound to the discredit of older societies. The mystery of Africa! Yes. Yet when one reviews the known and written history of Southern Africa, one finds that it goes back only a matter of three centuries.

In this history the author deals with the country's prehistory in an appendix and the book begins with the arrival of the Europeans and the establishment of the refreshment station for ships at the Cape by Jan Athoniszoon van

9

Riebeeck in 1652. From this point the author leads the reader through violent as well as peaceful times, through times of storm and times of calm, as well as times of progress and times of retrogression. Step by step he leads the reader along the road which South Africa has followed down the years. At times this road was strewn with thorns and pitfalls, at others it was covered in rose petals; there were times when the road became nothing but a track and was almost impassable and overgrown with high impenetrable barriers. The author goes on to show us how the interests of the inhabitants clashed at various times, and how this led to bloodshed. There was always something new taking place in this land of contrasts. News flashes of spectacular happenings went out regularly to the far corners of the earth. At other times even these were momentarily stilled, as the world's attention was temporarily diverted to other lands, peoples and societies. Of recent times South Africa is once again in the very forefront of world headlines, a fact which partially stems from the specific racial problems peculiar to South Africa and from the phenomenal development of her industrial potential, both of which attract attention. The decolonization processes, which focused the interest of the world on Africa, the creation of new countries and the gradual evolution of political and ideological relationships in the erstwhile 'dark' Africa, continue to attract the attentions of friend and foe alike.

Then there is the undoubted importance of the sea route round the Cape of Good Hope, the relationship between South Africa and her neighbouring states and the efforts being made by South Africa to solve her internal problems and to bring them to a satisfactory conclusion. At the same time one must acknowledge the determined way in which she is striving to overcome other stumbling blocks which impede her progress towards her ultimate destiny and which are of interest not only to South Africans but to countries beyond the borders of South Africa.

In this regard the old adage still rings true, namely that 'He who knows not the history of his own country, i.e. his *own* history, is not in a position to understand the present'.

He can have no insight whatsoever into the sometimes concealed, sometimes clearly defined tendencies and policies which give rise to current conditions and relationships.

The desire to paint a clear picture within the ambit of the foregoing was undoubtedly one of the prime objectives of the author in becoming absorbed, as he has been, in so many facets of South Africa and its fascinating history. For the effort which he has expended in setting down the fruits of his researches, conclusions and views, Major John Selby will undoubtedly be extended the credit he so richly deserves, by those who have the privilege of reading this historical work.

Pretoria, July 1972

Acknowledgements

I wish to thank Professor C. F. J. Muller, editor *Five Hundred Years*, and Professor C. J. Barnard, both of the University of South Africa, Pretoria, for their help, and Professor Monica Wilson of the University of Cape Town and co-editor of the *Oxford History of South Africa* for reading the drafts of my chapters on the native peoples and making many cogent comments. I also wish to thank Professor Winifred Maxwell for allowing me to quote from her articles on the 1820 Settlers in *Lantern* and from her 1970 Henry Hare Dugmore Lecture, and, also with Mr J. M. Berning, for introducing me to the Cory Library at Rhodes University, Grahamstown.

I wish to thank Miss Fiona Barbour of the Alexander McGregor Memorial Museum, Kimberley, for providing me with a wide range of introductions and for showing me round the Kimberley museums and near-by battlefields; and also Mrs Rita Snyman of the Grahamstown 1820 Settlers Museum for giving up so much of her time to explain exhibits, and for being so generally helpful; also Miss Anna Smith of the Africana Museum, Johannesburg, for introducing me to the Strange Collection; and Captain Owen Smedley-Williams of the South African National War Museum, Saxonwold, Johannesburg, for his help and hospitality. I want to thank Commandant S. Bourquin for showing me the Fort and the museums at Durban; also Mrs Daphne Strutt for giving up so much time for my instruction at the Local History Museum, Durban. I am indebted to Mrs Vivian Tedder for showing me round the Killie Campbell Collection, Durban, and for introducing me to the Colenso Papers and other original material; Mr S. Bosman for showing me the First *Raadsaal* and Fourth *Raadsaal*, Bloemfontein, and introducing me to Professor Dr O. Geyser of the Institute of Contemporary History of the

University of the Orange Free State, and to Captain Retief Oostheysen, curator of the War Museum, the Boer Women and Children's monument, and the graves of Free State heroes, including Emily Hobhouse.

I want to thank Mr Charles More for help with illustrations, and Commandant Dr Jan Ploeger, not only for writing such a splendid foreword, but also for reading the draft chapters of my book and making many valuable comments on them.

In England, I wish to thank Mr D. W. King and his Staff at the Ministry of Defence Library (Central and Army), and Lieut-Col. Alan Shepperd and the Staff of the Library of the Royal Military Academy, Sandhurst, for their great help.

Contents

Illustrations

Maps

Chapter 1

The Hollanders

By tradition the Portuguese navigator Bartholomew Diaz was the first European to round the Cape. From a study of old Italian maps the course of his voyage can be plotted. In the first week of December 1487 he was sailing along the arid Namid coast of South-West Africa and may have put in at what is now Walvis Bay. During the early days of the year 1488 he seems to have been blown off course by a raging south-easter, but turning northwards sailed his two 100-ton ships past an unseen cape to close-haul off the African coast near the present-day Mossel Bay.

The next European visitor was Vasco da Gama. In November 1497 he sighted land south of the mouth of the Orange River, and continuing down the coast landed at and named St Helena Bay, where he met yellow-skinned Hottentots. Like Diaz, when attempting to round the Cape he found himself faced with the necessity of sailing directly into the prevailing south-easter but by skilful seamanship managed to turn into it and land at Mossel Bay. Here he made the acquaintance of more Hottentots and during a stay of thirteen days bartered beads for cattle. Continuing north, da Gama is said to have given the name Terra do Natal to the coast by the Kei River on Christmas Day 1497, though this is not recorded in his log-book. Later the name Natal was used for the coastal area from the Kei northwards, past the Umzimvubu River to beyond present-day Durban. Up to this time there is no record of da Gama seeing any black people, but during the first weeks

21

of 1498 he came upon some north of the mouth of the Limpopo.

In the spring of 1503, owing to a navigational error, Antonio de Saldanha sailed his squadron into what is now called Table Bay, and during his stay climbed Table Mountain. It is said he was the first European to do so. The bay bore his name for a hundred years, but now one farther north is called after him.

Over the years other Portuguese sea-captains put in at Table Bay, but usually only in exceptional circumstances, since Mozambique on the east coast and the island of St Helena off the west coast both suited their sailing schedules better. In 1510 Francisco d'Almeida, Portugal's viceroy in the Indies, landed at Table Bay on his way back to Portugal, and became involved in an affray with local Hottentots in which he and sixty-five of his companions were killed. From then on the Portuguese tended to give the Cape a wide berth, for besides having unruly inhabitants its terrain was barren and it was subject to storms.

When the Dutch and British began to compete with the Portuguese, they viewed the Cape with more approval, for they urgently required an unoccupied half-way station on the trade routes to the East. In the early days ships of both nations called at Table Bay, and there was a friendly relationship between their seamen. One way in which the place was used was as a sort of *poste restante*. Under large stones inscribed with names and instructions, mail was left ashore for collection by passing ships.

The Dutch were the first to destroy the Portuguese monopoly of the Eastern trade and soon after they had done so the stranding of the *Nieuw Haerlem*, caught in the Cape south-easter on its homeward journey in 1647, caused them to occupy the Cape. A party of sixty from the stricken vessel were left behind to safeguard what was left of its valuable cargo of spices and sandalwood, and when these men eventually returned to Holland, nearly a year later, their two leaders submitted a report which strongly recommended the place as a port-of-call for Dutch ships. The organization that controlled the Dutch Eastern trade was the Dutch East India

Company,[1] a mammoth concern which in 1602 had received a charter which gave it a trade monopoly in the East. It had seventeen directors – the famous Council of Seventeen – and although based on Amsterdam had chambers which chartered voyages in five other Dutch cities, and depots in Malaysia, and in the East Indies, Formosa and Japan.

In 1650 on the strength of the document produced by the leaders of the *Nieuw Haerlem*'s rear party, the Council of Seventeen decided to occupy the Cape. When they sought a commander to establish a station there, Jan Athoniszoon van Riebeeck offered his services. He had been a passenger in the fleet that had taken off the rear party and cargo of the *Nieuw Haerlem* when it finally left Table Bay in 1648, so he knew the place and its possibilities. He had earlier been dismissed from the Company for private trading,[2] but was eager to re-enter the service. When asked for comments on the rear-party's memorandum,[3] he reported on it so competently and enthusiastically that he was immediately appointed to command the new refreshment station at the Cape. Thus, on 6 April 1652, it was Van Riebeeck's small ships,[4] the *Drommedaris* and *Goede Hoope*, that anchored in Table Bay when the first permanent European settlement at the Cape came into being. Van Riebeeck was required to meet the needs of passing ships for fresh water, meat, vegetables and ships' stores for the second half of voyages to and from the East, and also to provide facilities to turn ships on their sides to remove barnacles. The station was at first confined to the Cape Peninsula. There was a suggestion of cutting a canal from False Bay in the south to Table Bay in the north to produce an island stronghold, but this was not carried out: instead, a 6,000 acre area was selected with boundaries formed by the sea on the north and west, by Table Mountain in the south, and by a hedge of bitter almond trees along the River Liesbeeck in the east. Six redoubts were constructed along the exposed eastern frontier by the Liesbeeck to pro-

[1] *Vereenigde Nederlandsche Ge-Octroyeerde Oost-Indische Compagnie* (VOC), United Netherlands Chartered East India Company.

[2] Quite common in those days in the VOC and British East India Company.

[3] The *Remonstrantie* of L. Janszen and M. Proot.

[4] His other vessels, the *Reijger*, the *Walvis*, and *Oliphant*, arrived next day.

tect the garrison from attacks by Hottentots, and near the mouth of a freshwater stream,[1] able to provide water for the ships, a fort was built on Table Bay to protect the anchorage from an attack from the sea. Gardens were dug and orchards were planted by the freshwater stream near the Table Bay fort, fields were ploughed in the valley of the Liesbeeck, and a big barn[2] was built to store the grain.

Van Riebeeck proved to be a great commander. The officials who were left when the ships departed often lacked initiative, and it was only through his personal inspiration and enthusiasm that the fields were dug, the orchards planted and a start made with the construction of the fort and eastern redoubts. The large numbers of cattle and sheep required to provide meat for the passing ships meant that great efforts had to be made to barter for animals locally. As it was the firm policy of the Company that good relations should be maintained with the natives, Van Riebeeck gave great attention to his dealings with the local Hottentots. Into his own household he took Harry the chief of the Strandlopers[3] and his niece Eva, who was one of the first Hottentots to be baptized and become a Christian; she lived in the garrison for some time and formed a useful link between the officials and her own people. Harry seems to have been good at languages, for when he was taken to Batavia on an English ship he was spoken of as 'the Ottentoo who speaks English'. Van Riebeeck had him taught Dutch, but the man got himself into serious trouble by murdering a Company herdsman and stealing forty-four head of cattle. This deeply shocked Van Riebeeck, who had fed him at his own table and regarded him as a friend. Van Riebeeck's preoccupation with getting butcher's meat is illustrated by the constant records in his Journal of such transactions: for example, the entry for Sunday 3 October 1655 reads: 'after sermon thirteen or fourteen of the Chainouquas came with 27 fine cattle, of which 24 were bought for beads, and three

---

[1] This ran down where Adderley Street now is.

[2] *Groote Schuur:* Rhodes's house, now an official residence, was built near the site.

[3] Hottentots who lived by the coast on sea-food.

came with six sheep which were bought for brass and tobacco'. There are countless similar entries.

Although ships were few and far between – perhaps twenty-five Company vessels and a stray English or Frenchman a year – it soon became evident that the meagre offerings of the natives in cattle and sheep were insufficient. As a result with the permission of the Council of Seventeen, an attempt to produce more food was made by using free farmers employing slaves. In 1655 a few of the officials of the Company were allowed to try their hand at farming on their own account, and in 1657 nine Dutch and German families were established on small tax-free farms in settlements in the Liesbeeck valley. Slaves for these farmers were obtained from Madagascar and the East Indies, and the first lot proved good workers. A second batch from Angola, however, were not so satisfactory. They ran away and took refuge with the local Kaapmen horde and it required a small war to get the runaways back again. After this no more slaves were drawn from West Africa.

In 1657 the Council of Seventeen reduced the number of officials at the Cape and gave all the encouragement they could to the free farmers. More slaves were provided, the burghers were permitted to barter directly with the Hottentots, and an element of democratic representation was introduced by two free burghers being selected to sit on the commander's council.

Van Riebeeck did not restrict his attention to the Cape, for anxious to make the station capable of providing facilities for the ships at as small a cost to the Company as possible, he set about diversifying the economy. According to his Journal he started sealing, whaling, fishing, viticulture, tobacco-growing and other activities, and he dispatched several expeditions inland to seek products like honey, wax, ostrich feathers, elephant tusks, silver, gold, pearls, tortoiseshell, civet, amber and fine pelts. Thanks to his efforts, there grew up at the Cape a happy composite community.[1] When

---

[1] It is recorded in 1658 as consisting of: 50 freemen, the majority farmers and labourers with a few tailors, hunters, doctors, fishermen and carpenters; 91 paid officials of the Company, including a few soldiers; 22 women and children; 10 convicts; 16 slaves; in all 189.

Van Riebeeck and his family left in 1662, after he had been ten years in office, he was able to say in his final report that he was satisfied that the first difficulties with the Hottentots had been overcome, and that the station with its officials, free burghers and slaves was capable of provisioning the ships which passed to and from the East.

Not much of moment occurred in the time of Van Riebeeck's immediate successors as commanders or governors[1] at the Cape station. The first, Z. Wagenaer (1662–6), attempted the cultivation of rice in order to prevent the necessity of importing such large quantities from the East Indies. But the climate did not suit it. When the earthen fort collapsed during the winter rains of 1663, he suggested that it should be replaced by a stone castle, and this was approved. Wagenaer found that many of the free burghers were no longer working satisfactorily. He spoke of them as 'lazy and dissolute' and asked that they might be replaced by more diligent families. The Company did not immediately comply with his request, but the incompetent seemed to have been got rid of gradually, for a visiting commissioner was able later to describe those who remained as 'obedient and dutiful'.

After Wagenaer there were a number of short-term governors of one or two years. Under these, as war with England was either being waged or contemplated, the defences of the Cape were improved: good progress was made in the construction of the Castle which was finished in 1678, and the main bastion was named after the King Stadtholder William.

In 1679 Simon van der Stel began his long and distinguished term of office. At the time of his arrival the total population of the station was 766, but as only twenty-two families were actively engaged in agriculture, the Cape was by no means self-supporting, and large quantities of rice had to be imported annually. Van der Stel's main task, therefore, was to produce more wheat to feed the population and more meat and vegetables for the crews of the passing ships. In 1679, to

[1] Several had the higher rank of governor, particularly in time of war.

provide the additional supplies of wheat, he established a new settlement of free burgher farmers at Stellenbosch, so called because of the trees which he liked so much. The Stellenbosch settlement flourished from the start. By 1684 there were forty families who between them were producing over a third of the wheat grown at the Cape. It became, too, a well-organized community. A *landdrost* was placed in charge of the district and *heemraden* were appointed to settle disputes among the settlers. The success of Stellenbosch encouraged Van der Stel to establish more settlements in the same area. Some Hollanders and Germans, free burghers, settled north of Stellenbosch at Drakenstein, named after a commissioner who was visiting South Africa at the time. Next, came the Huguenots, the Protestants who left France, present-day Belgium and Holland following the repeal by the French King Louis XIV of the Edict of Nantes in 1685. The French eventually totalled some two hundred, and the first of them, who reached the Cape in 1688 and 1689, were settled on small-holdings at Franschhoek, near the Dutch and German families at Drakenstein. They were allowed their own minister and were taught in their own schools; but living among people of a similar type to themselves, they were soon absorbed.[1] This suited Van der Stel whose policy was to have a united settlement with one language (Hollands).

Among the many Company commissioners to visit South Africa during the twenty-year term of Simon van der Stel was Van Rheede, and he is considered to have left an indelible mark at the Cape. On a visit to a settlement in the Hottentots-Holland district he found much to criticize in the primitive buildings. He was particularly disgusted with one farmhouse and ordered it to be rebuilt. He stipulated that the new structure should have stone walls plastered with lime-white mortar, and that the house, pens, stables and other outbuildings should be protected by a surrounding wall. Everything was to be neat and practical so that the rebuilt farm could act as a model to show the free burghers how a

[1] Although French surnames survive, some were changed: for example, Crosnier became Cronje, and Gaucher became Gous or Gouws.

farmhouse should be built and how to protect their farms from wild animals. This is considered to have been the time when the so-called Cape-Dutch style of architecture was introduced to South Africa. Almost every year brought a commissioner to visit and report on the station's activities. In the time of Simon van der Stel their reports were usually complimentary to the Governor, for he was as active as Van Riebeeck had been. According to the records, besides increasing the production of foodstuffs, he started a saw-mill and opened a brickyard, he used his knowledge of wine-making to help the free burghers to improve the quality of their vintages, and he sent off expeditions inland in search of minerals. He even visited Namaqualand himself in 1685.

The term of office from 1699–1707 of Simon van der Stel's son, Wilhem Adriaen, was marked by trouble with the free burghers. Simon had established the burghers in settlements near Cape Town for the purpose of producing grain; he had not allowed them to become cattle farmers farther inland; but Wilhem Adriaen encouraged rather than discouraged free burghers to become cattle farmers. He issued many grazing licences and established a community of cattle farmers east of the earlier farming settlements under the jurisdiction of the *landdrost* of Stellenbosch. But although the cattle farmers of the interior were later to resist Company rule and rebel first against the Company and then against the British (and thereby alter the course of history), in the time of Wilhem Adriaen the troublemakers were among the established farmers nearer at hand at Stellenbosch, Draken-stein, Franschhoek and in the district of Hottentots-Holland where at Vergelegen the Governor had his own farm and vineyards. Because it was considered unfair for free burghers to have to compete with paid officials, it had long been the policy that officials who wished to farm should leave the Company's service. Wilhem Adriaen, however, could see no reason why officials should resign before becoming farmers. His father had farmed on his own account for most of his long term of office, and other governors and commanders[1] of the garrison had done the same. In spite of a VOC decree of 1688, he proceeded to grant a number of farms to members of his family and his friends, and he gave the valuable wine contract to one of his clique.

This jobbery caused great dissatisfaction among the burghers at the Cape and in the Stellenbosch area, and they prepared secretly a written protest, one copy of which they sent to Amsterdam and another to Batavia in the East Indies. When the news of the disaffection reached the Governor he immediately took vigorous counter-measures. He drew up a document averring that he was governing justly, and under pressure obtained sixty-three supporting signatures from burghers – which represented more than half their number. It is said that he obtained such results at the Cape by giving a magnificent reception to the dissidents at which he offered liberal supplies of liquor and smokes, and at Stellenbosch by making the signators notify approval under armed guard and at a table on which lay the local *landdrost's* pistols ready for use. After obtaining the supporting signatures, the Governor arrested those who still showed themselves recalcitrant, and imprisoned them in the castle. Four of their leaders he then dispatched on board ship to Amsterdam to answer charges of disaffection. One died on the voyage, but the other three answered the charges so successfully that not only were they set free, but Governor Wilhem Adriaen and some of his associates were recalled, and his brother was banished from all VOC possessions. Moreover, an instruction from the Council of Seventeen of 30 October 1706 forbade officials in future to own land or to trade. Thus, in this first tussle with the authorities, the free burghers had the advantage.

A prominent governor, whose term lasted from 1751–71, was Ryk Tulbagh. Tulbagh developed gardens at the Cape and planted some beautiful chestnut trees, which were much admired later by English visitors like Lord Clive and Captain Cook. His collection of plants won world-wide acclaim, and having received a gift of 4,000 books, he

[1] Simon van der Stel was raised from commander to the status of governor in 1691. Wilhem Adriaen van der Stel started his term as a governor.

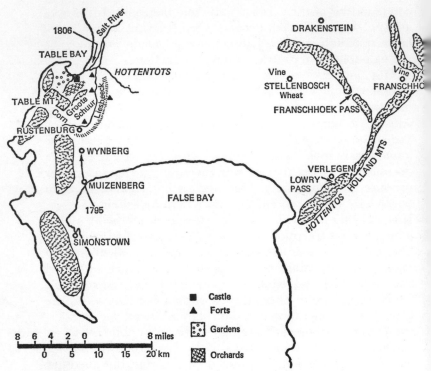

Map I   The Cape Area 1652–1806

established the first library at the Cape. During his term he
also consolidated into one single code the confused laws
which regulated the lives of the slaves. He retained severe
penalties for misbehaviour, but allowed them to work for
money to buy their freedom. When free they were treated as
equals of the white population. Although he attempted to
apply stringent health measures to incoming ships, a serious
smallpox epidemic struck the Cape in 1767. More than five
hundred people died, and it was not until 1770 that the
disease ran its course. There had been several epidemics of
smallpox during the hundred years of European occupation,
and on each occasion it had spread to the neighbouring
Hottentot hordes and killed off more of them than Europeans. The subsequent decline in number of the local

Hottentots weakened their resistance to encroachment on their territories. In contrast the negro Xhosa to the east were less vulnerable to the disease and continued to increase in numbers.

By the time Baron (Joachim) van Plettenberg was appointed Acting Governor in 1771, some cattle farmers had moved away far inland and were quite out of touch with the authorities in Cape Town. Van Plettenberg decided to go and see how they were faring in the outlying regions, and he seems to have planned his journey systematically, for before he set out he is recorded as instructing the *landdrosts* of the districts through which he would pass to have fresh draught-oxen and horses in readiness at convenient stopping places.[1] According to his diary, Van Plettenberg left the Castle with a small party of officials on 3 September 1778, and on his route north-eastwards at first encountered more springbok than people, for it was not until the tenth day after departure that he met a small horde of Hottentots. After three weeks of journeying they reached the upper reaches of the Gamtoos in the region known as the Camdebo[2] and here they saw some Bushmen's rock-paintings depicting men hunting game, with eland much in evidence. Van Plettenberg was pleased to discover that the White farmers were on good terms with the Hottentot families who lived among them. Continuing his journey to the Sneeuwbergen and the region of the headwaters of the Sunday River, he came upon a straw-thatched farm building which he describes in his diary as 'one large single low-walled room without partitions, which also served as a storehouse'. Although the farmers were hardworking, good-living people, always with a bible in their homes, he discovered they were not on such good terms with the natives as the farmers of the Gamtoos region: they complained that Bushmen and Hottentots stole their livestock and murdered their herdsmen. In the area of the Fish River, Chief Koba of the Xhosa and some followers including his two sons visited the Governor's camp and were entertained there. The border farmers had complained that the Xhosa had been crossing the Fish River recently in search of pasture, whereas in the past they had always stayed 'a distance of at

[1] Cape State Archives C 703, C 488.   [2] Map p. 44.

least one day's journey' east of the river. Accepting that the farmers considered the Fish their natural boundary Van Plettenberg asked Koba to get the Xhosa to stay in future to the east of the river. Koba agreed to do this, but later it was discovered that only the paramount chief Rarabe had authority to decide such a matter. Before returning to Cape Town, Van Plettenberg set up a beacon north of the source of the Fish River beyond the Zuurberg to mark the north-eastern corner of the territory claimed by the Company.

The period from 1778 to 1795 was one of turmoil and rebellion. A number of burghers, influenced by the democratic ideas emerging at the time of the French Revolution, used these as a justification for demands for freer treatment by the Company's officials and for direct representation in the Cape Government. They also asked for magistrates to be appointed in the outlying districts and for help in their struggle with the natives on the border.

Matters came to a head in 1779 when Carel Buytendag was reported for maltreating Coloureds[1] in his employ. The *landdrost* and *heemraden* at Stellenbosch recommended his banishment, and some Asians employed in the department of the Fiscal were sent to apprehend him and bring him to Cape Town. Here the Fiscal impressed him into the Company's military service and drafted him to Batavia. This so-called injustice towards Buytendag was not the spark which kindled the 'Patriot' movement, for the holding of its secret conclaves and the spread of its anonymous pamphlets had preceded the episode. But the affair did highlight the arbitrary treatment of burghers by some Cape officials. The 'Patriots' said little against Van Plettenberg, for they considered him a just man and he was popular; but they vigorously attacked the Fiscal and sent a petition to the Council of Seventeen, demanding that the Fiscal's powers of arbitrary arrest should be limited; and that in future only Whites should be permitted to arrest burghers. They asked too that there should be an equal representation of free burghers and officials on the Council of Justice and that they

[1] People of mixed blood, etc., see page 59.

32

1 Vasco da Gama, by Charles Gond (Castle of Good Hope)

Jan van Riebeeck

Sir Benjamin D'Urban, Governor of the Cape of Good Hope (Radio Times Hulton Picture Library)

2   Government House ('Tuynhuys'), Cape Town (Africana Museum)

The Great Trek
(Africana Museum),
Thomas Baines

might have the right of appeal to the Netherlands. Although it took some time, a number of these demands were met. After having been approved by Van Plettenberg, their request for equal representation on the Council was agreed in 1783, and the independent status of the Fiscal was abolished in 1792. The coveted appeal to Holland, however, was not allowed until later.

Over the year the cattle farmers spread further and further afield, and about 1745 it was decided to place the territory where the outlying farms were to be found under a *landdrost* and four assistant *heemraden*. By this time there were farmers beyond the Breede River as far as Mossel Bay,[1] and a *drostdy* was built near a crossing over the Breede at a settlement called Swellendam after the Governor from 1739–51 Hendrik Swellengrebel and his wife, whose maiden name was Ten Damme. In 1779, after his return from his journey to the north-east, Van Plettenberg, in answer to the requests he had received, appointed a *landdrost* and minister to the district on the upper Sunday River. Here the *drostdy* was established at the main settlement on the river and called Graaff-Reinet after Governor C. J. van der Graaff (1785–91). The district of Graaff-Reinet was made up of the far eastern part of the district of Swellendam and its need for its own officials is realized when it is noted that the new district was near the eastern frontier of the Cape Colony, about three hundred miles from Swellendam.

The officials eventually sent to Graaff-Reinet as *predikant* and *landdrost* were the Moravian minister Von Manger and H. C. D. Maynier; and neither was very popular, for they did not give the frontier farmers the support against the natives which they had sought. Von Manger, by teaching the Hottentot servants in a school he opened, caused them to get ideas above their station. Maynier was liberty, equality and fraternity personified. But he put a different interpretation on these ideas from that held by the cattle farmers of the frontier. They dwelt on liberty: liberty to do as they chose. He thought more about equality and fraternity, and even applied these principles to his dealings with the natives.

[1] Map p. 44.

c

Though he lacked sufficient police, he tried to establish the rule of law on the frontier where, as on most frontiers very little existed. He tried to stop burghers punishing their Hottentot servants unless official sanction had been obtained, regardless of the fact that some farmers had to travel many miles to his *drostdy* to obtain his official permission. He would not allow unauthorized commandos to ride out to rectify wrongful use of pasturages, or to retake stolen cattle – and the official commandos he led out himself usually failed.

In 1797 a precipitate unauthorized commando attack by the farmers invoked a devastating retaliation from the Xhosa who came in and destroyed farms and stole thousands of cattle. Maynier's first response on this occasion was to prohibit further commando attacks, and to try to get the Xhosa to restore the cattle by persuasion. When this policy failed he led out such a weak commando that it was able only to regain a fraction of the cattle that had been lost.

Eventually Maynier's weak policy towards the natives upset the border farmers irrevocably. They felt that the Company would neither support their pasturage rights nor allow them to defend themselves. In February 1795, when Commissionary-General J. A. Sluysken was in command at the Cape, they broke into open rebellion. At Graaff-Reinet a group of about forty mounted the tricolour cocade, and claiming they represented 'the voice of the people', marched on Maynier's *drostdy* and took it over. After Maynier had fled to Cape Town, Sluysken sent commissioners to parley with the rebels, but the farmers refused to have anything to do with the officials; instead, they elected a provisional government of their own. They also declared that in future they would enter Xhosa territory in search of stolen cattle whenever they considered it necessary, whether they had received official sanction or not. Four days later the farmers at Swellendam followed their example. Sixty armed burghers forced the *landdrost* and his *heemraden* to relinquish their posts, and then, having chosen new ones, the farmers established a revolutionary convention.

Now events in Europe were to alter the course of South Africa's history. In 1795 the forces of revolutionary France overran the Republic of the Netherlands and the Prince of Orange sought refuge in England. Possession of the Cape would enable revolutionary France to harry English shipping with India, so a strong fleet was quickly fitted out under Admiral Elphinstone to occupy the station before the French got there. The Prince of Orange had previously come to an agreement with the British authorities that their countries would help each other on the sea routes of the world during the war, so when the fleet set out, Admiral Elphinstone took with him a letter signed by the Prince asking Sluysken to receive the British as friends.

Sluysken and his officials were pro-Orange, but many of the burghers, like those at Graaff-Reinet and Swellendam, were republican, so when the British reached False Bay and asked permission to land Sluysken refused to let them do so. In vain the British offered good terms and depicted the horrors of French republicanism; Sluysken at first played for time, and then when he heard that his home country had become the Batavian Republic, made preparations to resist. The defences of the Cape were relatively formidable, and there were sufficient guns for the emplacements; but the manpower available was not impressive; it consisted of a few mercenaries, some gunners, some Hottentots and half-castes, and a number of not very staunch burghers, in all some 3,000 to oppose a British force of initially only 1,600, but later strongly reinforced. Sluysken evacuated Simonstown, and made his first stand at Muizenberg,[1] from which place, after a strong British attack, he was forced to retire on Wynberg. The British now made a double move. Their ships bombarded Cape Town from the north while their troops attacked the Company's forces on Wynberg Hill from the south. Again the defenders showed little determination. The mercenaries fled, and after a brief resistance many of the burghers, suspecting their officers were half-hearted, made off home, complaining of treachery. Deciding that further resistance was useless, Sluysken gave in. He capitulated at Rustenburg, north of Wynberg, on 16 September 1795, and the Cape passed into British hands.

[1] Map p. 30.

Chapter 2

The British: 1806–38

The British ruled the Cape from 1795 to 1803, first by means of a military government and then through a series of governors, in much the same way as the Dutch East India Company had done. Some of the higher Company officials and most of the lesser ones were left in their posts, and the structure of the administration was largely unchanged. There were few changes in the legal system, and Roman–Dutch law was applied to the British-born. On the economic side the British occupation brought advantages. Trade restrictions were relaxed so that burghers and merchants became better off, and although imports exceeded exports in value the difference was more than compensated for by the hard cash brought in by the British troops of the garrison and by passing ships. During the first British occupation about 170 ships entered Table Bay and Simon's Bay annually which was appreciably more than the eighty-six that had visited the Cape in 1794.

An early task for the British administration was to try to quell the rebellion at Graaff-Reinet. This proved easier than had been anticipated. A French squadron sent to help the rebels was blocked in Saldanha Bay and made to capitulate, after which a show of force caused the dissidents to surrender. In 1799, when Adriaen van Jaarsveld, who had been one of the rebel leaders at Graaff-Reinet, was arrested on a charge of forgery, a number of burghers besieged the *drostdy* where he was being held and released him. But again the appearance of troops sent up from the Cape was sufficient to cause the troublemakers to give in. After the first rebellion in 1795 the British had pardoned most of the offenders; but after the second in 1799 the penalties were more severe. Van Jaarsveld was arrested, tried on a charge of high treason and condemned to death, and the others were either sentenced to death, exiled, or given penal servitude. However, Van Jaarsveld died in prison and none of the other death sentences were carried out; also, by the time the Cape was handed over into the charge of the Batavian Republic in 1803, most of the prisoners had been freed.

Meanwhile, loyal citizens were well treated and there was much social activity under the aegis of the charming Lady Anne Barnard, wife of the local Colonial Secretary. The British authorities also made a serious attempt to secure peaceful relations with the local natives. A number of Bushmen were persuaded to serve as cattle-herders and those who would not co-operate with Europeans were chased away. Only in the Tarka area of the northern basin of the River Fish did they remain much of a menace to the farmers. Many Hottentots were also employed as cattle-herders, as servants, and as soldiers by the Government. Tribal systems were almost broken up locally and by 1799 there were only two hordes still occupying their own territories. The remaining small unattached and unorganized groups were placed by the authorities in the care of the missionaries, the first main mission station being established in 1803[1] at Bethelsdorp, six miles west of present-day Port Elizabeth, under the supervision of Dr J. van der Kemp of the London Missionary Society. The Xhosa on the eastern frontier of the province were more of a problem to the authorities than the Bushmen and Hottentots. The loose grouping of the tribes made treaties worthless because there was no paramount chief strong enough to enforce them. A major difficulty arose with those who had quarrelled with their paramount and fled westwards across the Fish River. They were occupying pastureland among Europeans in the Suurveld, and although their paramount Gaika (Ngqika) agreed that the Fish should

[1] This was in the time of the short period of rule of the Batavian Republic which continued the British policy towards the Hottentots.

be the border with the Europeans, and promised not to punish them if they returned, they would not comply. In the end the British allowed them to remain on the west of the Fish. By a treaty of 1799 they agreed not to raid European farms if they were permitted to stay, and the only action taken by the authorities was the establishment near the later Port Elizabeth of Fort Frederick whose garrison were given the task of keeping the peace on the western side of the river.

The British looked upon the occupation as a temporary measure. Uncertain of the value of the Cape even during the war with France, when peace came with the Treaty of Amiens in 1802 they decided that it was more trouble to look after than its strategic value justified, and they agreed to hand it over to the Batavian Republic, which from 1803 to 1806 ruled the colony through its Asiatic council in the Netherlands. The rule of the Batavian Republic was too short-lived for much to be accomplished, but J. A. Uitenhage de Mist, who was Commissioner-General at the Cape until 1804, introduced a number of reforms appropriate for a republican, including a greater degree of representation on the ruling councils and the long sought-after right of appeal by the burghers to the Supreme Court at The Hague. He also created the additional administrative districts of Tulbagh, sixty miles north-east of Cape Town, and Uitenhage, between the Gamtoos and Sunday rivers, the latter named after himself.

With the renewal of the war with France, Britain decided to reoccupy the Cape Colony, and on 7 January 1806 a force of 6,700 under General Sir David Baird landed two miles north of Cape Town and marched on the port. Some 2,000 mercenaries, burgher militia and Hottentot soldiers, were mustered to resist the invaders; but they made a poor showing. Half of the force retreated on Cape Town and surrendered immediately, and the other half fell back on Hottentots Holland and gave in after nine days fighting. In March 1806 the Governor, J. W. Jannsens, and the garrison left for

Holland and the British took over the Cape for the second time. To start with, the new occupation was still considered only as a temporary measure. But under a treaty of 13 August 1814 Great Britain, having restored to the Kingdom of the Netherlands (Holland and Belgium) the East Indies and most of the other Dutch colonies taken during the Napoleonic wars, took over permanently Ceylon, British Guiana, and the Cape. Although Britain did not, as is so often stated, buy the Cape from Holland, as a result of the above transaction £2,000,000 was made available for the fortification of the Belgian border against France, and £3,000,000 to help to consolidate the position of King William[1] in his enlarged kingdom.

As during the first British occupation, there was trouble with the Xhosa and the burghers on the eastern frontier. The tribes in the Suurveld, west of the River Fish, had begun marauding European farms again, and after an inspection of the frontier region it was decided to drive them across the Fish River, which was accepted as the frontier by both Gaika and Hintsa, the paramounts respectively of the two main groups of Xhosa. Thus, within a month of assuming the governorship in 1811, Sir John Cradock enrolled a large force of troops and burghers, and these, under the command of Colonel Graham, swept most of the offending tribesmen[2] over the Fish. Cradock next built a double line of block-houses to guard the frontier, and having garrisoned them with soldiers, established near the main military posts two new settlements, named appropriately Cradock and Grahamstown, near which were offered large farms at quit-rents with the object of consolidating the frontier by installing blocks of European settlers. Cradock's arrangements proved successful for a time in bringing peace to the frontier, but when the Colonial Office ordered the troops to be moved away to defend the harbours of the colony, the settlers on their own were insufficient to hold the line, and Xhosa tribesmen filtered back across the river and settled once more among the European farmers in the Suurveld.

[1] Hertslet, L. and E., *The Map of Africa by Treaty*, Vol. 1, pp. 359, 365.
[2] 20,000 Ndhlambis and Gunukwebes.

In 1815, during a second campaign to drive the Xhosa from the Suurveld, there occurred the affair of Slagtersnek which embittered relations between the frontier farmers and the British authorities. The farmers who for months had been out on commando against the Xhosa were shocked to hear that in their absence the authorities had been taking action against a recalcitrant member of their society living near the Fish River at Slagtersnek, half-way between the new settlements of Cradock and Grahamstown. A Hottentot herdsman had lodged a complaint with the *landdrost* at Cradock against his master Frederik Bezuidenhout, alleging ill-treatment. Bezuidenhout disregarded several summons, and after a delay was sentenced in his absence to a month's imprisonment for contempt. Shortly afterwards the under-sheriff, with an officer and a platoon of Hottentots of the Cape Regiment, was sent to arrest him. Bezuidenhout took refuge in a cave. When a detachment of the troops under a sergeant went to seize him, he resisted arrest and was shot dead by the sergeant while taking aim with his elephant gun. His relations and friends sought revenge. They raised an armed body of sixty sympathizers and invited help from Gaika and the local Xhosa. Back at Slagtersnek they confronted the *landdrost* who was accompanied by forty troopers. For a time it seemed that a pitched battle was imminent; but while they were parleying, news came that the Xhosa would not support the rebels, and on hearing this, most of them surrendered. Bezuidenhout's brother was one of those who fled. He was overtaken, surrounded and shot dead while his wife was helping him load. Thirty-nine were eventually tried for treason, and six were condemned to death. Of these, one was pardoned and five were hanged. The Slagtersnek affair disturbed the frontier farmers on several counts. They thought the officials had shown too much concern for enforcing the law at a time when all should have been concentrating on the war. They were offended at the use of Hottentot soldiers to arrest a White man. But above all, they considered a farmer should be allowed to punish a Hottentot servant as he wished.

. . . . . .

Although Cradock's plan to man the eastern frontier with soldiers was disallowed by the Colonial Office, his scheme to consolidate the border by means of introducing an increased number of European settlers was permitted, and was not only developed by successive governors, but incorporated into schemes for increasing the number of British settlers in South Africa, and for anglicization in general. In 1817, in a private venture, Benjamin Moodie brought some young Scots out to the Cape under indenture and these were settled successfully in Cape Town and Swellendam; but another immigration project for destitute boys at about the same time was not so satisfactory. These projects affected only the western districts, and meanwhile Cradock's Dutch settlers on the eastern frontier had begun to drift away. His quit-rent system had meant that farmers had to pay more for their land than under the old loan agreements, and it was hoped that they would be compelled to stay and engage in intensive farming. But few could be persuaded to remain long. To bolster up Cradock's failing scheme his successor as governor, Lord Charles Somerset, instigated the '1820 Settlers' project in the Suurveld district[1] around Grahamstown which eventually included the districts of Albany, Bathurst and Alexandria.

The urgency of the need to secure the frontier was brought home to the British authorities in 1819[2] when Makana the Xhosa prophet led the Ndlambi across the Fish, avoided Fort Brown and attacked Grahamstown. What saved the day for the puny outpost under Colonel Willshire was partly courage and partly superior armament. But there was dire peril for the neighbourhood, and to help protect it from further raids Somerset ordered Colonel Willshire to push forward the frontier to the Keiskamma, and then to annex the land between the Fish and Keiskamma and turn it into a no-man's land, forbidden to colonist and Xhosa alike. In due course this was carried out, and the appropriately-named Fort Willshire was built on the west bank of the Keiskamma

---

[1] The main district was named Albany by Lord Bathurst, the Colonial Secretary.

[2] Fifth Frontier War: the Ndlambi were rivals of the Gaikas.

to protect the neutral territory. Accepting also the value of trade as a harmonizer of relations on the frontier, Somerset organized periodic fairs at Fort Willshire where Europeans and Xhosa could legitimately exchange produce and goods. However, Somerset's main solution for the frontier problem was close-settlement of the Suurveld by Europeans or friendly tribes. He linked this with the social crisis in Britain, where following the Napoleonic wars there were many unemployed. The problem of redundant population and a desire to divert emigration to British colonies were together sufficient to persuade the British Government to apply a large sum of money to a state-sponsored and large-scale emigration scheme to the south-east coast of Africa.

Once the grant of money for emigration was through Parliament, matters moved quickly. Colonel J. G. Cuyler, the *landdrost* of Uitenhage, was instructed to carry out surveys in the selected area, and a plan was formulated to bring the families to Algoa Bay. It was eventually agreed that free victualling would be arranged from the day of embarkation and 100 acres would be allotted to each able-bodied male. Land was to be surveyed free and occupied for the first ten years free of rent. A deposit of £10 sterling per family unit of a man and his wife and two children under fourteen years would be repaid one-third on arrival, one-third on settlement and one-third three months later. In the original plan individual or independent settlers were not provided for. It was only later that land was promised to those who applied and would pay their own passage. The major scheme stipulated the arrangement of parties with ten able-bodied males as the minimum size; and for any group of a hundred or more a minister of religion salaried in the Cape was to be provided.

The peculiar feature of the organization was the wide initiative left to heads of parties, some clearly speculators. They could provide the deposits and prepare to build up a small empire in land if they drove a hard enough bargain with the labourers indentured to them. Based mainly on London, party leaders of this kind often went outside London to recruit. This helps explain why short of examining parish registers in Britain it is not easy to determine the provenance of individual settlers. James Erith, for example was a baker of Peckham, but drew his party from the Isle of Sheppey in Kent. William Wait of London collected some of his party from Somerset and others from Buckinghamshire. William Smith of London raised his party from Northamptonshire. Some parties were bound together by the nexus of religion. For example, the large group led by Sephton which settled at Salem fifteen miles south of Grahamstown were Methodists. Its members were nearly all London tradesmen; carpenters, weavers, one mathematical instrument maker, coach builders, sawyers, tallow-melters, chain-makers, shoe-makers, and one umbrella-maker. A mere handful of this characteristically London party described themselves as husbandmen. Yet this party, which planned its enterprise from the start as a communal one, established itself better on the land than most of the others. The bond of another large party, this time from Nottinghamshire, was neighbourhood. It was sponsored by the Duke of Newcastle and a group of country gentry who raised a considerable sum of money not only to pay deposits but to help with equipment. As late as 1837 the settlers of this group were writing to their patrons, and it had clearly preserved a sense of identity which disappeared from parties raised in a more haphazard way.

There were a number of war veterans among the settlers. One such was George Smith who led a party from Manchester. He had served in the Cape and had noted that the climate suited his constitution; he had been taken prisoner at Corunna, escaped after hair-raising experiences in France, and fought at the battle of Waterloo, where, in his own words, 'I was wounded in the belly and left hip, and pensioned after twelve years military service at nine-pence a day'. Men such as Smith were valuable residents for the troubled frontier.

Among settlers who later gained distinction were Thomas Pringle, Thomas Phillips, Robert Godlonton, the Rev. Henry Dugmore and Andrew Geddes Bain. Pringle was a writer in the romantic vein of Sir Walter Scott. His *Narrative of a Residence in South Africa* recaptures the blend of melancholy and expectation which most parties experienced on

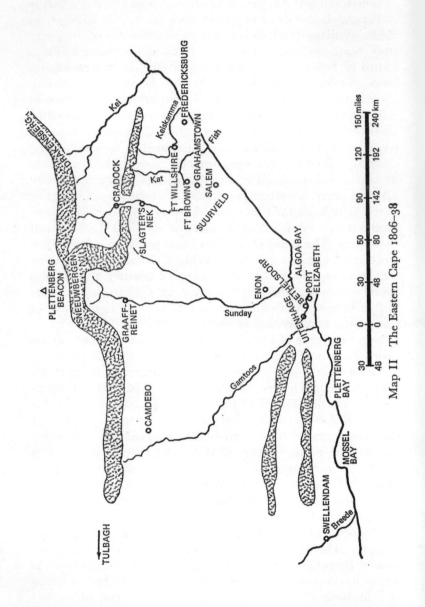

Map II The Eastern Cape 1806–38

arriving, while his ballad 'Makana's Gathering' has the narrative gusto of a true Border tale. Pringle was a born eyewitness. Most settler tales and fireside yarns made much of the amusing blunders of artisans turned farmers. He is the only writer who points out his own experiences of the converse, namely the value of skilled artisans when houses were being built and furniture had to be made. Pringle was a tough controversialist who exposed the shortcomings of the settlement. Along with John Fairbairn he set up *The Commercial Advertiser* in Cape Town and fought for and helped secure the freedom of the Press in South Africa. Thomas Phillips[1] came out at the head of his own party from Pembrokeshire in Wales, and became a senior magistrate. He was a prolific letter writer, and his letters give an invaluable account of the early experience of the 1820 settlers. Robert Godlonton was the editor of the *Grahamstown Journal* which had been founded by Louis Meurant in 1831 and which became a powerful agent of settler interests and the organ of settler opinion. The Rev. Henry Dugmore with William Shaw and others founded the Wesleyan Church in the Eastern Province, and later took a leading role in the life of the area. Andrew Geddes Bain, not to be confused with Thomas Baines the artist, was an explorer of note as well as a professional roadbuilder.

Thanks to the efforts of Colonel J. C. Cuyler, the *landdrost* of Uitenhage, and the interest of the Acting Governor, Sir Rufane Shaw Donkin, careful preparations were made to receive the settlers, the first of whom arrived in April 1820. By the time the settlers landed, their locations had been surveyed and a stores depot set up by the Bay where implements and seed could be purchased. A temporary tented town was also established alongside Fort Frederick, and Dutch farmers, led by Piet Retief, were ready at the Bay waiting to transport the settlers to their locations to the north. In June the village on the shore of Algoa Bay, where they landed,[2] was named Port Elizabeth after Lady Donkin,

---

[1] He presented a bible to the Voortrekkers who left Grahamstown on the Great Trek 1837.

[2] The place is now marked by the campanile tower in Port Elizabeth.

widow of Sir Rufane Donkin, who had died in India in 1818.

About 4,000 settlers, 2,400 of whom were males, grouped into sixty parties, arrived in twenty-one ships from London (Deptford), Portsmouth, Liverpool, Bristol and Cork. The first ship, the *Chapman*, dropped anchor in Algoa Bay on 9 April 1820, and the last arrival, the *Duke of Marlborough*, at the end of June. Once established, the settlers found Albany anything but an Eden. Despite the sweat of their brows, during four successive seasons they ate no bread from the corn they saved, for rust ruined the wheat. Then later, when it seemed they had tamed their wilderness, they were all but driven out by Xhosa raiders. However, a number of the more enterprising farmers turned to cattle and sheep, and by breeding merinos they established a flourishing trade in wool, so that by 1845 the annual wool clip had reached a million pounds in weight. Soon after the settlement was founded, many unused to working on the land defied the conditions of their contracts and left the countryside and moved to the towns; but this was not all loss, as valuable subsidiary industries were established. Stability was given to the area when some retired officers from the Royal African Corps were established well forward near the coast at Fredericksburg in the neutral zone between the Fish and Keiskamma rivers; this new settlement helped to consolidate the southern part of the frontier. Also, refugees (the Fingos) from the devastations caused by the forays set in motion by Shaka's Zulus were allotted territory to help strengthen the northern section of the frontier; and a large Hottentot settlement was set up on the Kat River in the basin of the Fish, with the same idea of settling on the frontier people friendly[1] to the Cape government.

Following on these measures the 1820 Settlement began to flourish.[2] Anglicization was carried forward. The number of English-speakers in Cape Province was doubled, and

[1] The Hottentots later went over to the side of the Xhosa, but the Fingos remained loyal.

[2] Although the settlement of 1820 did not secure the frontier the plan of establishing close-knit communities to guard it was a help and was repeated. In 1857 German legionaries were settled west of the Kei.

British sports, pastimes and institutions were introduced. Houses, churches and halls were built in the English style, and independent newspapers were started and an English language school was founded. With the influx of English settlers there were renewed demands for wider representation on the governing councils. These were met to some extent when in 1825 an advisory council was formed to which two colonists were allotted, and later in 1834 when seven colonists were appointed to the legislative council. The English jury system was also introduced and was well received. Other changes which met with less favour by the Dutch included the replacement of the *landdrosts* and *heemraden* by English-style magistrates and the curtailment of the powers of their valuable functionary the field cornet.

During the period 1806–34, supported by the European philanthropic movement then in full swing and encouraged by the British authorities, clerical and missionary activity in Cape Province increased rapidly, and made a tremendous impact on the social life of the colony. The Dutch Reformed Church and Lutheran Church, started during the VOC regime, had their congregation in Cape Town, Anglicans held services in Cape Town, Simonstown and Grahamstown, Wesleyans made good their footing in Cape Town and the newly settled Albany, and Roman Catholics ministered in the capital. The missionary stream had begun to flow in the last days of the Company, but at first only the Moravian Brethren and missionaries of the London Missionary Society of the Free Churches were represented in the field. Some of these went hopefully two by two, Dutch and English, to the region occupied by the Xhosa tribes under the paramountcy of Gaika and to the Bushmen in the Tarka region in the north-east. After 1816 they were joined by Wesleyans and members of the Glasgow Society. Robert Moffat established a Free Church mission station far afield among the Baralongs north of the Orange River at Kuruman, and he and his son-in-law David Livingstone gained reputations as explorers along with Thomas Baines the artist. Members of the Glasgow Society worked among the Coloureds established in

47

the region of the middle Orange River by Barend Barends,
Adam and Cornelius Kok, and ablest of all the semi-civilized
chieftains, Andries Waterboer.

The missionaries provided areas of law and order and
civilization wherever they went: for example, William
Anderson at Klaarwater, and John Campbell – artist as well
as missionary – at Griquatown near by. The French missionary Eugène Casilis established a station among the South
Sotho near Moshesh's (Moshweshwe) mountain-top capital
at Thaba Bosiu in Basutoland and gave valuable advice to
that famous chief. Nearer home the Moravians occupied the
old mission station at Genadendal and established posts at
Mamre in the west and at Enon near the eastern frontier.
Meanwhile, Dr Van der Kemp had turned Bethelsdorp into
a veritable Zion for the Hottentots.

At Bethelsdorp, working with Van der Kemp, was the Rev.
James Read who was to cause considerable offence to the
European settlers by his strong championship of the Hottentots. In 1812 he wrote to the headquarters of the London
Missionary Society in London accusing colonists of killing
and ill-treating their Hottentot servants. When this was
brought to the notice of the Colonial Secretary, the Governor
at the Cape was ordered to investigate, and if necessary
punish the offenders. In 1811 a circuit court had been
established to visit outlying districts and hear cases outside
the jurisdiction of the magistrates, so on the instructions of
the Governor the matter was brought before this newly constituted body. The court set about its task with great
thoroughness. Four months were spent in investigation, after
which, more than fifty settlers were summoned to appear and
some thousand witnesses were called. Of the seventeen
farmers charged with murder, one was convicted of assault,
two cases were postponed, three referred to Cape Town, and
the rest dismissed. Of the fifteen charged with violence seven
were found guilty. A single charge of murder was upheld
and only fines were imposed on those few found guilty of the
lesser offences; but the general effect of the 'Black Circuit' as
it was called, was unfortunate. Those against whom charges
had broken down were indignant at being falsely accused:

Dingane (reproduced from Peter Becker's *The Rule of Fear*)

3 Shaka

Moshesh (Africana Museum)

Cetshwayo

4   Kimberley Diamond Mine; an early picture

Witwatersrand main gold reef, the 'face'

all resented being brought to court 'by a parcel of Hottentots and missionaries'.

The missionaries generally gave much attention to the Hottentots who responded well to their evangelism. In 1809 Lord Caledon had issued his so-called Hottentot proclamation which, accepting that the Hottentots had become detribalized, made them subject to the laws of the colony. However, in an effort to encourage steady habits of work and curb their nomadic tendencies he also bound them to their European masters by registered yearly contracts, and issued them with yearly passes so that they could be traced if they wandered off. This arrangement had the virtue of civilizing the Hottentots and at the same time providing labour which was in short supply following the abolition of the slave trade in 1807; but it appeared to the liberal-minded missionaries as nothing more than another form of slavery.

The missionary who took up the cause of the Hottentots most strongly was Dr John Philip of the London Missionary Society, when he became the director and superintendent of missions in 1817 with his headquarters at Cape Town. John Philip was born in Fife in 1775 and was caught as a young man in the wave of evangelical revival. He had great sincerity and enthusiasm and, although centred at Cape Town, took no fewer than twelve long journeys to discover what life was like on the frontier and beyond. These included a visit to Moshesh at Thaba Bosiu. Dr Philip was particularly unhappy about Hottentot children being apprenticed to White farmers, and Coloureds being forced into White service. Although the contracts, and the pass-laws which bound them to their White masters, had a civilizing effect and instilled an understanding of the virtues of work, he disapproved of them, and worked tirelessly to change the laws controlling Hottentot labour. He was an active propagandist, and his *Researches in South Africa*, published in 1828, which stressed the worst features of the White–Hottentot relationship of the time, was widely read and much approved in philanthropic circles in Britain. He had a close relationship with Wilberforce and Buxton. He was on good terms with the members of the 1823 Commission of Inquiry sent out by the Colonial Secretary to review and report on all aspects of the administration of the Colony. He was only on fair terms with the Governor, Lord Charles Somerset, but he had the full backing of his successor, the philanthropic Sir Richard Bourke. Matters came to a head when Dr Philip received reports that Hottentots in the frontier area were being assembled in gangs for forced-labour for road making. Immediately he summoned his supporters to put pressure on the home government to repeal all the 1809–19 Hottentot laws, including Cradock's pass laws.

Dr Philip and his friends produced such a wealth of convincing arguments against the Hottentot laws that in 1828 the home government was prevailed upon to repeal them. It gave approval for a so-called Fiftieth Ordinance to be passed by the Cape Government, which cancelled the restrictive measures on Hottentots, and gave Bushmen, Hottentots, and all free Coloured people full rights to own land. At Dr Philip's insistence the Imperial Government also stipulated that the Fiftieth Ordinance could not be amended or repealed 'without the consent of the King-in-Council'. The Ordinance certainly raised the status of the Hottentots; but it also increased vagrancy and theft; and it made labour relationships chaotic. By 1834 it is calculated that between 8,000 and 10,000 of the 32,000 free persons of colour had become unemployed vagrants. Also, farmers were now not only harassed by Xhosa raiders, but were also likely to be robbed by bands of Hottentots from within the Colony. The repeal of the pass-laws allowed Hottentots to leave their masters: at worst to embark on a life of idleness and crime, and at best to loaf their time away at mission stations, where, with increased numbers, it was found more and more difficult to get them to understand the value of work. The new policy impoverished farmers already affected by the rise in rents brought about by the replacement of the loan system by quit-rents, and was further complicated because at this time South Africa's slaves were in the process of being emancipated. Emancipation was another cause of resentment in itself among the few who possessed slaves, for shares in the £20,000,000 compensation granted by the British Govern-

ment were so difficult to collect from London that a majority
sold their claims to agents at a loss or did not put in for them
at all. However, in the end the freeing of the slaves helped
combat Hottentot vagrancy. When emancipation began in
1834 it became essential to introduce some legal bond
between master and servant to replace the old master-slave
relationship; so in 1841 a 'Masters and Servants' law was
passed giving legal form to a new contract. This applied to
both erstwhile slave and Hottentot servant and bound them
sufficiently firmly to their masters to produce a workable
relationship.

During the governorship of Sir Benjamin D'Urban,[1] the
most significant event was the frontier war[2] of 1834. In the
preceding period an uneasy peace had been maintained on
the frontier by following a policy of giving monetary rewards
for good behaviour by the Xhosa, combined with an occasional sharp reprisal if they became aggressive. The nature
of the reprisals had varied, depending on what was permissible at the time. Under some governors, it was permissible
to follow back the spoor of cattle stolen and to retake the
cattle, or seize Xhosa cattle in lieu, from the kraal concerned;
under others, the farmers were permitted to take back only
their own cattle if they could find them; while under
philanthropically inclined governors like Bourke, this so-
called 'Spoor Law' was not allowed to be implemented at all.

In 1834 thousands of Xhosa warriors, operating in small
units, devastated wide areas of the frontier, and before the
authorities started serious counter-measures twenty-two
farmers or members of their families and eighty Hottentot
servants had been killed, and thousands of horses, cattle and
sheep had been stolen. Under the leadership of D'Urban and
Colonel Harry Smith,[3] troops and burgher commandos
counter-attacked and quickly drove the Xhosa back across
the river, and ended the war. Mopping-up operations,[4]

[1] After whom Durban was named.
[2] The 6th Kaffir War.
[3] In 1847 he became Governor as Sir Harry Smith.
[4] In the war and the mopping-up operations that followed Piet Retief and
his commando played an important part.

however, lasted many months. When hostilities ended D'Urban arranged a frontier settlement whereby all except well-disposed Xhosa tribes were expelled from the Suurveld (Albany) and the neutral zone between the Fish and Keiskamma rivers, and the area further east between the Keiskamma and Kei was annexed as the province of Queen Adelaide. D'Urban's arrangements pleased the colonists but met with stern disapproval from the missionaries and their supporters in London, who now included the Colonial Secretary, Lord Glenelg. Such was the strength of this opposition that in 1835 the frontier settlement was set aside, the tribes were allowed to filter back, and the old policy of peaceful persuasion was restored.

The liberation of the Hottentots, and the freeing of the slaves with what was considered inadequate compensation had both disturbed the frontier farmers. But it is generally considered that it was the reversal of D'Urban's frontier settlement which persuaded so many of them to cast off the Cape's authority and seek new territories in the north. This was because they were now convinced that the British authorities would not protect them from Xhosa raids, or allow them to protect themselves. Before discussing the Great Trek, however, something will be said about the Bushmen and Hottentots and the forays and devastations carried out by the northern Bantu-speaking tribes which emptied large areas and by doing so made them available for the disgruntled eastern frontier farmers.

The principal governors during the period 1806–38 were:

The Earl of Caledon	1807–11
Lieut-Gen. Sir John Francis Cradock	1811–14
Lord Charles Henry Somerset	1814–26
Sir Rufane Shaw Donkin (Acting)	1820–21
Maj.-Gen. Sir Richard Bourke	1826–8
Lieut-Gen. Sir Galbraith Lowry Cole[1]	1828–33
Maj.-Gen. Sir Benjamin D'Urban	1834–8

[1] The Lowry Pass was named after him.

Chapter 3

The Bushmen, Hottentots and Coloureds

The first people encountered by Europeans at the Cape were the Bushmen and the Hottentots. Bushmen are very short in stature and infantile in appearance, with flat faces, bulging foreheads and prominent cheekbones. Their skin is yellowish and wrinkled, and a fold to protect the eye from glare gives them a Mongolian appearance; also, their scalp hair grows in tight spirals that leave bare areas to facilitate sweating. The women have bulging buttocks and thighs which are said to store nutritive fat which can be used in time of food shortage – rather like a camel keeps water in a hump. They have very large nipples and their teats become particularly prominent when they are about to mate.

The Bushmen lived off fish or game, of which there were enormous herds in southern Africa. They supplemented this with berries, caterpillars, white ants and their eggs, ostrich eggs, wild honey, locusts and roots. Dr Robert Moffat records that on visiting a Bushmen settlement in a tree he was offered a bowl of locusts for refreshment and this was their staple diet. Recent studies of existing Bushmen settlements in the Kalahari show that vegetable foods still play a major part in the diet of Bushmen. The women use a stick tipped with bone to dig for roots, afterwards placing them in a skin bag. H. Lichtenstein writes of them digging up a species of lily with a mealy nutritive bulb, which, 'roasted in the embers, has very much the flavour of a chestnut'. He also states that, when they caught snakes to get the poison with which to tip their arrows, 'after cutting or biting off the head and taking out the bag of poison, the animal serves the Bosjesmans as food'. He gives a graphic account of how they caught various creatures.

'The banks of the Great river are full of pits made by the Bosjesmans to catch the sea-cow in its nocturnal wanderings; these pits are large and deep, with a sharp-pointed stake planted in the midst, and are most dexterously covered over with twigs, leaves and grass. The animal that falls in dies a death of the most horrible torture, for the stake driven deep into the body prevents his moving about in so confined a space, out of which he might otherwise, perhaps, be able to work his way by the exertion of his vast strength; nor is it much in the power of the Bosjesman himself with his imperfect weapons to release him speedily from his torments; in some places even the prudent elephant falls in this way into the hands of the Bosjesmans; nor are these people less subtle in ensnaring fish, for the sake of which they haunt the neighbourhood of the larger rivers; they make a sort of pointed basket of the twigs of trees which have very much the form of our eel baskets, and are used in the same manner.'

As hunters, their bows and poisoned arrows were effective up to twenty-five yards range, and they trained their dogs to drag animals out of their lairs. Highly skilled at tracing a spoor, they followed wounded animals until the poison had effect. Accounts by traders describe highly organized hunting excursions carried out by Bushmen. In these they would build across a valley a high fence with gaps marked by feathered sticks, between which deep pits were dug. When a herd of game was located amongst the hills, the Bushmen drove them down the valley up to the fence. Finding the fence unjumpable the animals sought out the gaps and tumbled into the pits, where they were killed by the Bushmen at their leisure. Such a hunt supplied sufficient meat, which would be dried in strips for future use. It also provided skins for clothing.

No matter how wide the territory or how far they had to scatter to find food during drought, Bushmen bands usually came together again to camp, 'settling for the night like migratory birds in the bushes'. Eighteenth-century travellers report coming upon them in clusters of shelters huddled together, each person making a small round hollow hole like a nest into which they individually coiled themselves. One of the jibes of the Bantu against them was that they slept together without regard to decency, but eyewitness evidence indicates that camps were set up in a proper manner with each married couple establishing its own shelter and fire. Boys from the age of puberty slept with other boys of the band, and girls of the same age with some single woman. As regards feeding arrangements, meat from animals shot was shared throughout the band, but each woman cooked for her own husband and children the berries she gathered and the roots she dug up.

Property that could be inherited did not exist except for rights over water, and the berries and roots of certain areas. There was no veneration of ancestors comparable to that general among the Bantu-speakers, and Bushmen appear as a present-orientated people who make little effort to hold the past in memory or teach their children history. On the other hand, the splendid rock paintings and engravings of the area are attributed to Bushmen. Some show them dancing, but most depict them in search of game, with their favourite subject the eland very much in evidence. Generally they paint animals naturalistically, but show people as stick-like figures. Every writer speaks of their dances, where the hunters mime animals, describing the courtship of an eland, or vultures devouring the carcass of a zebra. It seems as if the acute observation of animals necessary to a hunter found artistic expression in painting and dancing.

The Hottentots were nomadic, moving in search of grazing for their stock over the lowlands around the bays of the Cape. At first both the yellow-skinned herders and smaller yellow-skinned hunters were called Hottentots from the Dutch words *stotteren* and *tateren*, which described their clicking speech. In spite of their clicks, however, the hunters and herders did not all speak the same language;[1] though they do

[1] Some hunters (e.g. Naron) speak a language akin to Nama herders.

55

seem to be similar physically: P. V. Tobias[1] suggests they are basically the same sub-species, and that the shortness of the Bushmen evolved by natural selection because it was an asset for a hunter.

Hottentots had large flocks of fat-tailed sheep and long-horned cattle ancestral to the modern Afrikander strain. Their bands, referred to as hordes, were much larger than those of the Bushmen. Reports of the seventeenth century speak of a chief 'lying in Saldanha Bay with more than 16,000 followers', and in the nineteenth century hordes were recorded as consisting of from 600 to 2,500 members.

The herders killed their stock for meat only during rituals. Milk was their staple food, men drinking cows' milk and women and children ewes' milk. They also hunted game and fished, and collected berries, roots and honey, which last was used to brew mead. They gelded some of their oxen and rode them, fastening a bridle to a stick passed through the cartilage of the animal's nose. In this they were more advanced than the Bantu-speaking people of the north.

Camps consisted of a circle of huts usually surrounded by a fence of brushwood within which the cattle were enclosed at night; but the animals were trained to lie within a circle whether there was a fence or not. Camps were occupied by the men of one clan[2] together with their wives and children and servants, the last sometimes Bushmen. A number of such clans together with their adherents made up a horde, which was an independent political unit with a kinship base, but including some non-kinsmen. The clans within a horde sometimes moved separately and split off to form an independent horde of their own. The nature of all this can be discovered from studies in the last century in Namaqualand on the west coast where there is sufficient pasture for herds. It is less arid than the desert called 'Great Bushmanland' immediately to the east and still suited to fat-tailed sheep. In 1863 the Nama there consisted of seven hordes; the dominant clans of five of these claimed descent from brothers, and the

---

[1] P. V. Tobias in *Anthropos*, 57 (1962), 'On the increasing stature of the Bushman.'

[2] Descendants of a common ancestor of the male line.

clans of the other two were later offshoots from one of the five.

Hottentots are more attentive to history than Bushmen and are found to think in terms of lineages. For example, a chief near Saldanha Bay asked a Dutch captain whether he was descended like himself from a great family; and a Hottentot woman is recorded as saying, 'We Khoikhoin, if we are in trouble always go and pray at the graves of our ancestors.'

Disputes were heard before all the men of a camp assembled under the leadership of the senior kinsman of the clan. The chief of the horde, sitting with the heads of the clans, tried disputes between members of different clans and could sentence a man to death: but his authority was limited in that he could not interfere in disputes between members of the same clan. These were settled by the head of the clan without appeal to the chief of the horde. Although the authority of a Hottentot chief was less than that of the Bantu chiefs to the north, nevertheless, if arbitration in disputes is taken as the role of a chief, then the institution of chieftainship may be said to have emerged with these yellow-skinned herders of South Africa.

The Bushmen did not play a major role in the subsequent history of South Africa largely because they showed themselves unassimilable into the European community. There was, of course, some assimilation. There had been between the Bushmen and Hottentots before the Europeans arrived. Van der Stel on a journey to Namaqualand in 1685 recorded that every horde of Hottentots had Bushmen attached to them who were employed as hunters and honey-gatherers for the pastoral Hottentots, and acted as scouts and generally served their masters. The artist, Thomas Baines, shows something of the nature of their relationship in his nineteenth-century painting of a Namaqua Hottentot on a riding-ox with his Bushman – 'the possessive pronoun is revealing'.[1]

Some Bushmen bands remained wholly independent for a time; others attached themselves intermittently or permanently to Hottentots and Europeans. It was where land and game were plentiful that the hunters remained independent,

[1] Monica Wilson – p. 63, *Oxford History of South Africa*.

but where population grew more dense and game was shot
out by men with firearms, the bow-and-arrow Bushmen
hunters could no longer subsist. They stole cattle and sheep
and were themselves shot as thieves, or they became servants
of Hottentots and White farmers. When in bands, they often
proved such bad neighbours that both White settlers and
Hottentots turned on them without mercy and drove them
off. They fought back furiously and tenaciously, but many
were killed over the years, and the rest dispersed. They were
forced to withdraw deep into the interior to avoid extermination, and even there quickly disintegrated as formed bands.
Some elements, of course, were assimilated. Bushmen children were sometimes taken home by members of commandos
to be brought up and apprenticed as farm servants – 'tame
Bushmen' the farmers called them. Those Bushmen who
grew up on farms were absorbed into the mixed Coloured
community. Individuals like Andries Waterboer even became
chiefs of Coloured communities, so that it would be wrong to
imply that Bushpeople had no influence at all on the history
of South Africa. Moreover, there are still some existing
Bushmen bands. These are in South-West Africa, Botswana
and Angola, and are probably the descendants of remnants
of the vanguard of the great early Bushmen movement to the
south, who never got further south than these areas. In South-
West Africa, where there are the largest numbers, reserves
have been established, and attempts are made to teach
Bushmen a more static way of life and to provide school
facilities for them.

The Hottentots had more influence on the history of South
Africa than the Bushmen. Following skirmishes over the years
with the Europeans at the Cape, many of the local hordes
disintegrated. In 1707 Kolb noted that the Gunjerman
horde, whose land had been taken, lived now among the
Dutch. Once their land became unavailable they broke up
into smaller groups and attached themselves to the Europeans. No longer independent, they slowly ceased to speak
their own language or follow their own traditional way of
life. Dutch in the modified form of Afrikaans became their
language; European habits became their habits. Already

horsemen, they became skilled also in the use of firearms and fought alongside Europeans against the Xhosa on the eastern frontier of Cape Colony. By 1808, according to Moodie, a hundred men from one village of 800 inhabitants were serving in the Cape Regiment. Marais states that they sometimes outnumbered Whites on commando. In their own accounts it is recorded that remnants of Cape Hottentot hordes retreated eastwards, and having encroached on the Xhosa, emerged as the Gona of the Frontier region. Others, moving northwards to the neighbourhood of the Orange, became the Kora[1] tribe of those parts, encroaching on Bushmen territory. Meanwhile, the Nama horde on the west coast were pushed northwards across the Orange to areas where they still live in something like their old manner. Besides the Kora, the Bastards and Griquas and others of mixed blood formed something approaching viable communities on the Orange and in the Eastern Frontier area. They will be met with later, contesting control of the area with Moshesh's South Sotho remnants based on Thaba Bosiu in what was Basutoland and is now called Lesotho, and with the Voortrekkers as they surged north round the west flank of the Xhosa during the Great Trek period. Adam and Cornelius Kok of Hottentot origin and Andries Waterboer with Bushman blood were some of the leaders responsible for creating these Coloured communities athwart the Orange.

Many Hottentots moved away from the Cape; many more were killed off in smallpox epidemics and other European-brought diseases; but their descendants, and people partially descended from them, provide the bulk of the two million Coloureds of South Africa. These Coloureds, are Bushmen and Hottentots and descendants of Whites and Hottentots and various slave groups from Madagascar, Delagoa Bay and Indonesia. Also included in the Coloureds are the pure Malays.

---

[1] Khora, Corans, Coranna, Koranna are other names for them. Some of them were almost bandits.

Chapter 4

The Bantu

The Sotho language group of tribes lived mostly on the high plateau, and the Nguni group in the coastal sector; but of all the Bantu tribes and clans it was the Zulus in the eastern coastal sector, between the White Umfolozi and Tugela rivers, who had the most influence on the course of history. In the building of his Zulu empire at the beginning of the nineteenth century Chief Shaka waged total war against neighbouring tribes, destroying some and causing the mass migration of others. Once Shaka had conquered an enemy he aimed at removing any capacity for further resistance by eliminating the ruling family and, when expedient, by killing all the older men and many of the women and children. Usually uninjured young men were incorporated into Zulu regiments, and young women became Zulu wives. Those tribes which avoided destruction moved away to north or south or up on to the high plateau; and they caused more destruction and migration wherever they went. For example, Matiwane, Chief of the Ngwane, who lived a hundred miles north of Zululand, fled south-west and fell on the Hlubi. The Hlubi split. Some with other disorganized refugees moved down the length of the coastal plain and sought refuge among the Xhosa on the eastern border of Cape Colony. Here they came to be known as Mfengu or Fingos, from a word meaning 'beggar'. The other branch turned north, crossed the Drakensberg and attacked the southern Sotho tribes. Meanwhile, the Ngwane first occupied the territory vacated by the Hlubi; but in 1822 they were

60

displaced when Shaka invaded and drove them across the Drakensberg in the wake of the northern branch of the Hlubi. The Sotho community on the plateau, which bore the brunt of these Nguni invasions, was the large Tlokwa chiefdom. This was ruled by MaNthatisi, the widow of the deceased chief, pending the accession of her young son Sikonyela. The Tlokwa lived near the source of the Limpopo, some two hundred miles west of the original Ngwane tribal area, and on the other side of the Drakensberg – see map. The Hlubi and Ngwane drove the Tlokwa from their kraals and seized their grain and cattle.

For the next two years powerful hordes of Ngwane, Hlubi and Tlokwa, having been set in motion by the Zulus, devastated the southern high veld, dispersing inhabitants, colliding with one another, losing and gaining adherents and disrupting every Sotho community between the Vaal and the Orange. Thousands of inhabitants fled, some to the north where they caused destruction beyond the Vaal, others to the south-west where they obtained a footing among the Coloureds along the Orange in the settlements of Andries Waterboer and Adam Kok and Cornelius Kok, or joined Moshesh (Moshweshwe) on his mountain-top state in Basutoland, or took service with White farmers at the Cape, or went to live among the Xhosa on the Colony's eastern frontier. In most of the Vaal–Orange region itself old settlements were abandoned, stock destroyed, fields ceased to be cultivated, and in several places the landscape was littered with human bones. In certain areas demoralized survivors wandered round singly or in small groups, contriving to live on game or veld plants. Even cannibalism was widespread. This was the *Difaqane* or 'forced migration' period which fortuitously cleared much of the high veld of population and provided empty settlement areas for the Voortrekkers from Cape Colony when they moved north in the Great Trek in 1834.

By this time some sort of cohesion had come about. In the north, Sobhuza, a Nguni chief of the Dlamini clan, akin to the Hlubi, who ruled from 1815 to 1836, retreated to defensible positions in the mountains north of the Pongola, absorbed

Sotho as well as Nguni chiefdoms, created an army on Zulu lines and laid the foundation of what later became known as the Swazi kingdom – named after Sobhuza's son, Mswazi, who ruled from about 1840 to 1868.

Although Shaka was dead by 1828, his successor Dingane maintained law and order in a large part of the northern coastal sector. The Zulus had cleared of population an area to the south of Zululand in what is now Natal. The cattle had been removed and the grain destroyed; thousands of people had been killed; others had fled; some had been absorbed into the Zulu nation; community life virtually ceased. Only Bushmen bands managed to maintain some sort of existence in the foothills of the Drakensberg, and a few thousand Nguni in small groups in the bush, living on roots, game, fish and even, as on the high veld in a similar depopulated area, on human flesh. The Zulus' reasons for initiating and maintaining this devastation seems to have been to provide a buffer zone to the south between them and the advancing White people from the Cape. It had, however, the opposite effect to what they had planned. In the event, the Voortrekkers were tempted in over the Drakensberg from the north, and the British arrived by sea and settled near the coast.

To the south of the empty area, the Bhaca chiefs had brought together a group of clans under their paramountcy, and beyond them were Chief Faku's Pondo and the Thembu. To the south again lay the heavily populated Xhosa tribal area. Here there had been considerable disarray caused by tribal factions – and pressure from the Europeans of Cape Colony – but nothing like the destruction on the high veld.

On the high veld Moshesh gathered together remnants of victims of the *Difaqane* and formed a nation based around his mountain-top village on Thaba Bosiu in Basutoland. The Coloured states along the Orange, with the support of their resident missionaries, also managed to maintain their identity and hold off the marauders of the *Difaqane* by means of their superior skill with firearms, but some of these Coloured groups seemed little more than robber bands. A late arrival on the high veld was Mzilikazi, Chief of the Kumalo, western neighbours of the Zulus. Mzilikazi had served as a general in Shaka's army; but he quarrelled with his master and fled over the Drakensberg to spread his own trail of destruction. His followers came to be called Matabele or Ndbele. After making long treks north, and then west, he established a powerful military kingdom on the lines of Shaka's, first in the area of present-day Pretoria, and later further west on the Marico River.

The most significant figure among the Nguni on the coastal plain was Shaka, King of the Zulus from 1787 to 1828. Shaka was the son of Senzangakhona, a chief of the Zulu clan. His mother was Nandi, a member of the neighbouring Langeni. The chief had fallen in love while watching her bathing in a woodland pool. Young Zulu warriors were not allowed to marry, but all could release sexual tension by love-making with unmarried girls of other clans, provided phallic contact was limited. Fired by Nandi's beauty, the chief asked for this privilege, which was readily granted. Both parties paid too little attention to the rules governing casual intercourse, and three months later Nandi was pregnant. At first it was suggested that Nandi's menstrual irregularity was caused by an iShaka intestinal beetle. When this diagnosis was proved wrong and a child was born he was called Shaka. The union was regularized, for though young, Senzangakhona as a chief was already married, and Nandi was taken as a junior wife. However, she soon lost favour, and so was expelled with her child. Shaka's childhood was first spent among his mother's people. This was an unhappy period as there were recriminations because of the circumstances of his birth. Next they went to live with Mtetwa relatives on the coast, where Shaka worked happily as a herdboy and later joined the Mtetwa army.

Not much is known about Dingiswayo, the Chief of the Mtetwa. He is thought to have had contact with Europeans during a period of exile and learnt much from studying their ways. Certainly he became an outstanding leader and built up an empire by taking neighbouring tribes under his protection and making himself their paramount. This he achieved partly by force, but more often by negotiation. In the wars of conquest Shaka was one of Dingiswayo's most successful generals. His main opponents were the Buthelezi, who lived in the west near the Drakensberg, and Chief Zwide's Ndwandwe in the north. Against both these peoples the Mtetwa were successful; but Zwide was not sufficiently subdued to bring the Ndwandwe into the Mtetwa empire, even temporarily.

About 1816 Shaka's father died, and his appointed successor having been murdered, with the help of Dingiswayo Shaka became the Zulus' chieftain. From the start he acted vigorously, meeting out instant death to any who disobeyed him; and a half-brother, Dingane, returning with some idea of disputing the chieftainship, recognized how formidable Shaka was, dropped whatever he had in mind for the time, and made obeisance.

Dingiswayo's military successes were the result of the careful organization and training of his warriors. He had conscripted all the young men of his Mtetwa tribe into a standing army and placed them in regiments of the same age-group, each regiment wearing different dress and using shields with hides of distinctive colours. This appears to have given Dingiswayo an advantage over his neighbours, and was one of the means by which he built his empire. Shaka decided to follow his example. He inherited a rabble of 500, but as he was not content to remain the ruler of a minor clan like his father, he decided to create a large disciplined force to expand his inheritance. Thus Shaka called up the whole male population. Setting aside the older men and enrolling the young boys as baggage carriers and medical orderlies, he placed the rest in four regiments arranged by age, each regiment having, like Dingiswayo's, a different headdress and a distinctive shield. In Shaka's army this was usually a variation of black and white. Shaka's own shield was white with a black blob in the middle. Each regiment had its own military kraal under the control of its officers and one of Shaka's aged female relatives. At his own headquarters at Bulawayo was the military kraal of the uFasimba regiment, which was formed in 1818. This consisted of young warriors who had seen some service, and herdboys fresh from their years in the open. It became Shaka's favourite regiment. Shaka allowed only the older men to marry, and these formed the reserve. They were the only ones permitted to wear the headring donned previously by fully mature males prior to marriage. This ring, unique to Zulus, was made by sewing a fibre circlet into the hair and plastering it into place with beeswax. The ring was then greased and polished and the hair round it shorn. Restricting this popular distinctive adornment to the older men of the reserve caused a certain amount of discontent; but Shaka subjected his army to such iron discipline and vigorous training that it soon became without equal among the Bantu kingdoms.

Shaka's battle tactics were well conceived, and it was these, combined with the careful organization outlined above, which brought success. He evolved his tactics while still serving as a general in Dingiswayo's army. For an attack he formed up his strongest body as a *Chest* which closed with the enemy and held them fast. Then two flank formations like *Horns* moved out and surrounded the enemy, and ideally, when their tips met, attacked from the rear. The fourth body known as the *Loins* was placed in reserve behind the *Chest*, sometimes sitting with their backs to the fight waiting to be called for. A ploy he developed early on was to arm his men with stabbing spears. At first he used the traditional throwing spears for this purpose, but soon developed a short-bladed spear made by blacksmiths to his own design. Then he trained his warriors to close with the enemy instead of standing back, and hook the enemy's shield with their own, expose his chest, and stab him through the heart. Shaka also made his men relinquish their traditional sandals and go barefoot for greater mobility. He always sought to achieve surprise; he also made ingenious use of spies and smoke signals; all in all, he seems to have been well in advance of his time in generalship.

So long as Dingiswayo survived, Shaka was a loyal subordinate, limiting his own conquests to small local chiefdoms. Early on he overran and crushed his mother's Langeni tribe. Ordering the inhabitants to be brought before him he singled out those who had illtreated his mother and himself when they had sought refuge there after being expelled from his father's kraal. He dealt with these harshly, ordering some to be clubbed to death, and others to suffer the ghastly torture of impalation. Another tribe to be attacked were the Buthelezi whom Shaka had fought against when serving under Dingiswayo.

In 1818 Dingiswayo was persuaded to visit Zwide's kraal almost unaccompanied, and was made prisoner and put to death. This was a sad end for one of the greatest and most beneficent of the Nguni empire-builders; but it had advantages for Shaka, for very soon he joined the whole Mtetwa kingdom to his own. With this large extension to his dominions he became paramount of almost all the tribes of the northern coastal region. Only Zwide's Ndwandwe and their subject tribes remained outside his sway.

The Ndwandwe did not wait for the Zulus to strike. Instead, they invaded Zululand itself. The conflict to decide the hegemony of the northern coastal section was fought just south of the White Umfolozi River at Gqokli Hill. The Zulus formed a strong defensive circle all round the top of the hill and sent forward detachments to impede the enemy as they crossed the river. Unconsciously Shaka seems to have adopted similar tactics to Wellington at Waterloo, but using a battle circle instead of a square. The Ndwandwe managed to cross the river, but in spite of several gallant attempts failed to storm the hill. When it was obvious that they were drawing away, Shaka sent out the two *Horns* on either flank in traditional style and drove them from the field, and then over the river.

The period of Shaka's life which has just been described is not documented. The little that is known about it has come down by word of mouth, and must be treated with reserve. In 1824, however, Lieutenant Farewell, late RN, and Henry Francis Fynn paid a visit to Shaka's kraal and in his journal Fynn has described his experiences there. The distance from their base at Port Natal to Shaka's kraal at Bulawayo was over a hundred miles. The first half of the trek was tedious; but Shaka, having been warned of their visit, sent one of his chiefs to organize the second half, so that was more enjoyable. The chief, Mbikana, arranged each day's journey, and did not take the direct route but led them via the military kraals of Shaka's regiments. Fynn writes that he was astonished at the order and discipline maintained in the country through which they travelled. The military kraals showed, according to him, that 'cleanliness was the rule'. Messengers passed three or four times a day between Shaka and Mbikana, inquiring and reporting on the visitors' progress, until on nearing Shaka's vast capital the two leaders were told to move on ahead of the rest towards the royal kraal. On arrival, they were warmly received by Shaka himself. Then, having each been presented with a large elephant tusk, there followed a display of dancing and singing by several regiments of warriors and girls. Each of the latter carried a wand, and according to Fynn, were exceedingly well drilled.

On the following day Shaka received the White men's presents. These consisted of every kind of beads at that time procurable in Cape Town, and, according to the chief, superior to those he had previously got from the Portuguese at Delagoa Bay. There were also woollen blankets, brass lacquered bars, sheets of copper, pigeons, cats, dogs and a pig; but the most acceptable present appeared to be a full-dress military coat with epaulettes covered in gold lace. Though Shaka showed little open gratitude, he was clearly more than satisfied. He was very interested in the live animals, especially the pig; that is, until it got into his milk store and committed great havoc and set all the women in the seraglio screaming for help.

While at the royal kraal the visitors noted with horror that men were being taken off to be strangled. On a mere sign from Shaka, such as pointing his finger, the victim was seized by his nearest neighbours, his neck was twisted, and he was beaten with knobbed sticks. Each day a number were killed, or knocked senseless and their bodies carried to an adjoining hill and impaled. They visited this spot on the fourth day and found it a true Golgotha, swarming with vultures.

The sight of these horrors made them decide to leave as soon as possible; but when they announced their intention

67

to do so, Shaka insisted on Fynn staying for a time on his own. While Fynn was at the royal kraal after the others had left, an attempt on the life of Shaka occurred, and he was called in to dress the king's wound. The would-be assassins, who managed to escape, were thought to have been sent by Zwide, King of the Ndwandwe; but by this time Shaka was becoming unpopular even with his own people because of his cruelty. From the start, he had disciplined them through fear; but as the years passed he became more and more capricious, seemingly becoming mentally unbalanced. He forced his warriors to remain unmarried until they were forty because he believed they would fight better without home ties. He killed any who displeased him, and he sent out his armies to destroy without mercy even the women and children of neighbouring tribes. The trader Nathaniel Isaacs, who visited the royal kraal with Fynn, was of the opinion that Shaka by this time had no redeeming quality and was, 'in war an insatiable and exterminating savage, and in peace was an unrelenting and ferocious despot who kept his subjects in awe by his monstrous executions'. On the death of his mother Nandi, Shaka's mind seems to have given way completely, for besides other irrational edicts, he decreed that as a token of respect for the departed queen all sexual intercourse should cease, and that women found pregnant within the period of twelve cycles of the moon would be put to death along with their husbands. During the year following his mother's death, besides losses in war-like expeditions, a vast number of people were killed when they failed to comply with his edicts. Thus, many began to wonder how long they 'could continue to tolerate a king who craved not only the blood of his enemies, but also that of his own people'.

The end came in 1828 through the King's half-brothers Dingane and Mhlangana. While most of the warriors were away on a warlike expedition, the brothers with a few companions returned secretly to Shaka's new capital Dukusa in the south. Finding the King in the cattle-kraal, sitting wrapped in a kaross admiring his herds, they came up behind him and hid themselves behind a hedge to wait until he was alone. Then they fell upon him, plunging their assegais into his body. Turning in amazement at the unexpected attack and seeing Dingane's spear poised for a second thrust, Shaka staggered to the kraal gate leaving his bloodsoaked kaross on the floor of the cattle-fold. A few paces beyond the gate he stumbled and fell. He was dispatched by one of Dingane's companions, who thrust an assegai deep into the King's body.

The outstanding personality on the high veld was Moshesh. Moshesh's father was the chief of a Sotho clanlet living in the Caledon valley which had to pay a tribute of cattle to a local tribe. Moshesh first rose to fame in 1815, a year when South Africa was suffering from one of its periodic severe droughts. The drought had destroyed the crops and herds in the Caledon valley so that Moshesh's father was unable to produce the necessary tribute for his overlord, and Moshesh was sent on a raid on a distant tribe to get the necessary cattle. Everything went well for Moshesh on the expedition. He managed to cut out many head from his victims' herds, and bring them back safely; and on his return journey when he clashed with the overlord's warriors, he defeated them decisively, and freed his clanlet from bondage. Moshesh had proved himself and gained a footing, and a few years later, when the clanlet split into two factions, he took one of them away to new territory which had been given him by his father-in-law near Butha-Buthe hill to the east of the Caledon River.

Soon after Moshesh had established himself as chief of his own clanlet, news came of the approach of a marauding column set in motion in the *Difaqane*. What was worse, it seemed that Queen MaNthatesi, accompanied by her son Sikonyela and 40,000 Tlokwa, was advancing towards Butha-Buthe hill on the summit of which Moshesh had gathered his people and their cattle. They had heard terrifying tales of the Tlokwa and their queen, who was said to be possessed of an evil spirit and whose warriors drank from her huge pendulous breasts. Watching from his hill-top sanctuary, Moshesh saw the Tlokwa warriors approaching.

Dressed in black lion skins, black mantles and capes, and with black headdresses, they looked formidable indeed. Although Moshesh had fortified Butha-Buthe hill against such an attack, and was confident his stores of grain would outlast the longest siege, he realized that if the large force of Tlokwa persevered long enough nothing could prevent them reaching the top of the hill. Not even the boulders his people intended rolling down would stop their advance.

In the event, Moshesh came out of the affair well, for the Tlokwa were more interested in stocking up than fighting a pitched battle. They cut out some head of cattle from Moshesh's outlying herds and then swerved off into the sorghum fields and started harvesting the ripened crops. They were being followed by a Zulu impi and could not risk delay. Moshesh then used the diplomacy which was in the future to serve him well. Learning that the Zulu impi following the Tlokwa had intended to attack Butha-Buthe, he sent messengers with gifts suggesting they turn instead on the Tlokwa who by this time were laden with cattle stolen from his herds. The Zulus conveniently followed Moshesh's advice and the two marauding columns then fought it out between themselves and left Moshesh in peace.

Meanwhile, two of Moshesh's people had returned from an excursion to the south with news of a flat-topped hill nestling in the heart of an immense fertile valley, which would serve the tribe better as a sanctuary than Butha-Buthe. Delighted to learn of this natural fortress not far away, Moshesh moved all his peoples to it.

This hill, Thaba Bosiu,[1] had a large flat summit, 350 feet high, which was reached only by steep slopes terminating in sheer cliffs that were penetrated by four passes in the north and two in the south. The summit plateau provided about two square miles of pasture with perennial spring water, and Moshesh built his main villages there, and made it the heartland of his tribe. It became so secure that his fame spread far and wide as the great chief of the mountain.

On Thaba Bosiu Moshesh withstood a fierce attack by a

[1] Thaba Bosigo on modern maps.

Ngwane force, and even repelled the mighty Matabele, his warriors rolling boulders down on them as they tried to scale the cliffs. Soon bands began to settle round the base of Thaba Bosiu consisting of a rabble of emaciated, hunger-crazed *Difaqane* refugees and small local clans seeking protection. Moshesh welcomed them all, and even incorporated cannibals into his growing tribe.

Moshesh enhanced his standing by taking wives from many different local chiefly families, and he formed alliances with more distant chiefs like Shaka and Moorosi, paying tribute to the former to keep on terms with the powerful Zulus. Moorosi had once been a great chief, but had been robbed of most of his possessions during the *Difaqane*. He was an expert at raiding and cattle stealing and sought an alliance for the purpose of making joint forays. Early on they set out together on a distant raid on the Nguni Thembu, who lived far to the south on the coastal plain, almost in Xhosa country. The Thembu chief thought they were Zulus sent by Shaka, and went into hiding with his people in some bush-clad hills. Moshesh and Moorosi looted the deserted kraals, and finding the hill slopes teeming with cattle, goats and sheep, rounded them up. Soon a vast stream of captured animals were on their way northwards under escort, bound for Thaba Bosiu.

By the summer of 1829 an estimated five thousand people, drawn from a dozen or more distinct Sotho-speaking clans, were living on or in the immediate vicinity of Thaba Bosiu under Moshesh. Because of their mixed nature, they began to drop their clan names and refer to themselves as Basotho and to Moshesh's domain as Lesotho. For a long while Europeans, however, called them Basutos and the country Basutoland. Recently, as an independent state, it became Lesotho again.

About this time Moshesh's stronghold was subject to two attacks by bands of Coloureds. The first, by a Hottentot Kora group of bandits, was dealt with easily as the Kora conveniently got drunk the night before the attack in their camp at the base of the hill, and Moshesh's warriors were able to catch them unawares and kill all of them, except the leader

Hendrik Hendriks and his servant, who got away. The second attack by a band of mixed-bred Griquas had more serious consequences. These stole many head of Moshesh's choicest cattle, and when an attempt was made by Moshesh's men to reclaim them, the Griquas opened fire and killed a large number of his warriors.

The set-back caused Moshesh seriously to think. Even the formidable Thaba Bosiu would not be able to hold out against fire-power such as this. His next plan therefore was to try to come to terms with the Kora and Griqua, and he sent envoys saying he was willing to pay tribute in return for their friendship. The envoys never reached their destination. They were captured and killed by Kora brigands on their way, and Moshesh, having tried several times without success to make friends with his troublesome neighbours, sought another solution. He believed that if he could get hold of some horses and guns he could face the Coloureds on equal terms. Moshesh in fact had learnt to ride. A herd stolen by Moorosi had included a chestnut mare originally taken from a white man at Dordrecht, and one of Moorosi's men had taught Moshesh to ride. Eventually the Basutos became renowned horsemen and breeders of horses and ponies (Basuto ponies were used by the Boers in the Anglo–Boer war). It was about this time that Moshesh learnt that a friendly Griqua named Adam Krotz, whom the Kora bandits seemed to leave alone, might supply him with guns; but when Krotz was persuaded to visit Moshesh's kraal he refused to do so. Instead he suggested that it was because he was a Christian that the bandits did not molest him. He said that Moshesh would do better to get some missionaries to live at his kraal. They would ensure peace better than guns; they had done so already in some of the neighbouring Coloured states. Moshesh was disappointed about the guns, but took Krotz's advice and dispatched a request to the central missionary station at Griquatown for some missionaries to be sent to teach his people. In 1833 two members of the Paris Evangelical Missionary Society arrived in Griquatown to the west, and while they were there, Moshesh's request arrived. The missionaries, Thomas Arbousset and Eugène Casilis, took the news as a divine sign and hastened to Thaba Bosiu.

For the rest of his long reign Moshesh had the support of Christian friends and advisers living in his midst. Sustained by them he saw the strange agglomeration of peoples who formed his kingdom grow in size and prosperity. But trial and tribulation were by no means ended. Besides having to cope with squabbles and disturbances among his ill-assorted clans, two new mighty foes attacked him, the Boers and the British. Eventually Moshesh sought the protection of Britain and his state became a British Protectorate. This move enabled Basutoland to become one of the first self-governing, Non-White states in South Africa. With Swaziland, which was first under Boer and then under British protection, it became a prototype for the Bantu Homelands of the Transkei and Zululand.

In Xhosa country, on the eastern frontier of Cape Colony, no chief could control the large number of sub-tribes. The Xhosa tribes first on the frontier, like the Ndlambe and Gqunukwebe, who moved west of the Fish River, found the task of living alongside White people and absorbing Hottentot bands into their society more than they could manage. Also they were at enmity with Gaika the area chief, and Gaika, although he acknowledged Hintsa as paramount, acted independently of him. Thus, although according to Colonel Collins, as quoted by Moodie, Hintsa was able to maintain law and order in the territory immediately under his control 'without ever condemning any person to death', Xhosa country as a whole was in a state of civil war and confusion.

Sir Harry Smith fought against the Xhosa in the Frontier War of 1835, and afterwards was given the task of administering the new buffer state of British Kaffraria before the British Government disallowed its continuance. In his autobiography he describes the way of life of the Xhosa. According to his experience, the witch-doctors and rain-makers, who were in the confidence of their respective chiefs, acted as a kind of Inquisition. Whenever a rich or powerful

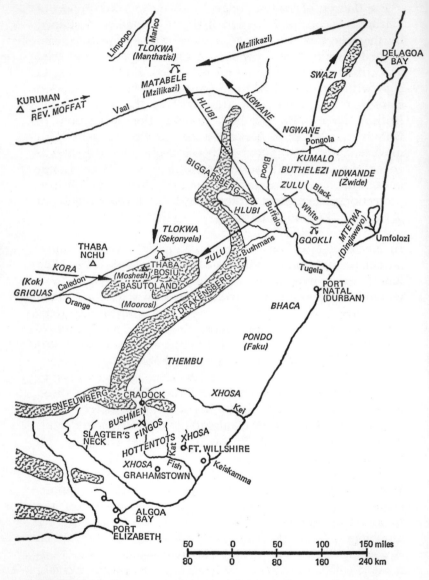

Map III   The Native Peoples *circa* 1830–60

person became obnoxious to the chief the witch-doctors called
a witch-dance to smell him out as one who was practising
evil magic, special care being taken to summon the individual
upon whom it was intended to fix the crime. An old woman,
completely naked, did the smelling out while the assembled
people danced round her. After a variety of gesticulations the
old woman approached the individual already named to her
secretly by the chief. As she approached him, she literally
smelled him, and then proclaimed him the culprit. If he were
rich in cattle and not particularly obnoxious the chief and
his councillors might be satisfied with 'eating him up' –
appropriating his herds. If the chief wanted to have him
removed completely, however, he would be tortured and
killed, one method employed for this being the customary
Bantu one of hurling the victim over a precipice. Sir Harry
Smith managed to get the people on his side by restraining
the witch-doctors, proving that the rain-makers were
charlatans, and abolishing unpopular traditional customs.
One of these was the festival of the rape of the virgins, at
which the maidens were assembled before the chiefs and sub-
chiefs so that they might chose those they fancied for a short
period before returning them to their families. Sir Harry
Smith had enlisted as his personal adviser a wise old man of
the Xhosa who had been Gaika's chief councillor. He told
Sir Harry Smith that by putting an end to this unpopular
festival, the British had a chance of winning the hearts of the
people. He added that many fathers of families had told him
that they would welcome its suppression. Its removal, therefore, met with much satisfaction, and strengthened the British
representative's hold over the border tribes for a time.

British Kaffraria did not last long, and although it was
reconstituted when Sir Harry Smith became Governor in
1848, real peace was a long time coming to the eastern
frontier and a long series of Kaffir wars continued at intervals.
In 1857, however, in the 'cattle-killing' episode, the Xhosa
so weakened themselves that eventual European dominance
was made certain. This 'cattle-killing' was a typical primitive
manifestation; but that made it no less tragic, and it was a
horrible, unnecessary affair, bringing death or misery to

thousands. According to J. A. Chalmers[1] and C. Brownlee,[2] who were both in the area, in March 1856 a number of past heroes were seen in a vision, first by a young girl and then by her uncle, a councillor of Chief Sarili. Much of the girl's vision was in traditional idiom, for she said she saw these men and the horns of beautiful oxen coming up through the rushes in a stream. In terms of Xhosa mythology, such a revelation demanded great sacrifices, and then it would bring untold benefit. If sacrifices were made, more past heroes would rise from the dead to provide the Xhosa people with an abundance of grain, cattle, wagons, clothes, guns and ammunition. First, however, all the present grain and cattle had to be destroyed; only then would the new abundance be sure to come. Then, too, a great wind would sweep the Whites into the sea. Paramount Chief Sarili next had a vision which confirmed that of the others and added additional predictions: he saw a famous horse long dead, and was told that the Mfengu and unbelievers among his own people would be destroyed, as well as the Whites.

Surprisingly, this was sufficient to start a wave of grain destruction and cattle-killing which almost destroyed the Xhosa people and weakened them for decades. At least 150,000 cattle were killed, to no effect except that by February 1857 the whole countryside was starving. In spite of mighty rescue operations by Governor Grey of Cape Colony, the population of this region dropped from some 104,000 to 37,000. One consequence of this disaster was that the British were able to consolidate their control over the area.

The Dlamini people, who are the dominant lineage in Swaziland, once lived in the region about Delagoa Bay. Their eighteenth-century ruler, Chief Ngwane II, set up villages on the north bank of the Pongola. In caves among tree-covered hills, he and later kings were buried, and annual pilgrimages are still made to their graves. The present Swazi King Sobhuza II is of the same line.

[1] Author of *Tiyo Soga* (Edinburgh 1877).
[2] Author of *Reminiscences of Kaffir Life and History*, 1896.

Ngwane II's grandson, Sobhuza I, built up a powerful tribe which he ruled in the manner of Shaka, any insubordination meeting with instant death. Sobhuza, however, also used the art of diplomacy like Moshesh. All around were mighty nations like the Mtetwa under Dingiswayo, the Zulus under Shaka and the Ndwandwe under Zwide; and Sobhuza devised a policy of avoiding conflicts with stronger tribes, and sending his warriors against weaker ones. To Dingiswayo he paid tribute; to Shaka he sent two of his own daughters as wives – and made no protest when they were murdered. After a brief attempt to hold the fertile lands along the Pongola against Zwide's forces, he realized they were too powerful and moved into what is now Swaziland. He settled his people along the valley of the Little Usutu close to the Mdimba mountains where Swazi royal kraals are still mainly built. Sobhuza further placated Zwide by taking one of his daughters, Tandile, as main wife, and it was from their union that sprang the line of subsequent Swazi kings.

The territory into which Sobhuza moved his people was already occupied by small Nguni and Sotho clans. These Sobhuza subdued and incorporated into his tribe. When Zulu impis attacked, he ordered his people to hide in mountain caves until they went away, and was prepared to sacrifice many of his cattle to the invaders. When Sobhuza's son, Mswazi, succeeded in 1840 the tribe already consisted of some seventy clans. Mswazi's name modified to Swazi became the title of the new nation. Mswazi made the tribe more powerful still by creating a national army in Zulu style and raiding successfully with it to the north. However, the Swazi still continued to be harried from the south, so Mswazi asked the British to intervene on their behalf. Meanwhile, the Boers were encroaching on his kingdom, and in 1860 the first land concession was granted to a Boer. From then on this policy of freely granting concessions of land, mineral rights and trading rights to the two European powers became traditional, with the result that Swaziland became a pawn between the Boers and the British. This situation, however, eventually developed to Swaziland's

77

advantage, for, largely because of it, Swaziland became one of the first independent Bantu national states.

After Mzilikazi quarrelled with Shaka he fled north, blazing a trail of terror and destruction. Along with 300 warriors and a few women and children he passed through Swaziland, and then over the Drakensberg. Brushing off some Zulu pursuers and persuading other Zulus to join him, he seized cattle and acquired fresh adherents as he travelled. Over the mountains, his band, which came to be called Matabele or Ndebele,[1] raided Sotho villages, captured young women and impressed young men in Zulu style. In 1823 the Matabele settled in Pedi country on the upper Oliphants River, a tributary of the Limpopo which reaches the sea in Portuguese territory at Delagoa Bay. This was away from the areas affected by the *Difaqane*, and might well have satisfied them permanently; but 1825 was another year of severe drought and to escape its effects Mzilikazi moved them south-westwards to the Apies River area, near present-day Pretoria. This was once a thickly populated area; but had been devastated during the *Difaqane*. From it, Mzilikazi extended his power in all directions, sending regiments north over the Limpopo to attack the Mashona, westwards against the Coloureds and south against Moshesh's people in Basutoland. But he remained insecure, for the Coloureds retaliated and, possessing firearms, hit back hard, while a Zulu army pillaged his villages. It was the Zulus he feared most, and in July 1832 he moved west to Mosega on the Marico River, to get farther away from them.

Robert Moffat, the missionary at Kuruman, visited Mzilikazi several times, and has given a description of the Matabele kingdom. On the first journey, when the royal kraal was in the area of the Apies river, Moffat's party came upon a Bushman band near the first Matabele outpost. They were occupying tree-houses thirty feet from the ground in a group of giant trees, and when Moffat climbed up to visit them he was offered some locusts from a bowl as refreshment. Later, Moffat was to discuss the Bushpeople with the King

[1] The Sotho version of Ndebele is Matabele.

who said there were only a few scattered bands in his territory and that, as they caused him no trouble, he left them alone. Also on this journey they passed villages ruined during the *Difaqane*, some of which had been substantially constructed with plastered walls. On inquiry, he was told that the destruction was the work of the Tlokwa,[1] the Zulus and Matabele, though the Matabele denied being responsible.

Moffat described Mzilikazi's government as tyrannical in the extreme. All the people, as well as what they possessed, were considered the King's. His word was law, and he had only to lift his finger and his order was carried out. Although Mzilikazi's rule resembled Shaka's, he appears to have been a more likeable person; it was not unknown for him to show compassion and pardon offenders, an action which would have been unthinkable to Shaka. He became embarrassingly fond of Moffat, and would do almost anything for the missionary provided it did not weaken his hold over his people. Even Moffat, who was very critical and described his rule as 'horrid despotism', seems to have realized that the King had to be cruel to hold his own and maintain the ascendancy of his tribe in the savagery of Africa at that time. He supplied the discipline without which no tribe could be stable in peace or successful in war. In Matabeleland law and order prevailed. Although they plundered others, there was little or no crime within the community. The King's word was law, yet government was administered with systematic uniformity. Mzilikazi successfully maintained his kingdom on the high veld until the arrival of the Voortrekkers during the Great Trek. After its start all the Bantu communities mentioned above were one by one to feel the full effect of the European presence in southern Africa.

[1] Or Mantatees after their queen MaNthatosi, mother of Sikonyela.

Chapter 5

The Voortrekkers

One of the most significant events in the history of South Africa was the exodus of some 10,000 Cape Colonists, men, women and children, from their isolated farms in the eastern frontier areas to seek new territories in the north, where they could be free and independent. This movement of peoples was not a casual and unorganized departure from the Cape Colony as a result of grievances of a more or less materialistic nature – although these must have contributed – but rather the climax of a gradual development towards national independence over a period of a century.

The Colonists of Dutch, Huguenot and German origin who were involved were spread over a vast area hundreds of miles from Cape Town, at that time the only centre of civilization. They had grown used to meeting their own requirements and had acquired the necessary skills to fend for themselves, both on their farms and while on the move in search of new pastures. Even in the time of the United East India Company these frontier farmers had felt indignant at interference from the government in Cape Town, and with the advent of the British there had been more to unsettle them. They resented criticism of their treatment of the Hottentots; they disliked the extension of anglicization; but above all they deplored lack of support against Xhosa raiders of their farms. G. M. Theal[1] records a frontier farmer as saying that during his father's lifetime and his own they had been 'clean swept' five times by the Xhosa and that they were

[1] Emigration Documents, p. 114.

worse off than they had been fifty years before, when at least they were allowed to seek redress. Sir Harry Smith[1] also considers that it was the 1834 raids and the revocation of D'Urban's settlement that proved the turning point. His sympathy is indicated when he describes the disgruntled farmers as 'brave, patient, industrious, orderly and religious people of Dutch, Huguenot and German descent, to the number of 10,000 who, having been shamefully abandoned by the British Government, settled themselves north of the Orange, across the Vaal and in Natal'. Piet Retief's Manifesto which he made on leaving the Cape Colony on 22 January 1837 also stressed the Xhosa raids. He writes: 'We complain of the systematic and incessant plundering that we have had to endure here on the part of Kaffirs and other Coloureds, and particularly as a result of the latest invasion of the Colony which destroyed the border districts and ruined most of the inhabitants.' But Retief also states that the main reason for their departure was a desire for freedom, for he says, 'We solemnly declare that we are leaving this Colony with the desire to lead a more peaceful life than we have led until now. We shall molest no people and deprive nobody of the least property. We are leaving the Colony with the complete assurance that the English Government has no further claim on us and will allow us without further assurance to manage our own affairs in future . . .'

By the early twenties a number of colonists had reached the Orange and settled alongside the Hottentots, the Griquas, the remnants of the Tlokwa under Sikonyela, the Baralongs of Thaba Nchu and the South Sotho refugees gathered around Moshesh's kraal on Thaba Bosiu. A few had even gone as far as the Vaal, and some hunters may have visited the Transvaal and learnt of empty lands there and in Natal. Many of these Trekkers, however, did not want to sever their connections with the mother colony, and in this way were different from the Voortrekkers who were to follow them in the thirties.

While the Frontier War of 1834 was still in progress,

[1] Autobiography.

scouting parties were spying out the land in various directions. A party that travelled north-west had to confess that prospects were poor; but another which went north reached splendid grasslands, open and rolling, which appeared to stretch beyond the Vaal almost to the Limpopo. Meanwhile, Pieter Lafras Uys and his friends had gone east through Xhosa country to Natal and reported that, although the route was difficult, being cut across by rivers, Natal was 'the best country in all Africa'.

The war delayed departure. Men like Piet Retief (1780–1838), who was on good terms with Governor D'Urban, were too busy fighting to make a start. And when hostilities ended, martial law on the frontier held things up again for a further period. But by November 1835 many would-be trekkers were on the move within the northern frontier, and the first two groups had set out, one led by Louis Trigardt[1] (1783–1838) and the other by 'Long' Hans van Rensburg, both starting from the Upper Kei area (TARKA). The original plan was that each party should get away as best it could, cross the Orange, and go through Griqua Philippolis to Thaba Nchu, the kraal of the friendly Moroka, Chief of the Barolongs. Although families under chosen leaders ventured forth alone, most of them not only owed some allegiance to one or other of the principals like Piet Retief or Hendrik Potgieter, but also usually came together on the journey so that a group of fifty or sixty wagons travelled north. They went forward, forming and scattering, crossing and reuniting, and all following the same direction. There was plenty of room and plenty of time.

Louis Trigardt the first of the Voortrekkers, was the grandson of a Swede and son of a Graaff-Reinet rebel who had been marched off to the Castle in 1799. He was the wealthiest in his group, owning ten slaves while the rest had only five between them. His diary suggests that he was a good leader, patient and kind. Trigardt and some of his neighbours got on the move northwards in May 1835. His ten slaves ran away back to the Colony and freedom soon after crossing the frontier, and since Trigardt had broken the law by taking

[1] Also written 'Tregardt' and Trichardt.

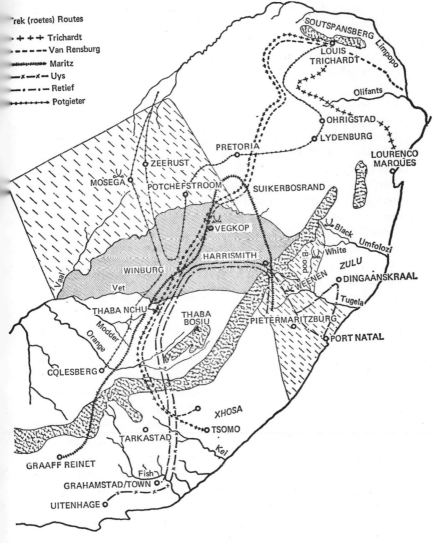

Map IV Trek (roetes) Routes

them, he forfeited all claim to compensation. His party of some fifty-two persons trekked on slowly to the Orange, and was joined by Van Rensburg's group. There were nine weapon-bearing men in Trigardt's band and ten in Van Rensburg's. There were also about thirty children with each. They moved slowly northwards together towards the Vaal. Five miles a day they went, since sheep could not do more, with long halts where water and grass were good, or when the ewes were lambing. Sometimes the two parties would keep close for mutual protection, but there was not much danger except from wild beasts. They kept well to the west of Moshesh's Sotho and Sikonyela's Tlokwa, and away from the Caledon Valley. They saw deserted kraals and dead men's bones; but not many men alive, for this was country ravaged by the Ngwane, Tlokwa, Zulu and Matabele during the *Difaqane*.

Sadly, after a time, there was such a serious quarrel between the leaders that Van Rensburg's group went off alone towards Portuguese East Africa. This led to tragedy, for on the way his people were set on by Tsonga warriors and annihilated. Trigardt's band continued towards the Soutpansberg, where they came across a friendly Venda tribe containing some half-caste children of Conrad Buys who had lived there when outlawed from the Colony. Trigardt stayed for about a year in the Soutpansberg, claiming any land he fancied and standing no nonsense about missing cattle. He would not allow the tribesmen to sleep near his settlement or approach him when armed; but he was ready to let them come and barter. Life was terribly isolated, and there were bouts of cattle sickness, but it was considered an improvement on the 'Frontier'. When gunpowder began to run low, efforts were made to get in touch with the Portuguese to the east. But replenishments were not forthcoming, and Trigardt then led the whole party down to Lourenço Marques. On the way several died of fever, and tsetse decimated the cattle. At Lourenço Marques they were treated kindly; but as a result of their privations many more died, including first Trigardt's wife and then himself. Finally a ship from Natal took off twenty-six survivors, all women and children.

Long before Trigardt's people had crossed the Vaal, Hendrik Potgieter's (1792–1852) party had set off north, along with Sarel Cilliers's, both starting from Colesberg near the Orange River. The combined group kept more to the east than Trigardt had done, and thus came in contact with the tribes in the Caledon area. They were cordially received at the Wesleyan mission station at Thaba Nchu by the resident missionary James Archbell and the Barolong Chief Moroka. Later, Potgieter met Moletsane, the chief of the Bataung and signed a treaty of friendship with him and Moroka. These peoples of the Caledon River area all spoke in awe of Mzilikazi's Matabele who lived in the Marico valley up north and preyed on all and sundry. They were glad to grant the Voortrekkers title deeds to land in exchange for a promise to protect them.

The Voortrekkers who settled temporarily alongside the Caledon tribes elected a Burgher Council and revived the traditional Dutch system of administration by *Landdrost* and *Heemraden*, which had been abolished by the Cape Government in 1828. Gerrit Maritz (1797–1838), whose group had set out from Graaff-Reinet, was chosen as Chairman and judge, and Hendrik Potgieter as Chief Commandant. At this time there was a difference of opinion among the Voortrekkers as to their final destination. In 1836, in an effort to retain control over those leaving the Colony, the Cape Government had passed an Act,[1] which gave criminal jurisdiction over all erstwhile subjects south of latitude 25°. Because of this Potgieter, who as Chief Commandant was at first the most forceful leader, was determined to find somewhere to settle beyond British jurisdiction. Therefore, although a number of Voortrekkers would have preferred to have moved towards Natal which had been so favourably reported on by Pieter Uys, because Natal was inside latitude 25°, Potgieter directed their attention towards the north. They had to wait for the arrival of Piet Retief from Grahamstown before they could attempt to settle in Natal.

· · · · ·

[1] Cape of Good Hope Punishment Act 1836.

85

In the north, the Voortrekkers soon began to encroach on territories dominated by Mzilikazi's Matabele, who were quick to react. In the same week that Potgieter with a chosen party of horsemen set out across the Vaal to search for suitable territory for settlement, the Matabele attacked and killed some members of Voortrekker families encamped on the south bank of the Vaal, and stole a number of their cattle. When Potgieter heard of this he returned quickly and set about arranging defences against further Matabele attacks. He remustered the northern and most vulnerable families in larger groups, and organized a number of strong laagers, with his own on Vegkop, a hill twenty miles south of the Vaal.

The laager at Vegkop was like an entrenched camp, fifty wagons in a ring lashed together by trek-chains with thornbushes piled in the openings and woven into the spokes of the wheels. Four wagons were drawn up in a square in the centre and roofed over with planks and raw hides, as a shelter for the women and children.[1] It was a strong place but had only forty men to defend it, so the women assisted. Each man laid out his spare guns for his wife to load, and while they waited the women cast bullets.

The little force on Vegkop had not long to wait. Early on the morning of 19 October a Bataung servant gave the alarm. After Sarel Cilliers[2] had offered up a prayer for victory, Potgieter rode out with some of his men to try and parley with the 5,000 warriors surrounding the laager. The warriors would have none of it. Leaping to their feet with a loud hiss, they trotted forward to attack. The Voortrekkers sprang from their horses, fired, mounted, reloaded and fired, again and again, falling back steadily as the enemy came on. Finally, they re-entered the wagon-ring and blocked the narrow entrance through which they had emerged. When

[1] Paul Kruger, later President of the Republic, mentions in his writings, that he took part in the battle of Vegkop at the age of eleven. In the fifth panel of the historical frieze inside the Voortrekker Memorial, Pretoria, he is depicted in the centre as a youngster with a powder horn. The boy who posed was a great-grandson of the President.

[2] Sarel Cilliers was an ex-Elder and became the Voortrekkers' most effective spiritual leader.

they were all back at their stations, Potgieter ordered them to hold their fire until the enemy were within thirty paces. Then they opened rapid fire. The Matabele swarmed round the wagons. They tore at the thorn-bushes but could not wrench them free. They tugged at the wagons but could not shift them. Those behind hurled their assegais high in the air to fall inside the laager. It was useless. The assegai was no match for the musket. The Matabele fell in heaps as volley after volley poured into them, and at length those left alive drew away; amid cheers from the defenders, cheers, however, somewhat dampened by the sight of their flocks and herds being driven off by the enemy.

Thus on 16 October the Voortrekkers won the battle of Vegkop, the first great victory in the epic story of the Trek. But although they stood victorious, they were in a sorry plight. Two of their number, both relatives of their leader, had been killed by assegais, and every third man bore a wound. Their draught animals had gone, they were short of food, and their nearest help lay far away south at Thaba Nchu. However, when a messenger was sent for relief, the friendly Moroka sent up oxen, and Gerrit Maritz furnished a guard of burghers from the large trek he had just brought to Thaba Nchu from Graaff-Reinet. With this assistance the Vegkop party were able to return slowly southwards. Tradition has it that Potgieter never forgot this act of grace on the part of the friendly chief. It is said that up to the time of his death he regularly sent presents to Moroka.

After Vegkop, Potgieter made several journeys to the north. He visited Trigardt in the Soutspansberg area, where he was convinced that the best settlement area was to be found because it was outside the jurisdiction of the Cape of Good Hope Punishment Act. But he realized that the Matabele would have to be subdued first; and finally he persuaded Gerrit Maritz and Pieter Uys to accompany him on an expedition against them. In January 1837 Potgieter's force crossed the Vaal and moved on the Matabele military post of Mosega on the Marico River, a tributary of the Limpopo. As they approached the Matabele kraals were barely discernible in the sorghum fields, and when they reached the first rows of beehive huts they were surprised to find no one astir. Then as they watched the kraal from their saddles, they saw a man crawl out of his hut to urinate beside its entrance; Potgieter raised his elephant gun and fired. This caused the warriors to come pouring out of their huts to attack, but as at Vegkop their spears were no match for Voortrekker muskets. The warriors were driven back time and time again, and many were killed. The remnants fled northwards along the valley of the Marico. By midday the entire population of Mosega was in flight and disorderly streams of fugitives were straggling away through the woods to the north.

The next main Voortrekker assault on the Matabele kingdom did not take place for several months. It came in October 1837, when Potgieter and Uys led the commando, first against the military settlement at Tshwenyane, north of Mosega, and finally against the royal kraal at Kapain along the Marico valley towards the north. Having dispersed the warriors at Tshwenyane fairly easily, and sacked the kraal, the Voortrekkers moved on against the larger forces gathering to guard the royal kraal.

The final battles of the campaign began on 7 October 1837, against this Matabele covering force. The Voortrekkers advanced in line with two groups of horsemen guarding their flanks. Slowly they moved towards the *Chest* of the waiting Matabele. Then the warriors attacked, their *Horns* spreading out and converging on the Voortrekkers' flanks. But Voortrekker horsemen on either side galloped forward to meet the tips of the *Horns*, and, firing from the saddle, blasted them asunder. Next they opened fire on the *Chest* of the Matabele crescent while the horsemen continued to shatter the *Horns*. The battle was brief but bloody. The Matabele lines buckled under the deadly musket fire, and some of the warriors broke away and formed up in groups behind. This manoeuvre, however, did not serve them well. The Voortrekkers surged forward and dispersed them, and then shot the warriors down as they scrambled away up the rocky slopes in the rear. Finally, the remnants went off in

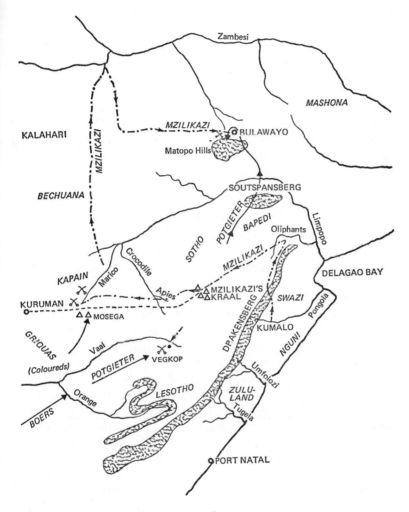

Map V The Voortrekker-Matabele War

headlong flight towards the safety of the river marshes, and from there back to the royal kraal at Kapain.

Potgieter's nine-day assault on Mzilikazi's last Transvaal stronghold at Kapain began on the morning of 4 November 1837. When the Voortrekkers reached its outskirts, they were puzzled to find before them, instead of Mzilikazi's massed fighting men, a huge herd of cattle, some being ridden. The cattle broke loose and charged the Boers, but the latter treated the animals just as they had the Matabele at Vegkop. They retreated and then turned and fired, and then retreated again and did the same thing. This had the required result. The bewildered animals turned and made off back towards the kraal, and finally dispersed to reveal ranks of warriors. These in their turn were driven back almost as easily as the cattle had been.

Kapain was the last battle of the war. Mzilikazi's women, children and old folk, with their animals and household goods, had already fled to mountain fastnesses in the north, and the final conflict was in the nature of a rearguard action to stop the Voortrekkers from pursuing them. In this it was successful, but at the cost of many casualties among the warriors. The Voortrekkers drove back the regiments guarding the kraal and then, until well into the night, they hunted down stragglers who were seeking safety among the sedge along the banks of the Marico. Returning, they set fire to the royal kraal, and then next morning they followed the Matabele right up into the rugged wooded regions of the northern Marico district. There, the Voortrekkers' horses being worn out and the terrain being so treacherous, Potgieter decided to turn back. But the result of the campaign on the Marico in 1837 was that Potgieter could claim by right of conquest all the open country north of the Vaal river from the mountains of the east to the Kalahari desert on the west. Meanwhile, Mzilikazi fled northwards across the Limpopo with his followers, and after a period of wandering a new Matabeleland was created at the expense of the local Mashona in the country which is now Rhodesia. Mzilikazi's royal kraal was established near present-day Bulawayo. He died in 1868 at the age of nearly eighty and was succeeded by Lobengula. The latter preserved a precarious independence until his people were conquered by the men of Rhodes's British South Africa Company in 1893.

By this time Piet Retief had set out from Grahamstown. At Grahamstown he had been joined by the Uys family from Uitenhage. The English settlers of the district were grieved to hear that their Dutch colleagues were leaving, and according to the *Grahamstown Journal* of 27 April 1837, because 'of the fraternal regard of the English settlers towards the Dutch colonists' a Bible was presented to the Voortrekker patriarch Jacobus Uys on their departure from the Colony on behalf of the British Settlers by Thomas Phillips, J.P.[1] (It is worthy of note that the presentation of this Bible was inserted in Panel 2 of the Historical Frieze inside the Voortrekker Monument, because, as is recorded, 'the Bible was to the devout Voortrekkers a shining light on their path'.)

In Transorangia at the time of Piet Retief's arrival in April 1837 the Burgher Council, formed in 1835 and now known as the Council of Policy, was still in being, and in June 1837 the Nine Articles of Vet River, a guidance for the government, not a constitution, were drafted and put into practice. But the leading personalities on the Council were at loggerheads, particularly the Potgieters and Uyses with the Retiefs and Maritzes. Finally, at meetings of representatives of the Voortrekkers in the neighbourhood of present-day Winburg, Maritz was confirmed in his offices as President and Judge, and Retief was chosen as Governor and Chief Commandant. With the exclusion of Potgieter and Uys, Retief became the leading figure among the Voortrekkers, and he directed their attention towards Natal instead of towards the north, which had always been Potgieter's goal.

Natal was almost empty of population because it was Zulu policy to have a lightly populated buffer-state as protection from southern enemies. The first known European settler at Port Natal was a Londoner, Vaughan Goodwin, who was set

[1] See page 45.

ashore with three others in 1699. Natal's first real settlers, however, were a party of traders and hunters who came to Port Natal to form a trading settlement for skins and ivory in 1824, having been encouraged by the findings of a survey of the area during previous year. The expedition was led by Lieutenant F. G. Farewell and Lieutenant J. S. King, both formerly of the Royal Navy, the other principal being Henry Francis Fynn; and there were at first some twenty-six settlers. In 1824 Farewell and Fynn visited Shaka at his kraal near the White Umfolozi River in Zululand and obtained a concession granting hunting and settlement rights over the coastal belt north and south of the bay of Port Natal. Following this, a settlement of sorts was founded. In 1835 the first missionary, Captain Allen Gardiner – also late RN – arrived. Having come overland to Natal to convert the Zulus, he went off first to see King Dingane (Dingaan) – for Shaka was dead – to ask permission to form a missionary station. This was refused, though later the Rev. Francis Owen was permitted to set up a mission-station at Dingane's kraal at umGungundhlovu. Meanwhile, the settlers at the Port, who had a large following of refugees from Zululand sheltering with them, persuaded Gardiner to form a mission there. He called it Berea, because he likened his experiences to those of St Paul, who was turned away from Thessalonica and then welcomed at Berea. Berea is still the name of the district[1] on the hill north of the port where Gardiner's mission-station was situated; but Captain Gardiner is remembered less for his missionary work than for the fact that it was he who gave the port-town its name on 23 June 1835, when he called a meeting of the settlers to form a proper settlement and draw up rules for its administration. Then, the site having been selected, it was named Durban after the Governor at the Cape, Sir Benjamin D'Urban. It was also decided to ask the Government to declare Natal a British Colony, but this was not sanctioned.

Retief realized that if the Voortrekkers were to settle peacefully in Natal, arrangements would have to be made with the

[1] Also the name of districts in other towns, viz. Pretoria.

British traders at Port Natal to forestall British intervention, and also with Dingane who was overlord of the area the Voortrekkers wished to occupy. In October 1837, therefore, he led a party to Port Natal, and he was heartened to be greeted in a welcoming spirit by both the missionary Captain Gardiner and Alexander Biggar, the leading settler – two men who were not usually in agreement. Next Retief set out to interview Dingane to find out his reaction to Voortrekkers occupying land on the borders of his kingdom – though by this time their wagons were already descending through the difficult passes of the Drakensberg and entering northern Natal. The Drakensberg provided the most serious physical obstacle to the Voortrekkers' advance, and in the annals of the Trek much is made of the surmounting of the mountain barrier. It is doubtful, however, whether the tracks through the mountains were quite as precipitous as the one depicted in Thomas Baines's famous and much reproduced picture given facing page 33.

Retief and his party arrived at Dingane's capital on 5 November 1837. On being asked their business, they explained that they had come from the Cape Colony to seek new lands to develop, and finding north Natal unoccupied sought permission to colonize it. Dingane received their proposition without enthusiasm. He said he had just heard reports that Voortrekker raiders had stolen some of his cattle, and he expressed himself surprised that after this outrage they should expect a grant of land. Retief had heard of the raid on the royal herds. It had been made by Sikonyela's Tlokwa disguised as Voortrekkers, and he explained this to the King. Dingane replied that if Sikonyela's men were the culprits, the Voortrekkers must go back and find his cattle and punish the thieves. Only then would he consider granting any territory.

On 27 November 1837 the party arrived back at the Voortrekker camp in north Natal, and arrangements were made for a commando to go into Sikonyela's country, accompanied by some of Dingane's herdsmen, to identify the stolen cattle. On arrival at Sikonyela's kraal the Voortrekkers played a trick on the chief. Among the gifts they presented were some handcuffs. These they persuaded him to try on. They then locked them tight and made him prisoner, surrounding him with their muskets at the ready to keep his followers at bay. Under the threat of being shot, Sikonyela confessed that his people had been responsible for stealing the Zulu cattle and agreed to restore them.

In January 1838, with a selected party of horsemen, Retief set off back to Zululand to return the cattle and negotiate a treaty with Dingane. The interview took place in the King's great cattle-kraal, where he was surrounded by his warriors. Dingane was not pleased to learn that Sikonyela had been released; he was also concerned to hear about Potgieter's successes against the Matabele. He made difficulties in drawing up the treaty; but eventually put his mark to a document which stated that as they had restored the cattle stolen by Sikonyela's Tlokwa, he, as King of the Zulus, would grant them territory in Natal.

On 6 February 1838 they returned to the great cattle-kraal to take leave of the King. They left their muskets outside and entered and sat down in a circle at the King's feet. After wishing them a safe return journey the King invited them to share some sorghum beer with him and his indunas. While this was being served, the surrounding warriors began to sing and dance, surging backwards and forwards. Each time they approached the group round the King they uttered wild cries in which there appeared signs of hostility, so that the Voortrekkers turned and looked at their leader Piet Retief nonplussed. Finally the wave of dancing warriors moved right up to the White men; and this time Dingane leapt to his feet, flung up his arms, and looking towards the sky cried out in a loud voice: '*Bulaláni abátagati*' 'Kill the Wizards.'[1] Immediately the warriors pounced on the Voortrekkers and dragged them away. Binding them with thongs, they hustled them off to the hill of execution outside the kraal, and having knocked them senseless with blows from the knobkerries, impaled them and left their bodies for the vultures.

[1] By calling them 'Wizards' the King was attributing them with evil magic. Acting as his own witch-doctor, he was perhaps 'smelling them out'.

Dingane next planned to annihilate the rest of the Voor-trekkers in Natal. These were encamped in the countryside watered by the rivers Bloukrans, Bushmans and Mooi, streams that run into the upper reaches of the Tugela River. Gerrit Maritz, in supreme command during Retief's absence, was near Bushmans river, Retief's own people were west of the Bloukrans, and most of the others were dispersed over a wide area, some nearly as far east as the Mooi on the Zulu-land side of Bushmans river. It was on the exposed eastern encampments that the Zulus burst at one o'clock on a moon-less night along a front of twenty miles. There were only three Zulu regiments engaged, for expected reinforcements never came up. But they did great execution. They almost wiped out the Liebenbergs, the Prinsloos, and the Bezuid-enhouts, and they beat down the Bothas' defences by driving their own cattle in upon them and following up fast. The Trekkers farther back, hearing the first shots, thought it must be Retief's party come back from Zululand. But when the fusillade persisted, and then grew nearer, they stood to arms. Stragglers began to come in: a Bushman servant, a wounded lad riding one horse with his braces knotted together for a bridle and driving seven others; finally three White men wounded. A band of Italian pedlars with their wagons were encamped a little distance from the laagers by Bloukrans River where many men, women and children were killed by the Zulus. Theresa Viglione, one of the Italian women, jumped on to a horse when she saw what was happening and rode off to Bushmans river to Maritz's laager to warn the rest of the Voortrekkers. Theresa's gallant deed saved the lives of many men, women and children, for Trekkers further up river, warned in time, were able to defend themselves.

When the news of the disaster reached the western en-campments, wagons were formed up in lagaars and rescue parties rode out. Sarel Cilliers was early in the field with five men. They arrived in time to save a party that had been caught by the Zulus before they could close their wagon-ring. Reinforced, and picking up stragglers as they went, they then came upon a dozen Van Rensburgs who had been driven from their wagons in the plain and were holding out desperately on a koppie. The Van Rensburgs signalled they were short of powder and shot. Whereupon the youthful Marthinius Oosthuisen volunteered to fetch ammunition from one of their abandoned wagons some distance from the koppie. He rode through the massed natives to the wagon and returned with a bag of powder and bullets, forcing his way through the Zulus. His heroism saved the Van Rensburg trek from extermination, for the combined groups were then able to drive the Zulus away. By this time the men of the other encampments had also driven off their attackers, so the Voortrekkers were able to pause and count their losses. These proved severe. Thousands of their animals had been taken from them, including many vital draught oxen; some 500 men, women and children including 200 Non-White servants had been killed; many more had been wounded; and this was not counting the hundred or so of Retief's men who had been killed in Dingane's kraal.

After the attack the scattered groups drew together for protection into three great laagers, chief of which was Maritz's on high ground overlooking Bushmans river. After some deliberation, suggestions that they should leave Natal were rejected and it was agreed that Dingane must be called to account for what he had done. In this decision they had the support of the English settlers at Port Natal, who agreed to make common cause with the Voortrekkers against Dingane. The first retaliatory expeditions, however, met with little success. A commando was led against the Zulus under the joint command of Hendrik Potgieter and Pieter Uys, who had come down from the high veld to throw in their lot with the people of the United laagers of Natal. The force travelled for four days unopposed and then came up with a large Zulu force at Italeni in broken country unsuited to an open style of fighting. Uys's men engaged the enemy to the right, Potgieter's those to the left. On neither flank did the Voortrekkers meet with success. Potgieter's men were beaten back so that they retreated in confusion. Uys's people were surrounded and cut off, and fought their way out with difficulty, losing Uys and eight others, including young Dirk

5 Early Pretoria: on the right the first Government Building (Raadsaal)

Early Barberton; Crown Street, 1887

6   General Piet Cronjé   Commandant-General Piet Joubert

General C. R. de Wet (third from right with watch-chain) and Staff

Cornelius Uys who gallantly rode back to help his father who had been unhorsed in the Zulu attack. When the boy saw what had happened, he turned back and spurred his horse to his father's side. Jumping down he stood over his father to protect him and shot two Zulus before he was killed.[1]

The English settlers' expeditions against Dingane's warriors were no more successful. Alexander Biggar's son Robert, at the head of a mixed force of nineteen Englishmen and 1,200 native auxiliaries, crossed the Tugela and fell upon the nearest Zulu kraal. But the auxiliaries quarrelled over the spoils. An intertribal stick fight took place on Zulu soil and the cause against the Zulus was advanced little. A second expedition was even less effective. On this occasion the force was trapped in a narrow place and two-thirds of the non-Europeans and Robert Biggar and all save three of the Englishmen were killed. The survivors fled to the Port, pursued by the triumphant Zulus. The auxiliaries hid in the bush, and the Europeans sought refuge on board the *Comet*, a little Cape coasting vessel that had put in a few days before. For nine days they watched the Zulus pillaging and destroying. Then, when the impis had withdrawn, the *Comet* sailed gloomily away with all the White inhabitants of Port Natal save a half a dozen who elected to remain. Finally however, when the Zulus had returned across the Tugela, Carel Landman and a strong detachment of Voortrekkers rode down from the north and took possession of Port Natal in the name of the United Laagers, and in this way it passed into Voortrekker hands.

Not long after the evacuation of Port Natal by the British, Andries Pretorius (1798–1853) arrived in Natal. Pretorius had been late in joining the Trek, but was an experienced commando leader, and under him Voortrekker fortune took a turn for the better. In December 1838 he collected together a force five hundred strong and, together with Sarel Cilliers, led it into Zululand. On Sunday, 9 December 1838, when the force halted for the day on the banks of the Blyde River,

[1] In the same year, in July, the patriarch Jacobus Uys died, so the family's loss was severe.

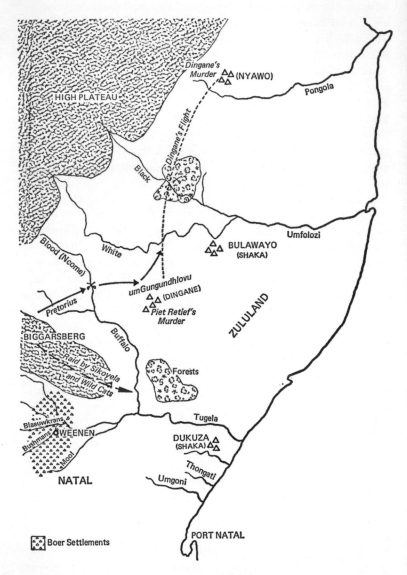

Map VI   Zululand at the Time of Piet Retief's Murder

Cilliers with the approval of Pretorius, prevailed upon his commandos to make together the following vow:

'My brethren and fellow countrymen, at this moment we stand before holy God of heaven and earth, to make a promise, if He will be with us and protect us, and deliver the enemy into our hands so that we may triumph over him, and that we shall observe the day and the date as an anniversary in each year and a day of thanksgiving like the Sabbath, in His honour: and that we shall enjoin our children that they must take part with us in this, for a remembrance even for our posterity; and if anyone sees a difficulty in this let him return from this place. For the honour of His name shall be joyfully exalted, and to Him the fame and the honour of the victory must be given.'

They promised also to build a church[1] to His name.

After leaving Blyde River there followed some days of rough going. On Saturday, 15 December, they encamped on the banks of the Ncome River, a northern tributary of the Buffalo and Tugela, meaning to keep the Sabbath there. It was a strong position, protected partially by the Ncome; and they made it even stronger by chaining the wagons together and mounting cannon.

On Sunday, 16 December, the Zulus surrounded the laager and attacked. But again the musket was more than a match for the assegai. Volleys from the Voortrekkers and shots from their cannon tore great swathes in the Zulu ranks and drove the warriors back through the river so that it became choked with dead and dying, and its waters stained red with blood. The final blow came when mounted Voortrekkers issued from the laager, and rode at the exhausted and dispirited Zulus, shooting them from the saddle. The extent of the Voortrekker advantage at Ncome River, soon to be called Blood River (Afr: Bloedriver), can be gauged by the casualty

---

[1] The little church of the Vow was built at Pietermaritzburg and a tiny modern church with a huge cross was recently erected near Dingane's hill of execution. The church in Pietermaritzburg is now the Voortrekker Museum. It has a statue of Piet Retief outside.

99

figures. No Voortrekkers were killed, and only three, including Andries Pretorius, were wounded, while the Zulu dead were numbered in hundreds. This great Voortrekker victory marked the turn of the tide in the war.

After the battle at Blood River, Pretorius's men moved on to Dingane's royal kraal at umGungundhlovu, only to find that the King had fled. The seraglio had been reduced to ashes, but copper and iron brought by White men earlier as presents still lay in the great cattle-kraal. They moved on next to the hill of execution – Hloma Amabutho. This horror spot abounded in vultures and was carpeted with bones and skulls. Among the first to be identified was Piet Retief, whose clothes, although made threadbare by months of exposure, were recognizable. Alongside was a leather bag containing the treaty he had concluded with Dingane. When the rest of the party had been identified, they were all buried in a communal grave.

Dingane, meanwhile, had moved his cattle and people across the White Umfolozi and taken refuge in a densely wooded region. While there, an effort was made to entice the Voortrekkers to follow so that the Zulus could stage an ambush in the forests. Pretorius's men did allow themselves to be led into the wooded area; but directly they were surrounded they put spurs to their horses and galloped back to safety. The British settler Alexander Biggar[1] and his native followers, who had accompanied the Voortrekkers, were less fortunate, for the Zulus managed to intercept and kill most of them, including their leader. After these encounters Dingane established his capital at a new umGungundhlovu, north of the Black Umfolozi. An attempt was then made by the British to re-establish relations between Dingane and the Voortrekkers, and an arrangement was arrived at whereby the Voortrekkers agreed to live at peace with the Zulus provided Dingane returned the firearms, horses and equipment taken from Retief's party and paid an indemnity of 19,000 cattle as compensation for the damage sustained during the previous year. By August 1839 the bulk

[1] A range of hills in central Natal is named after him (Biggarsberg).

of Retief's property had been returned, but only a very small number of the cattle. At this time the King's attention was concentrated on a campaign against the Swazis; also he was by nature a procrastinator and reluctant to part with so large a section of his herds. Failure to comply with the terms of the agreement, combined with other events which turned to his disadvantage, was to lead to his downfall. A number of Dingane's subjects were growing tired of his growing intolerance. A sub-tribe, the Qwabe, had already defected, and now Dingane's brother Mpande went over to the Voortrekkers with 17,000 subjects and 125,000 cattle and asked for help to turn Dingane off the throne.

In due course a combined attack by the Voortrekkers and Mpande's impis was staged, and the latter, moving into Zululand, brushed with the loyal Zulu army. Surprisingly, Mpande's followers were successful, and when Dingane's chief induna returned to report his failure he was berated by the King and accused of cowardice and negligence. He was arrested and later, in full view of his fellow indunas, strangled with an oxhide. This savage end to a popular leader shocked even those inured to Dingane's cruelties, and there were more desertions, and then plots to assassinate the King. His end came, however, at the hands of Silevana, chief of the Nyawo, a sub-tribe of the Swazi king into whose territory Dingane and his remaining followers had strayed when fleeing north. Informed that the bulk of Dingane's warriors were away on a foraging expedition, a strong force of Nyawo surrounded Dingane's kraal by night, and Silevana with three followers entered the seraglio unseen and took up position on either side of the entrance to Dingane's hut. At sunrise some Zulu warriors emerged to urinate, and the Nyawo fell upon them. Their cries for help alerted the entire settlement, but Zulus who resisted were quickly slain and the remainder accepted terms for surrender. Awakened by the screams, Dingane jumped up from his sleeping-mat and crawled out through the narrow entrance of his hut. He was in the process of getting to his feet when Silevana and his companion leapt on him. A spear was thrust into his side, another through his thigh, and he fell to the ground bleeding profusely. Then as he tried vainly to reach the gate of the seraglio, a third stabbing-spear was plunged into his massive body to kill him.

With their ally Mpande on the throne in Zululand, the Voortrekkers were able to move into Natal confident of a sympathetic reception. They passed down through the Drakensberg passes and spread out as their fathers and grandfathers had done in Cape Colony, so that by 1842 there was a scattered Voortrekker community of 6,000 men, women and children. The two main centres were at Weenen (Weeping) on Bushmans River, the settlement of the early tragedy, and Pietermaritzburg in the central area, named after Piet Retief, and Gerrit Maritz. The latter was made the seat of the republican government consisting of an elected Volksraad of twenty-four members, with legislative and executive functions. Meanwhile, local administration was carried out by military commandants and civilian *landdrosts* in conjunction with unpaid *heemraden* and field-cornets as it had been at the Cape under the Dutch East India Company. The leading personality was now Andries Pretorius, victor at Blood River. During 1840 he went up on to the high veld to negotiate with the rump of the Voortrekkers under Potgieter. As a result, the Natal Republic was united with the Voortrekker settlements centred on Potchefstroom and Winburg. These districts were allowed representatives in the Volksraad at Pietermaritzburg, and the enlarged council was made responsible for the entire Voortrekker community. There were squabbles between the elected members of the Volksraads and the leading followers of the Commandant-General Pretorius, and disputes over the allocation of farms to latecomers to Natal who were still arriving in considerable numbers; but by 1841 it seemed as if the dream of the Voortrekkers had at last come true, and that their long-sought independent Trekker Republic had been established.

Chapter 6

The Boer Republics or Afrikaner States

The South African Republic (Transvaal) 1852
The Orange Free State 1854

The policy of the British authorities concerning the extension of British interests in South Africa varied from time to time. It was always believed that Britain should hold the Cape peninsula because of its commercial and strategic importance on the sea route to Asia, but as to the need to control contiguous territory there were differing views. The two main factors involved appear to have been the need to restrict expenditure on the colonies and the pressure from the missionaries and philanthropists for an extension of British interests on the score of the need to protect the natives from the rapacity of White traders and farmers. In 1843, at the time of the annexation of Natal, the need to protect the natives was considered paramount. By 1852 and 1854, however, the difficulty of bringing law and order to native communities with the small military forces available was so far realized that the policy of supporting the natives against the Boers was given up. Instead, first the Boer communities beyond the Vaal (1852) and then those between the Orange and Vaal (1854) were granted independence, and afterwards treaties with Non-White chiefs and leaders were repudiated and alliances were formulated with the new republican Voortrekker states.

In 1841, after the establishment of Mpande on the throne of Zululand in place of Dingane, Andries Pretorius was able to set up something like a viable republic in Natal, centred on

Pietermaritzburg and linked with the Voortrekker communities around Winburg and Potchefstroom. The members of the Volksraad in Pietermaritzburg, which represented the three Voortrekker states, next sought recognition of their independent status from the British authorities. For a time it looked as if they might be granted independence, but eventually the pressure of missionary opinion caused the British first to refuse and then to implement again the Cape of Good Hope Punishment Act in an effort to restrain the actions of the Natal burghers against the natives who had flocked into the previously almost empty buffer-state.

The Natal burghers had ruled that except for five Bantu families for each farm, Bantu refugees and others not wishing to work for the Whites should proceed to special Bantu homelands; but these efforts to control the excess Bantu, who poured into empty Natal when peaceful conditions returned, combined with retaliatory action to check raiders from outside, brought the new Republic's authorities into conflict with the missionaries, the philanthropic movement in London, and finally the British authorities at the Cape. Andries Pretorius, believing that the Bhaca in the south were responsible for cattle raiding, sent commandos into Bhaca country, and these killed thirty tribesmen, recovered their stock, and made off with seventeen children whom they brought up as apprentices. This meant that the children were made bonded servants until they were twenty-five years old, which the missionaries and philanthropists classed as a form of slavery. Next, in order to deal with the excessive number of Bantu refugees from Zululand and the south who were settling around Boer farms, the Volksraad attempted to transfer them to unoccupied lands in the south. But the empty lands selected belonged traditionally to Chief Faku of the Pondo who was under British protection. When Faku refused to comply with the Volksraad's demand to admit the refugees, he was ordered to Pietermaritzburg to appear before the council. The council threatened to hang him if he did not submit; whereupon, Faku appealed to the British authorities at the Cape. The British supported the chief. They asserted that the Voortrekkers were still British subjects as they were south of latitude 25°, and that their acts of aggression against natives were the responsibility of the Crown. As it seemed likely that the Boer actions would lead to tribal uprisings, they sent a force first to Pondoland and then to Natal to look after native interests.

The force, consisting of 200 men of the 27th Regiment under Captain Smith, set up a fortified camp at Port Natal. The Boer leader Pretorius was approached, but he proved intransigent, demanding that Captain Smith should withdraw from Natal or he would resort to arms. What was more, to show he meant business, he seized the English draught oxen and drove them away. In retaliation Captain Smith staged a night attack on the Boer camp at Congella, south of Durban; but his force was greatly outnumbered, as many volunteers from the high veld had joined Pretorius. From concealed positions the Boers opened fire on the assaulting column, killing seventeen and wounding thirty more, and they forced the British to withdraw to the fort at the port. Here, although besieged for a month and suffering much privation, the British force managed to hold out. Meanwhile, a Natal trader, Richard King, had ridden south to Albany for help. Fording deep rivers and crossing hundreds of miles of hostile Xhosa territory, he reached Grahamstown in nine days, and within seventeen a relief force had arrived at Port Natal by sea and put the Boers to rout. Many Boers fled to Weenen, and then up to the high veld; but the few who remained invited the British Commissioner, Colonel Cloete, to Pietermaritzburg, where on 15 July 1842 they submitted to the authority of the Crown in return for an amnesty. For several years the annexation of Natal had been considered, but had been decided against on financial grounds. Now, however, there was more enthusiasm for Imperial expansion, and it also began to be thought that Natal might eventually pay its way. These facts, combined with pressure from the philanthropists who were convinced that the interests of the natives were better served under British control, led to Natal becoming a British colony in 1843. After this most of the remaining Voortrekkers left Natal.

At the time of the British annexation of Natal there were

Voortrekker settlements beyond the Orange, between the Vet and Sand rivers, around Winburg, and along the Modder. Beyond the Vaal were settlements in the neighbourhood of Potchefstroom, in the east at Lydenburg and Ohrigstad, and in the north at Schoemandsdal not far from the Limpopo. Following the British annexation of Natal many Voortrekkers moved back over the Drakensberg to join their fellows on the high veld, including eventually Andries Pretorius, the hero of Blood River.

Before the arrival back of Andries Pretorius the aims of the Trekkers on the high veld were confused. A number under Michiel Oberholzer wished to remain under the protection of Cape Colony. Others under Jacobus Snyman were accepting farms near the Caledon from Moshesh, thereby recognizing his right to the territory. The majority, however, and these were reinforced by those from Natal, wanted to bring about a united independent community under Hendrik Potgieter. This was because Andries Pretorius, by staying on in Natal and negotiating with the British authorities, had lost favour as a suitable leader for republican-minded burghers.

But Potgieter was more interested in finding new, better and independent territory for settlement in the far north, preferably within reach of the coast, than in consolidating the interior areas already occupied. To begin with he had designs on Mzilikazi's new country beyond the Limpopo, and in 1845 led another expedition against the Matabele, officially to recover two White children who had been reported as captured by them. The Boers entered Matabeleland (now Rhodesia) without much difficulty. Galloping into the first military kraal they surprised and dispersed most of its garrison, and they then proceeded deeper into Mzilikazi's territory, brushing aside improvised opposition and taking many thousand head of cattle. Potgieter next planned to capture the King by a sudden dash on the royal kraal, but in this he was unsuccessful, for Mzilikazi was many miles away. The Voortrekkers had taken a lot of cattle and had heard that the story of the captured White girls was untrue; but they were now 400 miles from their farms and the country was alive with rumours of approaching impis.

Reluctantly, Potgieter made the decision to return and, driving ahead the captured cattle, moved slowly back towards the Limpopo. Disaster, however, was to strike. On the first night on the way back, when the Voortrekkers had bivouacked on a hill near the Khami river, a Matabele regiment crept out of a hiding-place and massacred the native levies who with the captured cattle in their charge had lain down to sleep in the open at the bottom of the hill, while their masters with muskets beside them and the reins of their horses in their hands were at the top. At dawn the Voortrekkers found the mangled corpses of their servants and not a single head of cattle. At this stage Potgieter decided the horses were too exhausted to seek reprisals and led his men home; this was the last attempt against the Matabele by the Voortrekkers, for very soon afterwards a peace treaty was drawn up. The Matabele were glad to receive a promise of help from the Voortrekkers against the Coloureds who were skilled horsemen and could use muskets to good effect; the Boers considered it wiser at this stage to hold back, as they realized that their raids were turning world opinion against them. Their native policy was always offensive to the British and these raids made it even more so. Continuance might have brought back a more direct British control than even the *Cape of Good Hope Punishment Act* permitted; also, Moffat's famous son-in-law, David Livingstone – no friend of the Voortrekkers at any time – was recommending giving the natives firearms to protect themselves.

Meanwhile, in Transorangia there was great dissatisfaction among the Voortrekkers, even among those who wished to retain the British connection. This derived from the fact that the Cape authorities in 1834 had made a treaty with Andries Waterboer, leader of the West Griquas based on Griquatown, whereby he was recognized as being the ruler of the territories his people occupied, and given a small annual grant to keep law and order on behalf of the British. Similar treaties were drawn up in 1843 by Governor Sir George Napier with Adam Kok, another Coloured leader with his headquarters at Philippolis, farther east up the Orange, and with Moshesh, King of the Basutos, who claimed the

Caledon lowlands to the west of his mountain kingdom based on Thaba Bosiu. These treaties with the rulers of the northern border of Cape Colony allowed them jurisdiction over White settlers in their territories, of whom by this time there were a considerable number; and even the collaborators among the Voortrekkers did not relish the idea of being apprehended by a native.

There were a number of incidents, and a final one, in which Adam Kok was concerned, brought about a minor war between the Trekkers and the British authorities supporting their sponsored native rulers. In May 1845 two natives who were unruly were brought before a local Trekker leader, who had them flogged, whereupon Adam Kok asserted his authority by sending a force to arrest the man. The farmer was away, so the posse confiscated his guns and ammunition. The local Boers, on hearing what had happened, were indignant. They rose in arms and went into laager at Touwfontein, thirty miles north of Kok's capital at Philippolis, and from there rode out to war against Kok's Griquas and a small British force[1] under Major Warden which was supporting the Coloured chief. In their first encounter with the Griquas the Boers killed seven of the enemy for a similar loss to themselves; but they were not so successful against the British, whom they met at Swartkoppies, for in this skirmish they lost a score of their number and were driven off. When finally Sir Peregrine Maitland, who had succeeded Sir George Napier as Governor at the Cape, rode north to Touwfontein to try to settle the dispute, some of the unhappy farmers fled north to join Transvaal settlements, but the rest agreed to live at peace alongside their native neighbours. The chiefs in fact proved accommodating. Adam Kok set aside a part of the northern half of his principality for exclusive White occupation, and Moshesh offered the Trekkers a wedge of land near the confluence of the Caledon and Orange rivers.

To keep the peace Maitland installed Major Warden as a British Resident in the locality, and Warden set up his

[1] About three hundred men drawn from the 7th Dragoon Guards, the Argylls and the Cape Mounted Rifles, with three field guns.

headquarters at Bloemfontein[1] farm in the centre of Adam Kok's region of permitted White settlement. Warden managed to keep on fair terms with the various resident peoples of the locality of which he was in charge. By his famous Warden Line he demarcated the territory lying west of Basutoland accredited to Moshesh, and he was able for a time to maintain something like law and order in the area. Not that he was left unmolested. In March 1846, when the British were fully engaged against the Xhosa on the eastern frontier of Cape Colony in the War of the Axe[2], the Boers at Winburg, feeling it too good an opportunity to miss, formed a commando and attacked his post. On this occasion Warden was too quick for them. Calling out some of Moshesh's native levies to supplement his Coloured troops, he sent the commando flying, some back to Winburg, the rest over the Vaal to their friends at Potchefstroom.

In 1848 Sir Harry Smith, who as Colonel Smith under Governor D'Urban had defeated the Xhosa and attempted to consolidate the eastern frontier, was himself back as Governor at the Cape. After the War of the Axe had been successfully concluded, he scrapped Commissioner Andries Stockenström's[3] appeasement treaties and, returning to his discarded earlier designs, re-annexed D'Urban's Queen Adelaide Province under the style of British Kaffraria.

Having temporarily pacified the eastern frontier, Sir Harry Smith next turned his attention to Natal and Transorangia. With Natal he did not make much progress, for his suggested arrangements for the Boer settlers of the Pietermaritzburg and Weenen areas were so unacceptable that most of them – including Andries Pretorius – returned to the high veld. In

---

[1] Later the site of the town of Bloemfontein.

[2] A petty Xhosa chief entered a store in Fort Beaufort where he saw an axe, took a fancy to it and lifted it. He was caught in the act, accused of theft, arrested and put in gaol. The Xhosa pleaded for his release and when this was refused, and an attempt at rescue failed, hostilities began.

[3] Andries Stockenström was the son of the landdrost of Graaff-Reinet, Anders Stockenström. South African born, but of Swedish descent, he was an official on the eastern frontier for a period and used similar methods to Maynier; namely, persuasion and compensation for good behaviour instead of applying force.

Transorangia, however, he was more successful. During an official visit to Major Warden's post at Bloemfontein he saw Andries Waterboer, captain of the Griquas in the west, Adam Kok, the Griqua chief based on Philippolis in the south, Moroka, the friendly Baralong chief based on Thaba Nchu, and Moshesh, King of the Basutos in the east. By his strong personality and by offering increased annual grants it did not take him long to convince them of the advantages of remaining under British protection. Next he approached the Boer settlers of the neighbourhood. Those who had remained in the locality proved surprisingly tractable. After haranguing and cajoling them, as only he could, he received the impression that the majority of the people of Transorangia would welcome being brought under the protection of the British Crown. On 3 February 1848, therefore, he annexed the area under the title of the Orange River Sovereignty.

Meanwhile, Andries Pretorius had returned to the high veld. When he first heard about Sir Harry Smith's activities in Transorangia he was convinced that the Governor would not consider annexation without four-fifths of the burghers agreeing. He was appalled when he heard that it had actually taken place without being put to the popular vote at all. He immediately set himself the task of driving out the British officials and creating one large Voortrekker republic stretching from the Orange to the Limpopo. When he tried to raise a force to accomplish this, Potgieter refused to join in, and many of the Transorangia burghers were unenthusiastic; but he managed to enrol about 1,000 men mainly from the Transvaal and Winburg settlements and with these he marched south. He moved first against Major Warden's post at Bloemfontein. This time the Coloured troopers were unable to resist the large force of well-armed Boers, and Warden was first chased out of his post and then right across the Orange. The British magistrates in the area were also easily driven away, and Pretorius hoped that this quick expulsion of the authorities and his unopposed advance to the frontier with Cape Colony would induce Sir Harry Smith to withdraw permanently from Transorangia. He was soon to be disillusioned. First, Major Warden set up an impregnable armed camp on the south side of Botha's Drift, where he had crossed the Orange, and then Sir Harry Smith assembled a force[1] of several hundred men, set a price on Pretorius's head, called on local burghers and chiefs for support, and marched north.

When Pretorius's men heard of Sir Harry Smith's action many feared the consequences and began to desert and slink off home. With the remainder, however, Pretorius took up a strong defensive position in front of a deserted farm named Boomplaats on a ridge of hills a few miles north of Touwfontein. As it straddled the road, the position offered possibilities for an ambush of the punitive column as it wound its way north through the hills; but the British shook out into skirmishing order long before they reached Boomplaats, so Pretorius's plan was foiled. In the event the burghers opened fire and disclosed their position while still at extreme range, and their attacks on the column's flanks were easily beaten back. The British then brought their field guns into action, and after a systematic bombardment, charged and drove the Boers from their position. The Boers tried to make a stand in the cattle kraals by the farm and on some hills behind; but when British mounted men galloped forward round their flanks and threatened their line of retreat, they broke and fled. This was the end of the Boomplaats fight. Sir Harry Smith then led his column up through Bloemfontein to Winburg and quickly restored British authority in the Orange River Sovereignty.

The annexation of the area between the Orange and the Vaal in 1848 was as severe a blow to the Voortrekkers as that of Natal had been five years earlier; but attempts were now made to unite in one community the remaining free settlements beyond the Vaal. This presented difficulties, for the two main leaders, Potgieter and Pretorius, did not work

---

[1] This was made up of drafts from the 45th (Sherwood Foresters), the 91st (Argylls), the Rifle Brigade and the Cape Mounted Rifles. It had three field guns and was supported by some loyal burghers and over 200 Griquas led by Andries Waterboer and Adam Kok.

together in harmony. Because of this discord among the principals, as many as four commandants-general were eventually appointed. These consisted of Andries Pretorius for the Potchefstroom area in the south, Hendrik Potgieter for the Soutspansberg area in the north, W. F. Joubert for Lydenburg in the east and J. A. Enslin for Marico in the west. The dispersed nature of the settlements also meant that although there was nominally one Volksraad for the whole area there was little co-ordination between the parts. The result was that the Transvaal did not become a truly viable state for many years, and internal strife continued into the 1860s and later.

In the 1850s there came about a significant change in British policy which brought its compensation to the Voortrekker settlements of the high veld. The considerable financial cost of the many frontier wars to stem Xhosa intrusions on the eastern frontier led to retrenchment in other areas. Major Warden's already slender forces were reduced, and he was quite unable to restrain Moshesh's warriors from raiding Voortrekker farms in the area of the Caledon River, where they began to pay no attention to the Warden line of demarcation. Finally, an operation staged by Major Warden in 1851 against Basuto raiders ended in a British defeat at Viervoet, and there was a threat that the Transvaal Boers might ally themselves with Moshesh's people against the British authorities. In this situation the British decided to try to win the support of the Transvaal Boers, and negotiations were opened with them. Potgieter refused to parley, but Pretorius was more accommodating. Through his good offices a convention was held at Sand River where, on 17 January 1852, it was agreed that the independence of the community beyond the Vaal would be recognized in exchange for a commitment from its people not to ally themselves with the natives against the British. Thus came into being the state which was known as the South African Republic (Transvaal). It became a united state in 1852 and had its first constitution in 1858. Then, surprisingly, a further failure of British arms against Moshesh's impis led, after long

7 Dr Leander Jameson
(Radio Times Hulton
Picture Library)

Cecil John Rhodes
(Radio Times Hulton
Picture Library)

8   Lord Kitchener, General Ian
    Hamilton and Staff at
    Johannesburg (National Army
    Museum)

Lord Milner (Mansell Collection)

negotiations, to a similar arrangement being arrived at with the leaders of the settlements centred on Winburg. At a convention at Bloemfontein on 23 February 1854 it was agreed that a second Voortrekker republic should be established called the Orange Free State. Under the Sand River Convention of 1852 and the Bloemfontein Convention of 1854 Britain repudiated her treaties with the Non-White chiefs and allied herself instead with the two new republican Voortrekker states. Britain thus accepted Boer support against the indigenous peoples, and although she did not always adhere to this new policy, nevertheless, with the recognition of the two Voortrekker states in 1852 and 1854, it may be said that at the close of the period of the Great Trek the Voortrekkers had been successful in their aims of establishing independent republics on the high veld, if not in Natal.

The consequences of all this for the Bantu and Coloured peoples of Transorangia were somewhat different from what might have been expected. Moroka, chief of the Baralongs based on Thaba Nchu, gratefully accepted Boer support against the hostile Basutos, and a happy relationship continued until his death in 1880. The Boers found Moshesh's raiders of their farms as difficult to restrain as Major Warden had done. In 1868 they were beginning to gain control, although they never managed to occupy Moshesh's stronghold at Thaba Bosiu, when Moshesh asked Britain to annex his country and avoided defeat. Adam Kok sold his Griqua territory and its capital Philippolis[1] to the Boers in 1861 and was allowed by Governor Sir George Grey to move the remnants of his people to a depopulated area in the east, which became known as East Griqualand. Meanwhile, Andries Waterboer and later Nicolaas Waterboer, his son, based on Griquatown near the confluence of the Vaal and Orange, were left in something like peace with their missionary supporters until diamonds were found in their territory. Then, 'all hell was let loose', and once more, as had been the case of the Great Trek, the course of history was transformed.

---

[1] He was later to claim that he sold only the settlement at Philippolis and not the surrounding territory.

Governors of the period:

Sir Benjamin D'Urban	1834–8
Sir George Napier	1838–44
Sir Peregrine Maitland	1844–7
Sir Henry Pottinger	1847
Sir Harry Smith	1847–52
Sir George Cathcart	1852–4

Chapter 7

Conflict in the East – the Anglo–Zulu War of 1879

In 1868 there were still a number of independent native communities. In the north by the Limpopo were the Venda, north-east of Pretoria[1] were the Pedi, and in the mountains beside the Pongola, west of Delagoa Bay, were the Swazi. Moshesh's South Sotho state of Basutoland had been annexed by Great Britain at his request, but on the eastern lowlands of Natal were several independent groups like the Mpondo, the Thembu, the Mfengu, the Bomvana, the three Xhosa chiefdoms of Ndlambe, Gcaleka and Ngqika, and the newly created Hottentot settlement about Kat River. North of Natal and bordering Portuguese East Africa (Mozambique) were the Tsonga chiefdoms, and south of these the important Zulu kingdom. To the west of the two Boer republics were several Tswana[2] chiefdoms, and in the south, about the Harts, lower Vaal and Orange rivers, were independent Coloured bands under Nicolaas Waterboer and Adam Kok.

The Venda chiefs in the north had managed to reverse the tide of Afrikaner expansion. In 1859 Stephanus Schoeman appointed a Portuguese trader as superintendent of the tribes east of the township of Schoemansdal in the Soutpansberg district. This proved an unwise choice, for one of the

[1] Remnants of Ndebele (Matabele) remained on the high veld. Seventeen miles north-west of Pretoria there is still a Ndebele village which is a tourist attraction.
[2] The principal ones being the Baralong, Lete, Ngwato, Ngwaketse, Kwena, Kgatla and Tlhaping.

man's lines was exporting slaves from the area through Delagoa Bay; also, although his wife was an Afrikaner, he had no deep loyalty to the Afrikaner community. In his efforts to collect taxes he antagonized the Venda chiefs, and in retaliation they started raiding White farms. The Government of the South African Republic (Transvaal) endeavoured to restore order by sending its Commandant-General, Paul Kruger, to Schoemansdal with a small force. When this proved insufficient to master the Venda in their mountain strongholds, and President M. W. Pretorius was unwilling to send reinforcements, the Transvaalers withdrew, followed by the White inhabitants of the frontier zone; whereupon the Venda destroyed their settlements. It was not until the 1880s that the Afrikaners returned and re-occupied the area. Then General Piet J. Joubert, the new Commandant-General of the South African Republic, led a series of expeditions against the Venda and eventually subdued them, those chiefs not willing to stay and co-operate crossing the Limpopo and settling in Mashona country.

In the 1870s the Pedi chiefdom under Sekhukhune became the most powerful state in the eastern Transvaal. A counterpart of Moshesh's South Sotho kingdom, it had become the rallying point for the survivors of the northern Sotho chiefdoms destroyed in the *Difaqane*. By 1876 the Afrikaners in the Lydenburg district were alarmed at Sekhukhune's strength and disturbed by Pedi raids on their farms. In retaliation for the raids, President T. F. Burgers of the South African Republic led a force of Afrikaners and Swazi allies against the Pedi. Owing to strife within the Republic the Afrikaner commandos employed were very weak, and the result was that after some initial successes the force failed ignominiously before Sekhukhune's stronghold in the mountains. At this stage Sekhukhune seemed invincible. But the tide turned. Early in 1877 Burgers organized another punitive force and, adopting a different strategy, built forts at strong points on the borders of the plain so that the Pedi were prevented from coming down from the mountains to plant and reap their crops. This proved decisive, for Sekhukhune, troubled by

the pressure on the economy of his state, made a show of sub-
mission. It did not, however, end the trouble between the
White farmers and the Pedi, and two further expeditions
had to be staged to subdue them. In the first, at the time of the
British annexation of the Republic, a mixed force led by
British regulars stormed Sekhukhune's stronghold, took the
chief captive, and replaced him by his half-brother and rival
Mampura. In the second, when the new chief had proved no
more compliant than Sekhukhune, the now independent
Transvaal sent in commandos that drove Mampura out of
his kingdom. After the successful conclusion of the second expedition, the Pedi people were divided up into small groups
so that the Republic could consolidate its hold over them.

Swazi foreign policy in the reign of Sobhuza's son Mswazi
(1840–68) and his successor was based on the premise that
the Zulus who had tried to destroy the Swazi kingdom in the
time of Shaka and Dingane, and had continued to raid
thereafter, were the most serious menace, and that White
people should be treated as potential allies. Mswazi asked
Sir Theophilus Shepstone to use his influence with Mpande
to stop the Zulu raids, and entered also into treaty relations
with his Afrikaner neighbours in the Transvaal. He made
some concessions by allowing Transvaal farmers to settle
along the Pongola River as a buffer between his people and
the Zulus, and he allowed the Swazi borders to be defined
by a Transvaal boundary commission even though it meant
some contractions. He even admitted a vague Transvaal
overlordship. In the early part of the reign of Mbandzeni
(1874–89) Mswazi's policy was continued, and as has been
seen, regiments were sent to help both the Afrikaner and
British Governments to subdue the Pedi. By 1881, however,
Mbandzeni was becoming anxious about Afrikaner infiltra-
tion, and at his instigation, in the Conventions[1] that followed
the First Anglo–Boer War, a clause was inserted recognizing
his independence within defined boundaries. During the last
years of Mbandzeni's reign a number of concessions were
made to Afrikaner stock farmers seeking grazing and to

[1] Pretoria and London Conventions.

British prospectors in search of minerals. Attracted by their offers, Mbandzeni got into the habit of placing his mark on the documents they submitted in order to enjoy the rewards they gave. By the end of his reign he had given away almost the entire resources of his kingdom: not only the land and the minerals; but also the rights to operate industries, to collect custom duties, to build railways and to conduct postal services. Some of these were granted several times over to different people, and in 1889 they were capped by a super-concession which gave the holder the authority to collect all the king's private revenues, including revenues from earlier concessions, in exchange for a royal income of £12,000 a year.

The Transvaal was particularly interested in Swaziland. By 1889 Afrikaner expansion to the west had been shut off by the British in order to keep a 'passage' open to Matabele-land and Mashonaland in the north, and the only part of the east coast that was not under British or Portuguese control was the gap where Swaziland lay. As the danger of complete Transvaal control mounted, Mbandzeni asked for British protection. This was refused, and after Mbandzeni's death British negotiators offered the Transvaal control of Swaziland and the territories down to the sea provided it would enter into a custom's union with the British colonies. President Kruger and the *Volksraad* feared this condition would mean the loss of the Transvaal's independence and would not accept. For some years the country was administered jointly; but by 1891 the Transvaal had bought out all the concessions of political significance – including the super-concession – and the Republic's influence was dominant. In 1895 the Transvaal was allowed to assume control, but as it turned out, Afrikaner domination was brief, for after the Second Anglo–Boer War (1899–1902) the British Government separated Swaziland from the Transvaal and ruled it in much the same way as Basutoland. Thereafter came a revival of the power and prestige of the traditional Swazi authorities, and eventually Swaziland became an independent state like Basutoland (Lesotho).

At the southern end of the eastern coastal lowlands, on either side of the Kei river, was a deep frontier zone extending from the Fish river to the Mthatha (Umtata) where Whites and Blacks had fought or co-operated for a hundred years. But it was not a line of division between Black and White societies; many Bantu remained in the Ciskei west of the Kei and there were White residents in the Transkei east of the river. Nor was it a line of division between distinctive Nguni peoples. The Xhosa lived on both sides of the river, the Ngqika and Ndlembe near the Hottentot Kat River Settlement, the Gcaleka on the coast between the Kei and the Mthatha. Other tribes in this area were the Bomvana on the Mthatha side of the Gcaleka, and the Mfengu (Fingo), who were remnants of various Nguni tribes which Shaka had disrupted in Natal, and whose principal area of settlement now lay in the central Transkei region, south of the Thembu, who occupied the land stretching north towards the Stormberg. The Cape Government had appointed officials to live beyond the Kei among the Thembu, Mfengu, and Gcaleka-Xhosa, even though the river was the formal boundary; and in spite of the fact that they had no official powers that could be enforced, these men exerted great influence, for they all exercised judicial functions, and some even raised taxes. Traders, missionaries, and frontier officials, all favoured, for different reasons, the extension of British control over the Transkei. But further subordination of the area did not begin until the expansionist policies of the 1870s began to have effect. In 1875 the Thembu asked for British protection against the Gcaleka-Xhosa, with whom they were at odds. At the same time the Mfengu quarrelled with the Xhosa. War followed between the Xhosa and an allied Thembu and Mfengu force under White officers. In this situation the Cape Parliament, with the blessing of the British Government, first annexed Fingoland in 1879 and then the territories of the Thembu and Gcaleka-Xhosa in 1885. Thus a century after they had first begun to interact with Afrikaner farmers on the Fish River the South Nguni were finally subdued. The prestige of their chiefs had been seriously affected by the series of military defeats of the Frontier Wars and the lamentable consequences of the 'cattle-killing', so that the colonial magistrates were rapidly able to become effective administrators in their districts. Land was not appropriated for White settlement in the Transkei, yet the people had been civilized from contact over many years with officials, traders and missionaries, so that it is understandable why the Transkei became the first self-governing Bantu[1] homeland in 1970.

Farther north, on the eastern lowlands adjoining Natal, lay Faku's Mpondo chiefdom. In 1844 Faku made a treaty with Britain and was recognized as the ruler of the territory extending from the Mzimkhulu to the Mthatha rivers, and from the Indian Ocean to the Drakensberg. In fact, the Mpondo occupied only the coastal sector; the Bhaca, Xesibe and Mpondomise lived in the territory farther inland, and between them and the Drakensberg there was an area which was known as Nomansland, where the inhabitants were bands of Bushmen and a few small Nguni and Sotho subject communities over which Faku had little control. In 1861 Faku placed Nomansland at the disposal of Sir George Grey, the Cape Governor, who arranged for Adam Kok to bring down his Coloureds from the Orange River area where they had fallen on hard times, with the result that 3,000 Griqua arrived in 1863 and founded a new East Griqualand where they exercised some control over the remnants of Nguni and Sotho tribes settled near them. When Faku died in 1868, the Mpondos' dynastic quarrels produced anarchy throughout the whole area, whereupon the traders, the missionaries, and the White farmers who had bought Griqua farms in Nomansland, all asked Sir Henry Barkly, the High Commissioner, to intervene; at the same time the Nguni and Sotho tribes demanded British protection. At this stage Britain's main interest was in Port St Johns at the mouth of the Mzimvubu River, which German concession-hunters desired as a point of entry for German trade and political influence. In 1885, when one of the claimants to the Mpondo

---

[1] Although a number of tribes occupy the southern coastal region, the Xhosa dominate as regards numbers. In the 1970 census there were 3,930,087.

chiefdom appeared to be flirting with the Germans, Britain proclaimed a protectorate over the entire coastline to forestall German intervention. Inland, there was still discord for many years between rival claimants, as well as among the subject tribes, and it was left to Cecil Rhodes, when Prime Minister at the Cape (1890–96), finally to bring law and order to the region. Rhodes's representatives skilfully achieved this. Without even sending an armed force to the country, they persuaded the main claimants to agree to the annexation of East and West Pondoland. The Cape Government divided Mpondo country into several magisterial districts, and the powers of the chiefs were greatly reduced. By the end of the century the Mpondo, like the Xhosa and the Thembu, had been firmly subordinated to colonial magistrates.

The main centre of native unrest at this period was in Zululand and in adjoining Natal. On 31 May 1844 Natal, which had been annexed by Britain on 12 May 1843, became a district of Cape Colony under a lieutenant-governor. Apart from a few English traders and the small British garrison, the White population consisted of about 400 Voortrekker families who had remained in Natal after the annexation of the Republic of Natalia; and among these, at first, was Andries Pretorius. There were about 100,000 Bantu in Natal, most of whom had streamed into the country from Zululand after the British occupation. They were a burden and a threat to the Whites. They squatted everywhere, even on Boer farms, went about armed, thieved, and were reluctatnt to work for farmers. It was difficult to decide how to deal with them. Although Mpande was not as pugnacious as his brothers had been, it was feared that if they were forced to return to Zululand they would be severely punished, so after a commission had looked into the matter it was decided to concentrate them in a number of locations.

When the areas of the locations had been decided there followed serious objections from farmers that the Bantu had been allotted White land, including inhabited farms. Andries Pretorius had a large group close to him and wrote plaintively: 'As a result of these decisions such an inundation of murderous and rapacious people will be living in our midst that every one of us will have to leave our beloved homes rather than risk our lives and property.' Attempts were made to allot the original Voortrekkers farms away from the locations, but the surveys and grants took so long to complete that most of the settlers decided to trek out of Natal. Meanwhile, Voortrekkers in the Klip River who had bought their land directly from the Zulu king boldly set up their own administration. When as a result of this they were declared rebels by the Natal Government, they too left Natal. Eventually there were very few Afrikaners left in the colony.

The Bantu problem remained, but Natal was fortunate in having Theophilus Shepstone who proved an outstanding Secretary of State for Native Affairs. Possessing a forceful personality, he was able to control the chiefs and their peoples. Chiefs who revolted quickly forfeited their positions of authority, and for many years the Bantu in Natal did not dare to resist the Government openly. Nevertheless, the many thousands of Bantu were a constant threat to the handful of Whites, so an effort was made to encourage European immigrants. Owing to economic distress in Europe at the time, emigration to Natal was attractive, and the offer of cheap land and assisted passage brought 200 Germans in 1848 to cultivate cotton in what is now New Germany. A number of emigration schemes were also organized in England, with the result that between 1849 and 1851, 2,200 British settlers arrived, some of whom experimented with sugar cultivation on the north coast. In 1869 young Cecil Rhodes and his brother came and tried their hand at cotton growing, but having no success departed for the diamond fields. Besides those who arrived under definite schemes, numbers came out independently, and towns such as Richmond, Howick and Verulam were founded, and Durban and Pietermaritzburg had such an increase in population that in 1854 both achieved borough status. The value of land in Natal at this time is revealed in a letter[1] of one Robert

[1] Local History Museum, Old Court House, Aliwal Street, Durban.

Bushley who sold his parcel before he had even disembarked. He apparently received two pounds two shillings and sixpence for twenty acres.

As in Albany, when the British came, churches were founded and newspapers[1] started. The first church in Durban was attached to the Wesleyan mission and erected in Aliwal Street in 1842. The formal organization of the Anglican Church in Natal began in 1847. Among those who ministered in Natal was Dr J. W. Colenso, Bishop of Natal, whose liberal inclinations and unorthodox views regarding the scriptures resulted in his being deposed by Bishop Robert Gray, Metropolitan Archbishop of South Africa in 1863. Dr Colenso, however, appealed to the Privy Council, which pronounced the act of Bishop Gray null and void in law.

In 1858 some ninety Hollanders arrived. These settled near Stanger on the northern frontier and had the dual task of helping to defend the frontier and of growing sugar. Most of the other new settlers were British, and there was little chance of any other nationality attaining a majority. Over the years a limited form of representative government was granted, the electoral qualifications being high enough to exclude the Bantu from the franchise. In 1856 Natal had about 8,000 White inhabitants and in 1872, 17,500, but by then the Bantu had increased to 300,000 and Indians had begun to enter the colony. Although the cultivation of sugar-cane and cotton inevitably suggested Indian labour, there was a general opposition at first to importing Indians. The sugar industry, however, needed a steady supply of labour and was in danger of failing because the Bantu only wanted to work occasionally and were not dependable. In 1859, therefore, the Natal Government decided that indentured Indian labourers – who had been employed successfully in such places as Mauritius – should be brought to Natal. As far as the sugar industry was concerned this was a good investment, for production increased sevenfold in ten years; but as many Indians stayed after their time in the plantations, and as more and more entered the colony each year, a large Indian

[1] *The Natal Times*, 1852; *The Natal Mercury*, 1852; *The Natal Star*, 1859.

population[1] grew up, which produced another serious race problem.

The Bantu had been kept peaceful for several years by the skilful direction of Theophilus Shepstone, who made sure among other things that they had no access to liquor or firearms. But in 1873 trouble arose when Langalibalele, the chief of the Hlubi in the north, failed to comply with the arms regulations. The lieutenant-governor had ordered him to send eight men to Pietermaritzburg to register the rifles they had obtained in the diamond fields. Langalibalele only despatched five of the eight, and subsequently insulted government messengers sent to question him. The Hlubi's chief's impudence upset the other tribes and to remove a troublemaker the Natal Government sent an armed force to arrest him. The chief fled to Basutoland, his followers firing on the patrol that pursued, but the Bataung chief in whose village he sought sanctuary was afraid of the consequences of harbouring a runaway and surrendered him to the British authorities. Those Hlubi who continued to resist were then subdued and their land confiscated, and Langalibalele was brought to trial and given a term of imprisonment.

As a result of the rising of the Hlubi, the Colonial Secretary Lord Carnarvon, came to the conclusion that, instead of ruling through chiefs, more democratic methods should be employed, and he sent out General Sir Garnet Wolseley to reorganize native administration. Wolseley sought at first to try to give more natives the vote. In theory, those of long standing who had the property qualifications and had been discharged from living under native law could already vote. But none[2] applied to do so. They had too much to lose. For example, a man who entered European society was allowed only one wife. Realizing that the Bantu were not ready for a more democratic system, Wolseley decided to let things stay as they were. The only changes he made were to institute a High Court to hear appeals, to appoint a commission to

[1] The 1970 census gives 620,436 Asians, predominantly Indian.
[2] In 1893 there were three.

codify native law and to abrogate the marriage tax. It had been hoped that Wolseley's reforms would bring stability to Natal so that it might take part in Lord Carnarvon's intended scheme of federation of all the colonies in South Africa; and the measures he took, combined with the severe punishment which had been meted out to the Hlubi, might well have achieved this. But, owing to a crisis which now arose in neighbouring Zululand, it was not to be.

When the British replaced the Voortrekkers in control of Natal they took over the role of protectors of the Zulu people; and it was their interference in Zulu affairs in the time of Mpande's successor Cetshwayo that brought about the Anglo–Zulu War of 1879.

In 1856 many Zulus had been killed in an extremely bloody war of succession in which Cetshwayo defeated his younger brother Mbuyazi. At the beginning of the conflict, which took place in the area of the lower Tugela, John Dunn, hunter, trader and border agent, attempted the role of arbitrator; but he was surrounded along with Mbuyazi's followers, lost horse, rifle and all else, and narrowly escaped death. However, not long afterwards, he left his post as a border agent and became an adviser to the victor, settling permanently in Zululand and becoming a White chief under Cetshwayo's paramountcy, with many wives, followers and herds.

After the war of succession had been concluded Theophilus Shepstone visited Zululand to investigate the conditions prevailing there, and on meeting Cetshwayo, came to the conclusion that the new ruler was likely to make a troublesome neighbour. However, at the start the Zulu king not only sought but accepted British advice. At the time of his coronation, Cetshwayo asked for the presence of a British representative, and Shepstone attended with an impressive cavalcade, including a band and two nine-pounder field-guns. Also during the ceremony, the King agreed to pass new laws which ensured a fair trial for all criminals. After this good start relations with the Zulus deteriorated, at first due to the Voortrekkers in the north of Natal, to whom

Map VII   The Anglo-Zulu War, 1879

Mpande had promised territory beyond Blood River. The
Voortrekkers attempted to get Cetshwayo to sign a document
making the grant of the territory official, but the King
refused to do this, saying that his grandfather Shaka had
always asserted that by right of conquest the Zulus had
dominion of all the land from the Drakensberg to the sea.
With the help of John Dunn, the King drew up a memorandum setting out clearly the Zulu claims, and this was presented to Theophilus Shepstone. Unfortunately, Shepstone had
relinquished his post as Secretary for Native Affairs and
become, in 1877, the Administrator of the newly annexed
state of the Transvaal. His sympathies now were with the
Voortrekkers for whom he had become responsible. With his
new duties in the north he had no time to give to the matter.
He did not take any action on the receipt of the document
from Dunn and the King, and allowed the Voortrekkers to
occupy the disputed territory. It seemed as if war between
the Zulus and the Voortrekkers was imminent, but when the
Lieutenant-Governor of Natal agreed to set up a commission
of inquiry, it was temporarily avoided.

In the same year, however, there arrived on the scene a
figure who was to make war between the Zulus and the
Europeans inevitable, bearing in mind the manner of

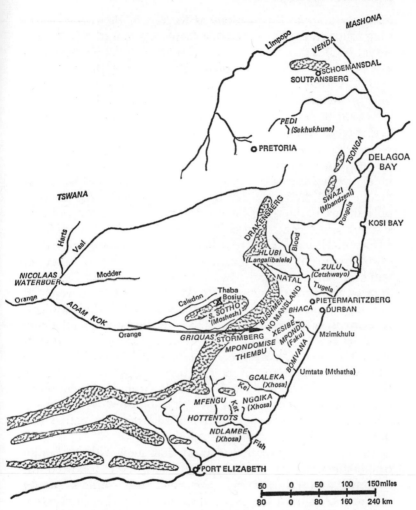

Map VIII Subjugation of the Native Peoples 1859–79

Cetshwayo's rule since the time of his coronation. In 1877 Sir
Bartle Frere was appointed Governor of the Cape and High
Commissioner for South Africa and given the task of creating
a confederation of the British and Boer states and Zululand.
When he obtained evidence of the tyrannical nature of
Cetshwayo's rule, which was now conducted in a manner

127

quite contrary to the agreement he had made at the beginning of his reign, Frere became firmly convinced that Cetshwayo, his indunas and warriors would have to be defeated in a war for the deliverance of the Zulu people, for in Frere's eyes Cetshwayo had become another Shaka, who would have to be removed from his throne before a civilized way of life could be brought to Zululand. Certainly there was some evidence to support Frere's view that Cetshwayo's methods were akin to those of his intolerant predecessors on the Zulu throne. For example, there was the affair which came to be known as the 'Marriage of the inGcugce'. When Cetshwayo was firmly established upon his throne he decided, with the support of his indunas, to reconstitute Shaka's entire military system, which had fallen into decay during the reign of Mpande. Hundreds of men had evaded military service on some excuse or another: for example, the number of witch-doctors, who had always been exempt, had increased greatly. Strong action was taken. Witch-doctors were reduced in number, the indunas were ordered to call all their subjects to arms, severely punishing any who disobeyed, and bring warriors regularly to the royal kraal for training; and firearms were bought from the Portuguese and any other traders who were willing to break the law against the profitable traffic in arms with natives. In this field, John Dunn managed to get hold of 250 weapons, though only a few were of good quality. The majority consisted of old muskets called disparagingly 'Birmingham gas-pipes'.

Shaka had been of the opinion that men without family ties made the best warriors, and Cetshwayo followed his example and reintroduced the rule that soldiers should remain single until the King decreed otherwise. Girls were governed by similar rules. In 1876 there were two regiments whose men had reached middle-age and were still unmarried. Cetshwayo therefore decided that they should choose brides from a young female regiment known as the inGcugce. A number of the girls refused to co-operate. Having made informal alliances with younger men, they did not like the idea of marrying forty year olds. Some fled to Natal. Others, trying to do so, were caught and put to death, their bodies being left on the main tracks leaving Zululand as a deterrent to girls with the same idea in mind. When news of this reached the British authorities in Natal, the Lieutenant-Governor sent a stiff message asking why Cesthwayo was behaving in this tyrannical way and not adhering to the promises made at his coronation. Worse, however, in the British view, was to follow. In July 1878 two women, the unfaithful wives of the sons of Chief Sirayo, fled and sought refuge in Natal. They were followed a few days later by their angry husbands with armed followers, who crossing the Buffalo and illegally entering British territory, seized the women by force, took them back into Zululand and put them to death. This incident again produced a reprimand for Cetshwayo, and an order to surrender the culprits for punishment; then, when the King refused to comply, details of his malpractices were passed by Frere to the authorities in London to convince them of the need to crush the Zulu King once and for all. About this time the committee of inquiry into the disputed territory gave its findings, and declared that the Boers should be allowed to settle, but not to possess the land. This meant that the Boers had been allotted the region in fact though not in name, and the Zulus, feeling greatly aggrieved, made preparations to fight for their rights. They were further aggravated when Frere demanded the disbanding of the Zulu army and the reaffirmation of their King's coronation pledges, but on John Dunn's advice were persuaded to wait on the defensive and force the British to make the first move.

The task of invading Zululand and forcing Cetshwayo to comply with the British demands was given to Lord Chelmsford, and he was allotted 6,000 British troops, 12,000 native auxiliaries and twenty nine-pounder field-guns. In the first instance he formed three columns to attack Zululand. None had any success. The northern column crossed Blood River and set up its camp at Kambula. While endeavouring to clear hostile Zulu from the plateaux of Hlobane a few miles east of the camp, a large detachment was attacked by a Zulu impi from Ulundi and cut to pieces. During the encounter

Piet Uys, the leader of the Boer commando which accompanied the British, was killed, as well as most of the Native auxiliaries with the detachment. However, the impi did not succeed in capturing the camp at Kambula. The southern column crossed the Tugela near its mouth and proceeded to Eshowe, where it was surrounded. It was later relieved with difficulty. The centre column crossed the Buffalo at Rorke's Drift and met with an even worse disaster. It set up its camp a few miles over the river at Isandhlwana, and when Lord Chelmsford with a part of the force went forward on a reconnaissance, an impi attacked and killed most of the men left guarding the camp. There had been almost 1,800 men at Isandhlwana at noon – 950 Europeans mostly from the 24th Regiment, and 850 Natal Kaffirs. By late evening fifty-five of the Europeans and 300 Natal Kaffirs were still alive, having escaped back into Natal.

The warriors of Cetshwayo's umCijo regiment were the heroes of this great Zulu victory. The impi came down from the Nqutu plateau in the fashion of Shaka's warriors of old. The *Right Horn* approached from the north, the *Left Horn* encircled the south and the *Chest* moving at a slower trot advanced in between. The encampment was set up on a ledge to the east of Isandhlwana Mountain. Although it was not entrenched, there were sufficient soldiers to man the two sides facing the Zulu attack. But 'the knuckle' between the north and east faces was entrusted only to native auxiliares and artillerymen; and the umCijo regiment struck at this vital place. Driving back the auxiliaries, the warriors broke through and attacked the thin red lines of the 24th Regiment alongside from front and rear simultaneously. In this way the whole camp was overrun and its guardians slain. However, the detachment of the 24th left in the buildings at Rorke's Drift in the rear was to redeem the honour of the Regiment.[1] Under Lieutenant Chard of the Royal Engineers it gallantly resisted all the attacks made by a large Zulu force under Cetshwayo's brother.

[1] No less than eleven Victoria Crosses were given to the defenders of Rorke's Drift, including one to Lieutenant Chard. There is still a John Chard Decoration awarded in the South African Defence Force.

Three months later Lord Chelmsford tried again and was more successful. This time there were only two columns. The southern one crossed near the mouth of the Tugela, but proceeded so slowly that it achieved nothing. The northern started from Dundee and crossed the Buffalo and Blood rivers well to the north of Rorke's Drift. It turned south before reaching the Umfolozi river, and joined the track leading directly from Rorke's Drift to Ulundi. While in the area of the upper White Umfolozi the deposed French Emperor's son, Louis Napoleon, the Prince Imperial, who was on attachment, was killed in an ambush. This later caused an international incident, but did not unduly delay the progress of Chelmsford's column at the time. After crossing the Umfolozi, Chelmsford formed his men into a great square and marched on Cetshwayo's capital. The King's impis attacked the square before it reached the royal kraal at Ulundi. On this occasion the fire from rifles, Gatlings and nine-pounders proved overwhelming. The Zulus unwisely surrounded the square, which was in the open, and charged. They were literally mown down, the nine-pounders sited at the corners of the square and firing grape being particularly destructive. When the Zulu survivors started to withdraw, Chelmsford loosed his cavalry from within the square. The 17th Lancers and King's Dragoon Guards galloped out and completed the rout. After the battle the King hid for a time in the hills in the north. Later, he was captured and deposed.

By this time General Sir Garnet Wolseley had taken office as High Commissioner, and Governor of Natal and the Transvaal Colony. Since the disaster at Isandhlwana had temporarily put a stop to the British Government's willingness to increase its South African responsibilities, Wolseley's instructions were not to annex Zululand but rather to arrange a peace settlement that would prevent a revival of the Zulu kingdom. The solution he adopted was an ingenious one. He banished Cetshwayo and divided Zululand into thirteen separate territories under separate chiefs. These chiefs included descendants of Zwide and Dingiswayo; Hamu,

Cetshwayo's cousin who had joined the British in the war; Zibhebhu who was a descendant of a brother of Shaka's father Senzanqakhona, and who had quarrelled with Cetshwayo; and finally the inimitable White chief, John Dunn. Each of the thirteen chiefs was made to undertake not to create an army, and to accept the arbitration of the British Resident. Unfortunately, the military defeat and Wolseley's settlement began a process of disintegration. The chiefs appointed by Wolseley were challenged by rivals and sharp disputes arose. It was not long before there were appeals for the restoration of Cetshwayo, whose cause was supported by the fiery South African prelate Bishop Colenso. In 1882 Cetshwayo was allowed to visit England where he was lionized by a sentimental public and given presents by Queen Victoria; but although he was allowed to return in 1883, Zibhebhu's territory in the north was excluded from his control, and so were the territories along the Natal border in the south. These latter, known as the Zulu Reserve, were brought under close British surveillance. Civil war followed between Cetshwayo and Zibhebhu in which Zibhebhu gained the upper hand, Ulundi being destroyed for the second time. Cetshwayo fled. He died in 1884. His surviving councillors chose as his heir his oldest son Dinizulu, a boy of fifteen, and they turned for support to the Afrikaner farmers who had been infiltrating into the northern part of Zululand during the previous two decades. The farmers recognized Dinizulu as paramount chief and helped him triumph over Zibhebhu. In return, they claimed a Boer Republic in north-western Zululand, centred on Vryheid east of Utrecht, and asserted also that the rest of the country, except for the Zulu Reserve adjacent to Natal, was subject to their protection.

Britain reacted against this extension of Afrikaner power in Zululand. After Afrikaners from the so-called 'New Republic'[1] had followed a Zulu chief into the Zulu Reserve and shot him, there were negotiations, with the result that in 1886 Britain recognized the 'New Republic', but with reduced boundaries, and the government of the 'New Repub-

[1] Afric: 'Nieuwe Republiek'.

lic' dropped its claim to a protectorate over Zululand. Then in 1887 the 'New Republic' was incorporated into the South African Republic and Britain annexed the rest of Zululand, dividing it into districts and appointing magistrates. When Dinizulu and his councillors tried to prevent the magistrates from taking powers out of the hands of the chiefs, he was arrested, convicted of treason and exiled to St Helena. Later he was allowed to return as the local headman of the Usutu district. In 1897 Zululand was incorporated into Natal, and in 1902 boundary commissions delimited extensive locations reserved for Zulu occupation. The large numbers[1] of Zulu living in the locations of Zululand marked out the territory as suitable to become a Bantu self-governing homeland like the Transkei. The first stages in this development occurred in 1971.

[1] According to the 1970 census there were 4,026,058 Zulus in South Africa.

Chapter 8

The Discovery of Diamonds — the First Anglo–Boer War, 1881

The conflicts in the east had not been resolved before serious ones arose in the west. In 1867 diamonds were discovered in Griqualand West in the neighbourhood of Hopetown on the Orange, a few miles from where it joins the Vaal; also on the east bank of the lower Vaal, and farther north on both sides of the lower Harts River. This area was an arid frontier zone sparsely populated by a few thousand people who recognized several different political authorities. The inhabitants included Tswana tribes like the Barolong and Tlhaping,[1] and some Afrikaner farmers of the Orange Free State with their Bantu and Coloured dependants. There were also British missionaries and traders, and transients on their way to the north; but the most important from the point of view of the diamonds were the Coloureds.

In 1803 the missionary William Anderson induced the mixed crowd of Bastards and Hottentots which had followed Barend Barends and the Kok brothers out of Cape Colony to settle in what became Griqualand West, from where his unruly protégées turned out luckless Bushmen. In 1813 another missionary, John Campbell, renamed the Bastards 'Griquas', and called their main centre Griquatown. His own name was given to another of their centres, and the whole large northern territory on both sides of the Harts and Vaal rivers became known as the Campbell Lands. At first Campbell appointed Barend Barends and Adam Kok as

[1] Of the Sotho language group like the Basutos (S. Sotho) and Pedi, (N. Sotho).

134

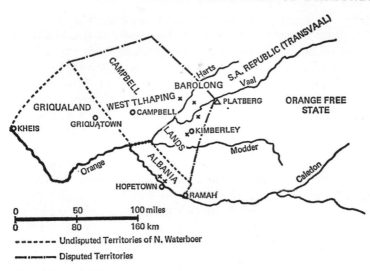

Map IX   The Disputed Diamond Area, 1871

captains, and furnished them with a code of laws, law courts and coinage. But later, Andries Waterboer of Bushman origin, the ablest of all the semi-civilized chieftains, came up from Cape Colony and was elected captain of the republic under the guidance of the missionaries. In 1834 Sir Benjamin D'Urban, Governor of the Cape Colony, made a treaty with Waterboer; he gave him a small salary and recognized him as an ally. Since that time, however, the West Griqua chiefdom had declined. Nicolaas Waterboer, who succeeded in 1853, was a weaker man than his father. The land dried up, the game was destroyed, diseases attacked the livestock and the Griquas became demoralized by cheap brandy peddled by traders from the Cape.

When diamonds were discovered, there were several claimants to the area. The Orange Free State considered that all the land east of the Vaal was part of its inheritance from the British Orange River Sovereignty, and that the rest of the Campbell Lands to the west of the Vaal had been included in the land purchased from Adam Kok in 1861 before he left with 3,000 of his Griquas for Nomansland in

135

Mpondo country on the coastal lowlands. The Transvaal Republic thought it owned the land east of the Harts and north of the Vaal. But the widest claims were made by an able Coloured lawyer from Cape Colony called David Arnot, on behalf of his client Nicholaas Waterboer. It was agreed that Waterboer's people had rights over that part of Griqualand which lay west and south of Griquatown, and also over the small territory known as Albania, north of the Orange River beyond Hopetown. Arnot, however, claimed the Campbell Lands as well, and so included in Waterboer's territories all the areas where diamonds had been discovered. His claims were based on the principle that Kok's people had only occupied the Campbell Lands as tenants, and therefore could not legally alienate them without Waterboer's consent, which had never been given. Therefore, according to Arnot, Nicholaas Waterboer's state still had as its boundaries the lines agreed under the various treaties made with his neighbours over the preceding years, namely:

(1) a southern line of the Orange River from Kheis, sixty miles west of Griquatown to Ramah, fifteen miles east of Hopetown – by reason of the 1834 Treaty with Governor D'Urban.

(2) an eastern line from Ramah, running east of Kimberley to Platberg on the Vaal – by reason of the 1838 Treaty with Adam Kok.

(3) a northern line from Platberg across the Harts River to Kheis again – by reason of the Treaties of 1842 and 1863 with Mahura, a Tlhaping chief.

It was in 1869 that the first diamond rush took place, its focus being the so-called 'alluvial diggings', most of which were on the north side of the Vaal above its junction with the Harts, in the area claimed by the Transvaal. President M. W. Pretorius reacted by putting pressure on the Tlhaping and Hottentot leaders to acknowledge the sovereignty of the Transvaal; but when the *Volksraad* granted a diamond-mining monopoly to a single company, the diggers formed an independent administration from among themselves and defied the Republican Government. Although Pretorius then hastily cancelled the monopoly, and gave the diggers assurances that they would be allowed self-government, they had been permanently estranged.

The next rushes took place in 1870–71 to the 'dry diggings' in the area later named Kimberley after Lord Kimberley, who was the Colonial Secretary from 1870–74. This area was claimed by the Orange Free State, and President J. H. Brand instructed a *landdrost* to assume authority. He issued regulations to resolve a dispute between the diggers and the companies which had bought farms on which diamonds were present; he also recognized diggers' committees which had already been formed as subordinate local authorities.

After Governor Sir Philip Wodehouse left South Africa in 1870, British interests were in the hands of a forceful Cape Colonial Secretary named Richard Southey, who was a keen expansionist, believing that Britain should block the western expansion of the two Afrikaner republics, protect the indigenous people, promote British trade by keeping the way to the north open, and generally to preserve British paramountcy. He reckoned the situation in West Griqualand offered him a chance of adopting such policies. Southey asked Arnot to send him a full statement of Waterboer's territorial claims; he put pressure on colonial newspaper editors to support them; he also arranged for petitions to be signed by colonial traders asking for British annexation of the diamond fields. With the documents from Arnot, he pressed the case for annexation, both with the authorities in Cape Town, and in London. Because of the evidence he submitted, his superiors came to the conclusion that the Afrikaner republics were about to destroy a Coloured community. Consequently they authorized a magistrate to be sent to the diggings under the obsolescent Cape of Good Hope Punishment Act of 1836. They also instructed the new Governor, Sir Henry Barkly (1871–7), to annex the territory claimed by Waterboer when he reached South Africa, provided that the diggers and indigenous peoples wanted it.

On his arrival Barkly took firm action. He immediately sent up troops to support the Cape magistrate. He also suggested that President Brand of the Orange Free State and

President Pretorius of the South African Republic should submit their claims to arbitration by a British tribunal. Brand refused, seeking international arbitration instead, but Pretorius surprisingly permitted the Transvaal's claims to be adjudicated by R. W. Keate, the lieutenant-governor of Natal – and agreed to abide by his decision. In the subsequent proceedings Keate came to the conclusion that Waterboer's territory extended as far east as Platberg, which vindicated Arnot's claim for his client on the east. On the strength of this, Barkly assumed that Waterboer's claims for the northern boundary were also valid, and in 1871 annexed all Griqualand West, including the Campbell Lands, as a Crown Colony. Pretorius was not unduly concerned,[1] but Brand was appalled and for many years continued to press the Orange Free State's claim to the Kimberley area. Eventually he achieved some result from his endeavours, for in 1875 a Land Court was set up to unravel once again the tissue of conflicting claims to territory in Griqualand, and this time it was ruled that Waterboer's claims to the Kimberley area were invalid. In spite of this the British Government would not agree to part with the land, and the Orange Free State had to be satisfied with a sum of £90,000, said to be the amount of damage it had sustained. Britain's attitude embittered some Free Staters and Transvaalers. It brought the two Afrikaner republics closer to each other. It also ensured that the Free State would have no part in the confederation scheme which Lord Carnarvon was trying to introduce.

In 1880, after rebellions among the indigenous peoples had been suppressed, Griqualand West was incorporated in Cape Colony. Although the Coloureds had been allotted farms, they very soon sold their land. By the end of the century they had ceased to exist as an organized community, and the few who remained worked for the Whites. The annexation had considerable effect on the subsequent development of South Africa, for it marked the first stage in the consolidation of British control of the southern part of the corridor along the

[1] The Transvaal *Volksraad* was; and it led to Pretorius's resignation, although the area eventually was left to the Republic.

western borders of the two Afrikaner republics. Control of the northern part of this corridor was later assured following disputes in the area after the first Anglo–Boer War of 1881, and then the two republics were encircled.

In the period from 1874 to 1880, which led up to the First Anglo–Boer War, Benjamin Disraeli, who was the Conservative Prime Minister, gave a free hand to Lord Carnarvon, his Colonial Secretary. Carnarvon was an avowed imperialist and regarded it as his task to unite South Africa under the Crown. In May 1875 he sent a despatch to Sir Henry Barkly, proposing that a conference of representatives of the White communities should be held to discuss native questions, the control of arms, and confederation; and he suggested the names of the individuals who might represent the colonies at the conference. This despatch had an unfavourable reception in Cape Colony, for the ministry of John Molteno, which was the first under responsible government, construcd it as imperial interference; in particular, the naming of the representatives to the proposed conference gave umbrage, because Carnarvon had included John Paterson the leader of the Eastern province's separatist movement which Molteno had been trying to scotch. Because of all this the Cape refused to send a representative. At this time, also, the British authorities were not on good terms with the Transvaal. President T. F. Burgers, who had succeeded M. W. Pretorius, wanted to modernize the state; and in order to gain access to the outside world without crossing British territory he planned to connect it by rail with Delagoa Bay. But when he tried to raise funds for his projects, the loans were under-subscribed, and he was convinced that this unsatisfactory response had been the result of British Government pressure. Thus the Transvaal, too, sent no one to the conference. When the conference met in London in August 1876 only Brand, representing the Free State, and Shepstone for Natal were present. The reduced meeting discussed various native problems, passed some non-binding resolutions and then dispersed. Brand had seen to it that confederation was never discussed, and Molteno, though in London, would not attend. In separate discussions, the latter said that he would not even sponsor the federal relationship that Carnarvon desired between Cape Colony and Griqualand West which was meant to be the first step towards his wider federation.

By the time the London conference ended, Carnarvon was preparing a more dramatic method of gaining his ends. The rival claims of Portugal and Britain to Delagoa Bay had been submitted to the President of France, McMahon[1], and in 1875 he gave his answer in favour of Portugal. This decision, combined with Burgers' attempts to construct a railway to the bay, aroused the fear that the republic might become too powerful. Carnarvon therefore decided to deal with the Transvaal while it was still weak and promote his confederation policy by forcibly bringing it into the British Empire. Pretexts were at hand to assuage the British public. There were missionary complaints of the Afrikaners' treatment of the natives, and traders and bankers were concerned about their investments in a bankrupt state. Also there were serious threats from the Zulus and Pedi to the Transvaal's security. Carnarvon discussed the situation with the principal British 'trouble-shooter' of the time, General Wolseley. On Wolseley's advice he despatched Theophilus Shepstone to the Transvaal, ostensibly to report on the situation, but armed with discretionary powers to annex the Transvaal Republic if he was convinced this was desired by the majority of the White inhabitants, and could be achieved without bloodshed. It has been suggested that Britain's wish to annex was strengthened by the discovery of gold in the Transvaal; but certainly the Colonial Secretary was sincere in his belief that annexation, and afterwards federation with the other colonies, was to the advantage of the people of the Transvaal in particular and those of South Africa in general.

Shepstone arrived in the Transvaal capital escorted by twenty-five mounted policemen and a small secretarial staff which included Rider Haggard, the author. President T. F. Burgers and Vice-President S. J. P. Kruger were against annexation, but some members of the Government seemed

[1] The Portuguese in Lourenço Marques still celebrate McMahon Day.

in favour, though they were hesitant to show their hand. Then suddenly, after three months of negotiation, Shepstone boldly decided on shock action. On 12 April 1877, he formally proclaimed the annexation of the South African Republic and took over the administration of the bankrupt state. For a people so devoted to freedom as the Transvaalers, there was at first remarkably little opposition to the annexation. The Boers' multifarious creditors and the British residents in the Transvaal were delighted with the change; the natives were pleased to exchange Boer rule for that of the more liberal English; even the Boers were too stunned by the *fait accompli* to do much at first. But although there was no physical opposition to the annexation, the Executive Council of the Republic at its final session instructed Paul Kruger, who had emerged as a principal representative of the conservative Afrikaners, and the State Attorney, Dr E. P. J. Jorissen, a Hollander whom President Burgers had originally imported to establish the educational system, to go to England to protest. Supplied by Shepstone with an inaccurate account of the state of public opinion among White Transvaalers, Carnarvon declined to discuss the deputation's request for a referendum on the annexation. On their return, Kruger and Jorissen reported to a well-attended meeting; it was decided to produce evidence of the attitude to the annexation by the customary Voortrekker method of signed petitions; and later, in 1878, Kruger and Piet Joubert went to London again with papers purporting to show that 6,591 Transvaalers were opposed to the annexation and only 587 were in favour of it. However, Sir Michael Hicks Beach, who had succeeded Carnarvon at the Colonial Office, declined to reopen the question.

Meanwhile, the natural leaders of the Transvaal Afrikaners built up the morale which had been at so low an ebb in 1877 and prepared their people for armed resistance. The discontent became more articulate when Shepstone was replaced by Colonel Sir Owen Lanyon, who proceeded to run the country as if it were a regiment, so that 'the government of the Transvaal became a timorous despotism, remote from the people, obsessed with making ends meet and dependent on small military garrisons stationed in the main towns'.[1] Lanyon's superior was Sir Bartle Frere, Governor, British High Commissioner and Governor-General designate of Carnarvon's proposed federation. Bartle Frere was sympathetic to the Transvaalers' aspirations. He had brought on the Zulu War partly to woo them. He advised the British Government by the newly opened telegraph cable to grant the Transvaal a modest degree of self-government without delay. Bartle Frere's period of office, however, proved to be short-lived. The disasters of the Zulu War were held to be his responsibility. He was sharply censured by the British Cabinet. Disraeli even spoke of impeaching him. Presently he was withdrawn to more limited duties as Governor of the Cape. With his departure went the last chance of a settlement in the Transvaal.

Frere's successor as High Commissioner, and therefore in charge of the Transvaal, was General Sir Garnet Wolseley. This jaunty and ambitious soldier was every bit as much a martinet as Lanyon. Disraeli once confided to Queen Victoria that Wolseley was an egotist and a braggart, but then shrewdly added that Nelson was too. Having sought and received confirmation of the Government's policy, Wolseley proceeded to announce it to the people of the Transvaal in bombastic fashion. 'So long as the sun shines,' he said, 'the Transvaal will remain British territory', and he added, 'the Vaal River would flow backwards through the Drakensberg sooner than the British would be withdrawn.' The protests of the Transvaalers now grew shriller. In January 1879, Kruger and Joubert reported on the second London mission to a large public meeting which took a resolution to work for independence; and in December a public meeting at Wonderfontein resolved to boycott British traders and all official institutions. Kruger, however, decided to hold his hand. Soon the troops brought in to fight the Zulus would be withdrawn. Soon, too, a new and more sympathetic Government might rule at Westminster. Gladstone in opposition was not only denouncing the annexation of Cyprus; he was also condemning the acquisition of the Transvaal. There seemed

[1] De Kiewiet, *Imperial Factor*.

142

little doubt that the vehemence of his oratory would sweep him into power.

Gladstone and the Liberals did return to office in 1880; but Gladstone found it difficult to redeem his election pledges; his policy towards South Africa became indecisive. This is to a large extent explained by dissension within the new Government. In the Transvaal, as in Ireland, the Liberals had to decide whether to meet a nationalist movement with coercion or concession. Forster, the Secretary of State for Ireland, and the humanitarian imperialists wanted to support the natives against the rapacious Boers; the Whig Peers, notably Kimberley and Hartington, were determined to uphold British prestige and supremacy. On the other hand, Gladstone, Chamberlain,[1] Bright and Dilke all sympathized with the Transvaal's demand for independence and inclined to concession. Indeed, all that united the groups was a desire to keep imperial expenditure in southern Africa to a minimum. To Kruger's inquiry as to when the Transvaalers might hope to receive independence, Gladstone replied: 'Our judgement is that the Queen cannot be advised to relinquish her sovereignty over the Transvaal.' This was long-winded; but not ambiguous. The Transvaalers saw now that they would have to fight for their freedom.

Britain was by this time unprepared for such a struggle, and Wolseley was largely responsible. He had spent his last months as High Commissioner arranging for the troops used in Zululand to leave; and while doing so was assuring everyone that the Boers would never fight. By the time he had handed over to his friend and protégé Sir George Pomeroy Colley, only three battalions remained in the Transvaal, and these were scattered in isolated garrisons all over the country. Colonel Lanyon in Pretoria was still in command. He, too, underestimated both the seriousness of the Boers' disaffection and their military capability. Indeed, his judgement was astonishingly wide of the mark. Through October and November 1880 he minimized the significance of the

---

[1] Chamberlain later changed his views – and his party. He joined the Conservative–Unionists, and was Colonial Secretary before and during the Second Anglo–Boer War of 1899–1902.

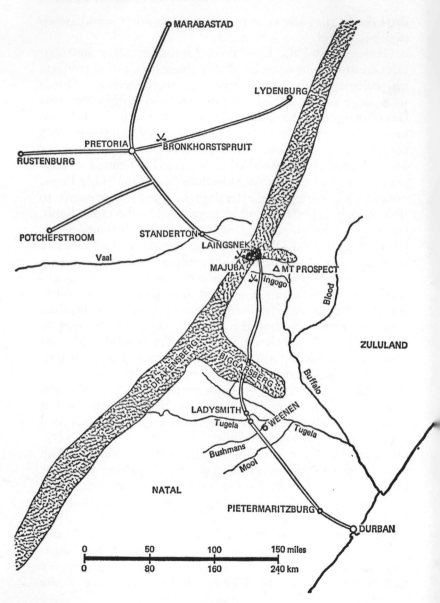

Map X   The First Anglo-Boer War, 1881

growing signs of unrest, and even when, on 4 December, he realized that an armed rising might be imminent, he dismissed it with the comment: 'They cannot do much for their commissariat will be limited'. And in a letter to Colley a week later he wrote: 'I don't think we shall have to do much more than show that we are ready, and sit quiet and allow matters to settle themselves . . . the Boers are incapable of any united action, and they are mortal cowards, so anything they may do will be but a spark in the pan.'

Potchefstroom, the capital of the south-west region, saw the start of the uprising. The local magistrate had ordered the costs for an action to be paid by seizing and selling the wagon of the burgher concerned. Commandant (later General) Piet Cronje, one of the malcontents of the district, thereupon organized an improvised commando which rode into the town on the morning of the sale, settled down grimly in its central square, and pulled the sheriff off the wagon when he put it up for auction. Then, amid triumphant shouts, they restored it to the burgher. From this incident grew a general rebellion of the burghers against British authority, the investment of the garrisons, and the appointment of Kruger, Joubert and ex-President M. W. Pretorius to govern the Transvaal in the place of the British.

Potchefstroom was also the cause of Colley's premature attack at Laingsnek. The garrisons at Pretoria, Rustenburg, Marabastad, Lydenburg and Standerton had sufficient food and ammunition for two to three months. At Potchefstroom matters were by no means so satisfactory. There the garrison of 120 infantry and artillery, and a small detachment of mounted men, were ill supplied with food. Not more than a month's supply could be counted on. They had been hastily moved from Pretoria to deal with the riot over the wagon; two officers and about twenty men had already been killed or taken prisoner out of the small isolated force; and it was known that a strong, active, and very energetic body of Boers under Piet Cronje were closely investing the place. As Colley himself wrote: 'Our weak point is Potchefstroom. Unless I can in some way relieve the pressure on it before the middle of next month, I am afraid that garrison must fall into the Boers' hands.'

Earlier British attempts to reinforce the garrisons had failed. The first was an internal affair within the frontiers of the Transvaal when Colonel Anstruther led a column from Lydenburg in the east to reinforce Pretoria 190 miles away. The Boers learnt of the move from spies, and Frans Joubert's commando ambushed the column at Bronkhorstspruit, thirty-six miles short of Pretoria. Although warned against being stopped on the road and well aware that fighting was about to break out at any moment, Colonel Anstruther took few precautions. Neither did he hurry to reach Pretoria; he proceeded very slowly with his force of 250 of the 94th (Connaught Rangers), three wives and two children of the men, and numerous baggage wagons. He received his orders on 27 November, but by Christmas week the column was still well short of its destination.

The men were in holiday mood, and as the column approached the small watercourse called Bronkhorstspruit the regimental band was playing, 'Kiss me mother, kiss your darling daughter', and the soldiers were roaring out the choruses cheerfully, and in between munching the peaches they had acquired at the last halt. When the colonel, on ahead, was approaching the slope down to the spruit, he caught sight of mounted men on a ridge in front and, turning, saw more men amid the cover on both sides of the road. Apprehensive, he called a halt; and not long afterwards a burgher with a white flag rode up. The emissary delivered a note to the British commander. Signed by the rebel leaders Kruger, Joubert and Pretorius, it told him to turn back, for an advance on Pretoria would constitute an act of war. It is thought that Anstruther was given only two minutes to decide. In any case, having delivered his warning the horseman rode away. Unwilling to recognize or accept orders from the rebel junta, Anstruther decided to ignore the summons, but before the British troops could open out from their column, or the bandsmen reach the wagons for their weapons, the surrounding Boers opened fire. All the British officers were picked off at once and within a few minutes 120 dead and wounded men lay sprawled across the road. The Boers lost only two men killed and five wounded. Colonel Anstruther was hit several times, and after murmuring that he 'had better leave a few men to tell the story', ordered his bugler to sound the 'cease fire'. He was later to die of his wounds. After the shooting stopped, the Boers treated their victims well, setting up makeshift hospitals and releasing prisoners on parole. They were particularly concerned to discover that one of the women in the wagons had been wounded. The dead were buried by the side of the road where they had fallen, and legend has it that the peaches in their pockets took root and grew into a grisly line of fruit trees.

The next attempt to relieve the Transvaal garrisons was made by General Colley with a force from Natal, but by the time he was moving off from Newcastle, Commandant-General Piet Joubert with General Nicolaas Smit as second-in-command, and several commandos numbering 2,000 burghers, had moved south and set themselves across the British advance in a strong defensive position at the pass Laingsnek along the line of hills on the border of the Transvaal and Natal. When Colley approached Laingsnek, mist hid the Boer position and he halted four miles away at Mount Prospect Farm, which was to become his camp and headquarters, waiting for visibility to improve. The road from Natal into the Transvaal curled round, rising not very steeply, through the barrier of hills at Laingsnek. On the west of the road was the dominating Majubu Hill with O'Neill's farm at its foot. On the east was a flat-topped ridge stretching towards the source of the Buffalo River. Directly the mist cleared, the whole crest of the ridge was seen to be alive with Boers, and Colley decided to attack them, planning to send his cavalry[1] against a detached hill on the east, from which cross-fire could be delivered, and his infantry,[2] covered by fire from his field-guns and rocket-tubes, in a frontal attack on the ridge. Everything went wrong. When the first troop of cavalry failed to reach the top of the hill, the second refused

[1] A sprinkling of men from the 1st King's Dragoon Guards and the rest mounted infantry.
[2] Mainly the 58th Regiment (Rutlands, later Northamptons).

even to try; and the infantry, exposed to cross-fire from the hill as well as fire from the front, were repelled with heavy casualties.

The next engagement came as a result of Colley's efforts to protect his line of communications back to Newcastle. Dispatches and mail carried by mounted natives had been attacked, and were only saved from capture by the rapid flight of the bearers back to camp. A convoy being expected from Newcastle, Colley decided to lead a column to escort the post half-way to Newcastle and then return with the convoy. He marched south with a small force, left a company to guard the drifts over the Ingogo River and established the rest on the low plateau of Schuinshoogte, where the post had been ambushed earlier. Here surprisingly, for it seemed unlikely the Boers would strike again in the same place, he was attacked by a strong force of Boers who crept up on the British under cover of boulders and tambookie grass. By afternoon the situation seemed hopeless. Then help came in the form of a heavy rainstorm. Towards sundown the incredulous British found the Boers had disengaged. With the darkness of night and the noise of the storm protecting them, both detachments got away with the loss of eight men swept to destruction in the swollen waters of the Ingogo at the drifts.

Laingsnek had been a repulse; Ingogo a success of sorts as the detachments had managed to get away; but the final engagement of the war was a signal disaster. Having failed to take the ridge dominating the pass on the east, Colley decided to occupy Majuba which controlled it on the west. He chose a mixed detachment of infantry[1] with some sailors and led them by night past O'Neill's farm up on to the top of the flat-topped mountain, which was found to be unoccupied; 365 men established themselves on the top of Majuba just as dawn was breaking, and on the orders of the commander formed a thin defence line around its perimeter. The first shots occurred when the 92nd opened fire on a party of about thirty Boers who rode up from the north unconscious of the British on the hill. Had a heavy fire been opened they would

[1] 58th and 92nd (Gordons).

probably have all been killed, but not being sure what General Colley wanted, the officers ordered their men to stop firing. Meanwhile, firm news of the British occupation of Majuba had reached the Boers headquarters from another source. The wife of the farmer living on the western slopes saddled her pony and galloped down to the Boer camp and told Joubert that she had seen the redcoats ascending the hill. Joubert was unconvinced and declared they must be mountain goats. He was soon set right, however, when Mrs Joubert, who like many of the burghers' wives had accompanied her commandant husband to the war, sarcastically inquired: 'Since when have mountain goats been dressed in red tunics?'

The first reaction of the Boers was near panic. Some even inspanned their wagons with the intention of abandoning their defence line to seek safety from the barrage of shells likely soon to fall among them. However, the realization that no cannon had been taken up Majuba, together with an impassioned harangue from Joubert, made them change their attitude. A hastily convened council of war called for volunteers to dislodge the British. When ninety-two young Boers, including Christiaan Rudolph de Wet, responded, General Nicolaas Smit was given the task of leading them to take the hill.

Divided into three commandos, these first volunteers saddled up and rode off to Majuba's north face, where terraces offered easier access to the top. They were not to be alone. Older burghers, who were good marksmen, stationed themselves around the western base of Majuba to give covering fire. The subsequent engagement proved a military triumph for the Afrikaners. Following instinctively the basic principle for a successful attack, namely fire and movement; they killed,[1] wounded or captured 280 of the 365 British on Majuba, and they drove the remainder off the hill for the loss to themselves of only two dead and five wounded.

After Majuba the Boers set out to destroy the British camp at Mount Prospect; but as at Ingogo, the weather intervened. Torrential rain began to fall and a thick mist shrouded their

[1] Including Colley.

objective. Satisfied with their success on Majuba, they returned to their defence lines. Bad weather saved Mount Prospect from destruction, but it did not prevent the camp from becoming an unhappy place of recrimination. Private soldiers blamed the officers for bad leadership; officers denounced the men as cowards. After four days this was changed by the arrival of General Sir Evelyn Wood with reinforcements. Inspired by him, the Natal Field Force was soon anxious to try again. But this was not to be. The British Government had been attempting to come to terms with the Boers before and during Colley's operations. Now, after Majuba, they were adamant on peace at almost any price. General Wood, to his disappointment, was not allowed another 'brush with the Boers'. Instead, he was set the task of working out peace terms with their leaders, Kruger, Joubert and Pretorius, at O'Neill's cottage at the foot of Majuba Hill.

Chapter 9

Rhodesia Founded, and the South African Republic Surrounded

Under the terms[1] of the Pretoria Convention of 1881 at the end of the war between the Transvaal and Britain the state acquired complete self-government subject to Her Majesty's suzerainty. The Convention also defined its boundaries, gave to a British Resident powers over the native population, and entitled Britain to move troops through the country and to control external relations.[2]

In the years following the signing of the Convention, Britain had need to try to enforce its agreed articles, the first occasion being when Transvaal subjects began to move over the Western boundary line of their state. This threatened the corridor to the north, over the southern end of which the British had gained control when West Griqualand had been annexed. The new Afrikaner westward expansion occurred between West Griqualand and Mafeking to the north. Farmers from the Transvaal first occupied lands beyond the agreed western boundary of the state. Then they entered into agreements with the leaders of the peoples living there and became embroiled in their quarrels. In the south of the region the farmers gave help to Coloureds under Taaibosch, with the result that they gained the upper hand over a local Tlhaping tribe. Then, in return, the Coloureds allowed the farmers to set up an independent republic in their midst

---

[1] These terms were modified at the London Convention in 1884 which did not include the term 'suzerainty.'

[2] Clause IV in the London Convention – it was to become the most disputed clause.

called Land Goshen. Almost the same thing happened farther
north when the Transvaalers, after helping one Barolong
tribe in a dispute with another, were allowed by the victors
to set up an independent state near Mafeking[1] called
Stellaland. Both states were soon in a condition of anarchy
and because of this seemed likely to be incorporated in the
Transvaal. Therefore, as they were well beyond the boundary
of the Republic, which had been fixed at the London Convention to the east of Mafeking, and as they also lay athwart
the desired corridor to the north, the British authorities
decided to take action. First, a British commissioner was
sent from Cape Colony to try to restore law and order. He
managed to do so in Stellaland, but was unable to control the
'wild men' of Land Goshen, and Kruger, growing impatient
at the continued anarchy beyond his western border, issued
a proclamation taking Land Goshen under Transvaal protection. Kruger's action provoked a strong British counter-
action. Germany had just proclaimed a protectorate over
the coast of South-West Africa, and the area of the dispute
lay in Bechuanaland, which offered Germany a link to the
Transvaal, so the British Government dispatched a force of
5,000 men under General Sir Charles Warren not only to
restore order but to hold the area. Warren's force proved
formidable enough to carry out its tasks without bloodshed;
the settlers offered no resistance; Kruger withdrew his claim;
and the natives who lived south of the Molopo River and
west of the Transvaal border readily accepted British protection. In 1885 the area was annexed as the Crown Colony
of British Bechuanaland; ten years later it was incorporated
in Cape Colony.

In the area immediately north of the Molopo the Tswana
tribes had not been subjected to so much pressure as those
south of the river. However, following the advice of the
missionaries and the traders living amongst them they also
agreed to accept British protection. During the 1890s the
boundary of this new Bechuanaland Protectorate was
extended to take in the whole homeland of the Tswana
peoples. In 1966 it blossomed into the self-governing inde-

[1] Around the farm Rooigrond.

pendent state of Botswana. Closely linked economically to the present Republic of South Africa, it was, along with Basutoland (Lesotho) and Swaziland, a model for the self-governing Bantu homelands created by the Republic within its own territory like the Transkei, the Venda homeland in the north, and Zululand.

Meanwhile, in the independent Boer republics a national Afrikaner consciousness and culture was developing. In 1875 a group of intellectuals at Paarl, thirty-five miles north-east of Cape Town, introduced the concept that the Afrikaners were a distinct nation, occupying the distinct fatherland of South Africa and speaking the distinct language of Afrikaans; and that they had, as their destiny under God, the task of ruling South Africa and civilizing its heathen inhabitants, the majority of whom they were convinced had arrived in the country only in the sixteenth century, at the same time as their own people. The founder and first leader of the organization at Paarl was the Revd S. J. du Toit, a *predikant* of the Dutch Reformed Church. He and his followers produced a newspaper called *Di Patriot*, printed in Afrikaans for the first time, which was used along with other publications to disseminate a nationalist mystique. In 1879 du Toit launched the political organization known as the *Afrikaner Bond* which quickly struck roots in the central and eastern districts of Cape Colony. Then in 1882 Jan Hofmeyr, who edited a Dutch paper in Cape Town, began to dominate the *Afrikaner Bond*. Hofmeyr had very different views from du Toit as to the role of the *Bond*. Whereas du Toit's nation was to be Afrikaner, Hofmeyr wanted to include any White people who were truly South African.[1] Also, whereas du Toit had no confidence in the Cape parliamentary system, Hofmeyr favoured working within this and other existing colonial institutions. In the end Hofmeyr prevailed because the Afrikaners of Cape Colony preferred his ideas to du Toit's more revolutionary ones.

[1] This dichotomy has been present throughout the history of the country; from time to time leaders emerging following the line of either du Toit or Hofmeyr.

In Cape Colony from 1884 onwards the *Bond* under Hofmeyr became an important political party, often holding many seats in both houses of the Cape Parliament, and, although Bond members never took office as a party, they were able to exert considerable influence on the policies of governments.

A British member of the Cape Parliament who worked very closely with Hofmeyr was Cecil John Rhodes.[1] The son of an English clergyman, Rhodes migrated to Natal for health reasons in 1870 at the age of seventeen. He moved to Kimberley and by drive and business acumen gained control through his De Beers Consolidated Mines of the whole producing and marketing sides of the diamond industry. He also founded Consolidated Gold Fields, which was later one of the major gold-mining concerns in the Transvaal. Having amassed great wealth and entered politics, Rhodes considered it his role to promote the expansion of the British Empire in Africa from a base in Cape Colony. Using the corridor to the north recently acquired by the annexation of West Griqualand and the two sections of Bechuanaland, Rhodes planned the subjugation of the new territory of the Matabele beyond the Limpopo, where Mzilikazi had taken his people when he had been driven from the high veld by Hendrik Potgieter. Rhodes then envisaged a further expansion northwards to link up with a southern British drive from Egypt and the Sudan.

Hofmeyr and Rhodes found they had much in common. They agreed that the British Government should be restrained from interfering directly in the internal affairs of South Africa, and that the future of the country depended on the co-operation of Boer and Briton. They agreed in regarding the African tribesmen as barbarous people who were too uncivilized to participate in the democratic political systems of the colonies and republics. In general terms, too, they agreed that a union of the states of South Africa, under the protection of Britain, was desirable. At first, Hofmeyr was reluctant to support Rhodes's plans for northward expansion, because they seemed to intrude upon the preserves of the

[1] Prime Minister from 1890 to 1896.

South African Republic. Ever since they had driven Mzili-kazi across the Limpopo in 1838, the Transvaalers had considered that they had a special relationship with him and his successor, Lobengula. In 1887 Lobengula put his mark to a treaty presented by the Transvaal Government, stating that he was an ally of the Republic and would admit a Republican consul and allow him to exercise jurisdiction over Transvaal subjects residing in his kingdom. The treaty seemed to be clearing the way for Transvaal penetration and ultimate control of the lands across the Limpopo. But this development was checked by Cecil Rhodes with the help of the High Commissioner[1] and the co-operation of his political colleague Jan Hofmeyr. Robinson sent John Moffat, the son of the missionary Robert Moffat, to obtain Lobengula's mark to another treaty which gave the High Commissioner control over his treaty-making and concessionary-granting powers. By this time Hofmeyr had come to regard the Transvaal as a major obstacle to harmony in South Africa and supported Rhodes's expansion schemes by promising *Bond* support for any ministry Rhodes was able to form, on the assumption that Rhodes in return would promote the interests of the Afrikaners of Cape Colony.

For twenty years the Matabele under Lobengula lived as had their forefathers under Mzilikazi: the people rigidly disciplined and the young warriors going off raiding each year into Mashonaland to the east. The relationship between the Matabele and the Mashona was a strange one. Mzilikazi regarded the Mashone as suitable prey for occasional forays, but like game-birds on a well ordered shoot, only in season. They were thus culled at intervals but never completely destroyed. A suitable area was chosen for each raid and, when it had been despoiled, sufficient survivors were left to replant the crops and build up the cattle herds. Then it would be left untouched for a period until it recovered. The forays took place each winter, the area being chosen by the King himself casting a spear in the desired direction. It is difficult to estimate the extent of the devastation caused by the Matabele

[1] Sir Hercules Robinson (1881–9) and Sir Henry Loch (1889–95).

raids on the Mashona. Some say that it was exaggerated by Rhodes and his lieutenants to justify their intervention in the country, but it is certain that the Mashona put up a poor resistance. 'We had only to shout as we approached,' said one warrior, 'and the cowardly dogs climbed the hills and rocks and hid themselves.' An American observer classed the Mashona as cowardly and cringing, 'lacking even the redeeming quality possessed by many savage races – courage'. For the Matabele, on the other hand, the raids satisfied their blood-lust, and brought a rich dividend in grain and cattle.

Towards the end of the century changes came about in the pattern of life, when Europeans began to press in on the Matabele kingdom from three sides: the Germans from the west, the Portuguese from the east, and the Boers and British from the south. The lure was the reputed mineral wealth to be found in the territories which the Matabele dominated. Soon representatives seeking concessions became a feature of Lobengula's court at Bulawayo, the most persistent being those who represented Cecil Rhodes and the British.

Rhodes did not make any personal contact with Lobengula, instead he sent a series of negotiators to act on his behalf. His first representative was the missionary at Lobengula's court, John Moffat, whose father had been so friendly with Mzilikazi. Concession hunters had been thronging into Matabeleland, and in 1888 there were thirty of them camping in the vicinity of the royal kraal at Bulawayo, all trying to get mineral rights for themselves or the countries they represented. They came to be known as Lobengula's 'Foreign Legion' or 'The White Sharks', and to gain advantages had begun to offer considerable bribes. John Moffat, however, held his own among them, and managed to persuade the King that Britain was a worthier friend than Germany, Portugal or the Transvaal. On 11 February 1888 he persuaded Lobengula to sign a treaty of friendship which pledged the King to cede none of his territory without Britain's consent. It was about this time that E. A. Maund became so disgusted with the goings-on of the concession hunters at Bulawayo that he left for England with two of

Lobengula's indunas to petition the Queen against the concession seekers troubling the King.

The initial spade-work done by the missionary was
followed up by the efforts of a team headed by Charles Rudd,
the others being Frank Thompson and Charles Maquire. In
September 1888, armed with an introductory letter from the
High Commissioner at the Cape, they reached Bulawayo.
Rudd gave the King a sweetener of a hundred gold sovereigns
at his first audience and then began to press him to come to
terms with Rhodes. Day after day he continued raising his offer
until the King began to show an interest. He was helped by a
timely visit from the administrator of the new British Protectorate of Bechuanaland. Lobengula was always impressed
by pomp and circumstance, and the administrator, Sir Sydney
Shippard, was wise enough to appear dressed in a smart frock
coat and with an imposing escort of troopers of the Bechuanaland Border Police. Their arrival added weight to Rudd's
argument that Britain was the most powerful of the rival
countries and therefore his most worthy friend. Anyhow, it
was sufficient to persuade him that it would be to his advantage to grant Rudd a concession and get rid of the other
troublesome concessionaires. On 30 October 1888, therefore,
he put his mark on a document which granted Rhodes's
company the right to all the metals and minerals to be found
in his kingdom, together with full powers 'to do all the things
that might be deemed necessary to win and procure the same'.
In return Rudd promised to pay the King £100 a month, to
supply him with a gunboat on the Zambezi, and also provide
1,000 modern rifles and 100,000 rounds of ammunition.

Both sides were at first content with this arrangement.
Lobengula believed he had got rid of the other concessionaires, that only a few miners were likely to dig in Mashonaland, and that the new modern weapons would enable his
men to raid more effectively. Rudd, on the other hand,
recognized that Lobengula had opened up his kingdom to
exploitation on a large scale. John Moffat realized this, too.
When he heard, he was indignant at the way his friend had
been hoodwinked about the significance of the treaty. 'I feel
bound to tell you,' he wrote to Rhodes, 'that I look on the

whole plan as detestable, whether viewed in the light of policy or morality. When Lobengula finds it all out, as he is sure to do sooner or later, what faith will he have in you?'

Leaving Thompson and Maquire behind at Bulawayo to keep Lobengula sweet, Rudd returned to Kimberley to break the good news to Rhodes, but he had hardly done so before Lobengula changed his mind. Lobengula's warriors had become almost mutinous on hearing about the Rudd concession. They threatened to kill Maquire, who immediately fled, and at their instigation Lobengula repudiated the concession and ordered the execution of the induna who had advised him to sign, together with more than three hundred of his household. Rhodes had just returned from London, where he had been trying to negotiate a Royal Charter for his British South Africa Company to exploit the concession, when he heard the unwelcome news of its repudiation and the flight of the last of his negotiators, Thompson, who had now followed Maquire. As usual, he reacted swiftly to the crisis. He sent his old friend Dr L. S. Jameson up to Bulawayo with instructions to use all his charm 'and everything else he could think of' to persuade Lobengula to recognize the Rudd concession again.

Within a month of Thompson's flight, Jameson was at Bulawayo and soon got into the King's good books by treating his dropsy and gout, and telling him that all great men suffered from the latter. Then, as at the time of Rudd's visit, lucky chance played a part in the form of a deputation from Britain, bearing a letter from Queen Victoria, escorted to Matabeleland by troopers in full dress. Impressed again by the pomp of Britain as evidenced by its official representatives, Lobengula began to weaken, and in December 1889, grudgingly gave permission for Rhodes's company to dig for gold at Tati in the south of his kingdom. Then, in an unguarded moment, when he had partaken too freely of sorghum beer, he added that if no gold was found – and no gold was – they might prospect in Mashonaland, provided they took a route round Matabeleland so as not to provoke the young warriors. To ratify this Lobengula would accept delivery of the rifles and ammunition mentioned in the Rudd concession – and so in fact he renewed it.

It had been a neat performance by Jameson, for by February 1890 he was able to return to Kimberley with the news that Lobengula would permit the passage of the company's mineral prospectors into Mashonaland. He had not told the King that there would be several hundred of them, or that permission to dig would result in the occupation of Mashonaland by Rhodes's men. Meanwhile, Rhodes had with some difficulty managed in October 1889 to obtain a Royal Charter for his company, which gave it the monopoly of exploiting the minerals of Mashonaland and all the functions of government there. This was a considerable achievement, as there were many in Britain who were against such power being given to a profit-making concern. The most vociferous were Henry Labouchère, the editor of *Truth*, and the representatives of the missionary societies, and these were to hamper the British South Africa Company's endeavours for many years to come. But now at least the stage was set for the legendary march of Rhodes's Pioneers.

The column consisted of 380 Europeans from all ranks of society, but having in common a high degree of determination and courage. Half were prospectors and half Company police taken to guard the column on its northward march and to keep order in Mashonaland. There were also a large number of native servants and labourers, and many transport animals and wagons. There seem to have been several who could be termed leaders. Frank Lawson was the contractor who organized the column. F. C. Selous, the famous hunter, plotted the route to avoid Matabele settlements in accordance with Lobengula's stipulations. Colonel Pennefather was column commander, and A. R. Colquhoun administrator in Mashonaland. But the most important person present was undoubtedly Dr Jameson. Having already played an important part in gaining the concession from Lobengula, he was to take over the post of administrator from Colquhoun and lead the settlers in the troublesome times ahead.

On 27 June 1890 the column crossed into Matabeleland,

and by 11 July had reached Tuli, where the Pioneers stopped to build a fort. On leaving Tuli they moved slowly eastwards along a track laboriously hacked out by native labourers under the supervision of Selous, who determined the route by compass and sextant as at sea. They were now in territory where they might expect an attack on their western flank from Lobengula's young warriors. It was the low veld bush country, well suited to ambushes, and everyone was aware that in Bulawayo Lobengula was being pressed by the warriors to let them attack the column. Nor was the country easy to traverse in spite of Selous's skill in choosing the best way. There was a series of rivers athwart the route, and although it was the dry season, each crossing presented difficulties. Crossings divided the column for hours at a time and made it vulnerable to attack.

Fortune, however, favoured the Pioneers. Somehow Lobengula restrained his warriors from attacking while the Pioneers were on the low veld, and on 17 August 1890, they reached the steep scarp of the Rhodesian plateau where they were safer. Almost as if by a miracle, they found a long valley leading up on to the plateau and thankfully named it Providential Pass. At the top they built another fort and called it Victoria in honour of the Queen.

From then on the way was easier, for they were now in open park-like country, and moving out of range of the Matabele impis. Just short of their chosen destination, however, at Umfuli on 6 September 1890, they almost failed to get across the last river-bed on the route. One pioneer wrote that in fording this river, which had a sandy bed and steep banks, the oxen had become so weak that 'the men placed the yokes on their own necks and pulled as though they were cattle'. Then, on 13 September 1890, in the region of their goal, the Pioneers, having chosen a suitable site for settlement, ran up the Union Jack where modern Salisbury[1] now lies, and disregarding Lobengula's claim to sovereignty of Mashonaland, they took possession of the country in the name of the Queen. Thus, without the loss of a single life,

[1] The settlement was named Salisbury after the Prime Minister at the time.

9 Boer Generals Meyer, Botha and Erasmus (National Army Museum)

Boer commando on Spion Kop

10 President M. T. Steyn of the
Orange Free State (Information Office, Pretoria)

John X. Merriman

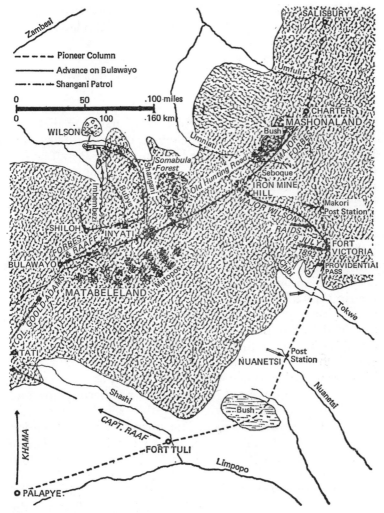

Map XI   Foundation of Rhodesia

Rhodesia was born, and the Transvaalers cut off from the north.

President Paul Kruger of the Transvaal was not pleased to see the British occupy what was to become Rhodesia, but he was much more concerned with Afrikaner expansion to the east which, besides providing fresh land could lead to the sea and permit an independent link with the outside world. After 1887, when Britain annexed Zululand, the only portion of the south-east coastline not under European control was Tongaland. This included Kosi Bay, half-way between Delagoa Bay and the inlet at the mouth of the Umfolozi; and Kosi was considered a possible harbour. If the Republic was to reach Tongaland, it had to absorb the intervening territories, including the Swazi kingdom whose independence had been guaranteed under the London Convention of 1884. Consequently, in 1889 Kruger had let the British Government know that he would not oppose Rhodes's plans for the north, if Britain would give him a free hand in the east. In March 1890 the High Commissioner, Sir Henry Loch, accompanied by Cecil Rhodes, met Kruger and offered him a strip through Tongaland for a railway to Kosi Bay, provided his country would enter into a customs union with the South African colonies and abandon its claims to the north; but this offer was refused because Kruger was not willing to enter into a customs union. Loch then appointed Hofmeyr as his representative to negotiate with Kruger, as Hofmeyr was by this time committed to Rhodes's northern plans and anxious that the South African Republic should enter into a South African customs union. The outcome was a convention which, as already mentioned, led to the incorporation of Swaziland; but the Transvaal would still have nothing to do with a customs union, so failed to get its seaport. Then in 1895, the British Government closed the last gap; it annexed Tongaland and the neighbouring chiefdoms. After this the South African Republic was completely hemmed in.

Chapter 10

Doctor Jameson

After the occupation of Mashonaland by the Pioneers, Dr Jameson remained as administrator for the Chartered Company. For a year or so there was no trouble from the Matabele, and the prospectors came to the conclusion that their neighbours were not the 'dread Matabele' of whom they had been warned. In 1891, however, Lobengula began to realize that he was losing control when one of the chiefs north-west of Salisbury refused to pay his annual tribute. Lobengula sent an impi that killed the chief and three of his indunas. Jameson remonstrated through the Company's representative at Bulawayo, and received the reply that the chief had said he was no longer subordinate to Lobengula because of the White men in Mashonaland. Lobengula, however, claimed the chief was still his slave, and that was why, when rebellious, he had been killed.

This showed a difference in standpoint between the King and the Company. The King considered he was still overlord of Mashonaland and could raid as of old, and punish those who did not obey him. On the other hand, Jameson believed that the collection of tribute and punishment for offences in the territory occupied by the Whites should be the responsibility of the Company on behalf of the King. Jameson tried to make an arrangement for the Matabele to refrain from raiding east of the Umniati and Tokwe rivers, and to keep away from the post-road to the south used by the settlers; but the King would not agree to such restrictions, and further intrusions occurred.

The first was in a camp north of Victoria where the raiders frightened the Mashona so much that the overseer could hardly persuade them to continue working. Next, in August 1892 a Matabele impi seized some Mashona women near Nuanetsi post-station, held up a European trader and took some of his things. In September warriors stopped and robbed Europeans on the way from Victoria to Charter. In November they seized a subordinate chief south of Victoria, and, claiming that he had not paid his tribute, took him off to Bulawayo where, it was said, he was skinned alive. In 1893 intrusions continued, and the telegraph line between Salisbury and Cape Town was cut several times. The line had only been completed in 1892 and the settlers were naturally delighted at being in touch with civilization. Although the natives did not understand the significance of the line, they interfered constantly, some to acquire wire for personal adornment, others from a general urge to destroy.

In July 1893 came the first intrusion into a White settlement when, after warriors had raided some kraals near-by, they entered Victoria. When the Mashona sought sanctuary with the Whites, the warriors demanded that they should be handed over. The Whites refused and eventually the Matabele raiders were driven off, but they took with them several head of cattle. Following earlier raids, Jameson had remonstrated with Lobengula. This method having failed, he now decided to use force. He was supported by almost all the Whites in Mashonaland, including the missionaries; but he had also to get the consent of Cecil Rhodes, the managing director of the Company, and Sir Henry Loch, Governor at the Cape and High Commissioner.

Loch was an expansionist and had long been interested in the north; but he was bound by a ruling from the British Government that he should not sanction an attack without its prior assent. The Colonial Secretary, Lord Ripon, considered that force should not be used unless British subjects were threatened, and advised Loch and Jameson to try to come to terms with the King. The specific points at issue were, a demand by the settlers for recompense for the cattle stolen, and a counter-demand from the Matabele that the Mashona being protected by the settlers should be handed over. At this stage Lobengula did not appear to have control over his warriors, and both Loch and Jameson felt that they would have to persuade the Imperial Government to let them move against Matabeleland. They therefore set about creating a war atmosphere to establish a picture of native aggression, so that columns could be set in motion to move into Matabeleland. Loch was particularly anxious that his troops should take part because he did not wish the Company to become supreme in the new territory. With this in mind he began explaining to Lord Ripon by telegram how necessary it was to protect Bechuanaland – which was an Imperial responsibility – and he suggested the employment of the Bechuanaland Border Police against Lobengula. Meanwhile, both Loch and Jameson prepared their columns.

The desired news of more Matabele aggression was not long in coming. On 21 September the British agent in Bechuanaland reported two Matabele impis advancing, one eastwards towards Victoria, the other southwards against Bechuanaland. Loch did not question the truth of these reports – which were probably exaggerated – and wired the information straight to Ripon, who thereupon left the decision to the High Commissioner. Then came two incidents in quick succession. On 2 October an impi entered Company territory and took some Mashona cattle, and on the next day reports came in that Matabele were massing on the borders. After hearing of the theft of cattle Loch did not give permission for the columns to advance; but on receipt of the news of the massing of warriors on the border, he delayed no longer. On the morning of 5 October 1893, he sent Jameson the message the administrator had been awaiting. It read: 'Whatever your plans are with regard to the advance of the columns, they had better now be carried out.'

The columns advanced on Bulawayo from three different directions. The Salisbury column of 300 horsemen moved to Charter, and from there followed a route well south of the main one and away from thick bush and forest to avoid ambushes. The slightly larger Victoria column advanced north-west and met the Salisbury column at Iron Mine Hill, where it came under the latter's commander, Major Forbes. Dr Jameson was present, but the direction of military operations was in the hands of Forbes, an officer seconded from the 5th Inniskilling Dragoons. The Bechuanaland column was composed of a few regulars from the Cape, the Protectorate's mounted police and 4,000 warriors of Chief Khami. At Tati it was joined by Captain Raaff and some of his Rangers. It moved on Bulawayo from Tati in the south, but was slower at getting on the move than the others. All three columns had Maxim, Gardner and Nordenfelt machine guns. Forbes also had a seven-pounder, and they all took native levies with them. The northern joint column first encountered Matabele after crossing the Shangani River sixty miles east of Bulawayo. It had laagered for the night, and was attacked just before dawn. The Salisbury column on the north side met the main force of the attack; but their machine-guns and seven-pounder inflicted such heavy casualties that the warriors soon withdrew.

After advancing, a similar battle with the settlers again in laager was fought near the source of the Imbembezi River, thirty miles east of Bulawayo. Again the Salisbury men bore the brunt, but the machine-guns and the seven-pounder proved even more deadly than before. It was learnt after the Matabele had been driven off that the Imbezu regiment alone suffered 500 casualties; the settlers only had three dead and ten wounded, all in the Salisbury column.

When the royal kraal at Bulawayo was reached, it was found to have been evacuated, and the few stone buildings blown up. A specially organized force, which included men from the Bechuanaland column, which had now arrived, was sent in search of Lobengula, who had fled to the north. Not only did it fail to catch up with the King, but the men of a forward patrol under Major Wilson were all killed after a gallant stand on the banks of Pupuspruit. This Matabele victory restored to some degree the martial pride of the Matabele warriors, which had been shattered at Shangani and Imbembezi. But it did not affect the campaign; for by this time all Matabeleland had been won. Rhodes, who had come north to meet the victors, greeted Jameson as a hero; he was soon planning to use his stalwart lieutenant in a similar role against the Transvaal.

In the Transvaal the flow of British and other miners into the Rand gold-fields had created serious political troubles. There was a cultural gulf between the older farming community of the South African Republic centred on Pretoria and the newer mining community of Johannesburg. The Afrikaners resented the presence of the foreigners who had entered their country to dig for gold. Many of these were British, and they recalled that it was the British element that had assisted Shepstone's annexation of their country in 1877. They were not willing to allow the newcomers or *Uitlanders* much political power lest they changed the State's institutions to suit themselves. Consequently the *Volksraad* took steps to prevent *Uitlander* influence. In 1890 it limited *Uitlander* franchise to those who were naturalized and had lived in the Republic for fourteen years. At the same time it created a lesser house (the Second *Volksraad*), for which naturalized citizens could vote two years after their arrival. But this body could only deal with matters relating to Johannesburg and the mining industry, and its bills had to have the approval of the First *Volksraad*. The newcomers therefore understandably had a strong grievance concerning the nature of the franchise.

President Kruger was elected for four successive five-year terms. He was inclined to rule personally and generally was permitted by his colleagues to do so. Making full use of his right to take part in debates, his forceful personality usually brought about the compliance of the *Volksraad* to his demands. To improve the efficiency of the administration, he placed Hollanders and Afrikaners from Cape Colony in charge of the main administrative departments, and one Hollander. Dr W. J. Leyds[1] became State Secretary and a member of his inner circle. However, in spite of these appointments there was considerable inefficiency, for the lower levels of administration were manned by local Afrikaners who were often

---

[1] Leyds was replaced as State Secretary by F. W. Reitz a Cape Afrikaner; in 1898 the Cape Afrikaner Jan Smuts became State Attorney.

167

appointed with little regard for qualifications,[1] and sometimes as a result of nepotism. This administration was considered by the *Uitlanders* to be one of the causes of the high
cost of living, and thus another cause for grievance.

Also the cost of some goods and services used by the
mining community was affected adversely by the Government's policy of granting concessions involving monopoly
rights. The water supply of Johannesburg was operated by a
concessionaire, and water was much more expensive than it
should have been. The same applied to spirits, and also,
particularly, dynamite. The dynamite concession changed
hands several times; but the price of this commodity essential
to a mining community remained inordinately high. There
was also a grievance because the State, whose official language was High Dutch, did not support schools for English
speakers.

The high cost of living was accounted for to some extent by
the customs duties in force. These charges were an integral
part of the Transvaal's railway and customs policy. In 1872
President T. F. Burgers wanted to modernize the republic
and connect it by rail with Delagoa Bay so as to be free from
using British railways and ports. His efforts came to little as
he could not raise sufficient money to carry through his
railway projects. Later, President Kruger wanted to prevent
the railways from the British ports extending their lines into
the Transvaal before the Delagoa Bay line reached Johanes-
burg. The task of constructing its 250 miles of track within
the Transvaal had been given to the Netherlands South
African Railway Company,[2] which had already completed
fifty miles of light railway along the Witwatersrand. The
Company was held up because the fifty miles of track from
Delagoa Bay to the Republic's frontier had been allotted to
an American firm, which was more interested in reselling the
concession at a profit than in constructing the line. This
section, therefore, did not get properly started until the
Portuguese lost patience and expropriated the American
company. Even then, shortage of money delayed completion,

[1] They had had in fact no opportunity for more advanced education.
[2] N.Z.A.S.M.

and by the end of 1889 Kruger realized that the Rand mining companies could not be kept waiting any longer and that at least one British line would have to be extended and used. The railway from East London was linked already with a line through Bloemfontein in the Orange Free State to the drift over the Vaal near Vereeniging. It only had to be extended to Johannesburg, a matter of some fifty miles. This task was also given to the Netherlands South African Railway Company. Lack of finance delayed building, but eventually a loan from the Cape allowed operations to start and the line reached Johannesburg in 1892. It enjoyed a brief monopoly until the Delagoa Bay line reached the Rand in 1895.

Just as it had resisted federation, so the Transvaal consistently refused to enter into a customs agreement with the British colonies, as the Orange Free State had done, for fear of losing its autonomy. It required as much as possible in dues and manipulated the rates over the internal sections of the railway lines to ensure that the one from Delagoa Bay worked to carrying capacity. This manipulation of rates brought about the Drifts Crisis in 1895, soon after Joseph Chamberlain became Colonial Secretary. The Cape Government tried to undercut the Delagoa Bay line, and the Transvaal Government replied by raising its rates for the section of the Cape line within the Republic. To side-step these high dues, the Cape arranged that goods should be unloaded at the drifts over the Vaal near Vereeniging, and sent on by ox-wagon to the Rand. It was a blunt weapon thus resorted to by the Cape, for the ox-wagon could only be used in summer, when the veld was green. The Transvaal chose to parry the thrust by a display of state power; it closed the fords across the Vaal by presidential proclamation. Chamberlain was not the man to stand for this. He arranged with the Cape Government for a joint colonial and imperial military expedition and sent a strong protest, whereupon the drifts were reopened. This had unfortunate results. It made the British authorities forget the lessons of Majuba. They came to the conclusion that the threat of the use of force would gain their ends.

In 1892 new disagreements arose between the British authorities and the Transvaal Government, this time over the way the latter was treating the foreign mining community in its midst. The aggrieved mine-owners had founded the Transvaal National Union; and its members held public protest meetings, bombarded the British Government with petitions for reform, and entered into political relations with opposition leaders in the Transvaal *Volksraad* like Lucas Meyer and General Piet Joubert. In 1895 Rhodes threw the resources of the Consolidated Gold Fields into this movement, and some of the other mining magnates, notably the Wernher-Beit group, gave their support. Although there was talk of revolution, there was no firm leadership. Many *Uitlanders*, including J. B. Robinson and Barney Barnato[1] stood aloof. Barnato indicated that he supported President Kruger by presenting him with a pair of stone lions. The old man was delighted and set them up on either side of the steps of his stoep.

The leaders of the National Union included Lionel Phillips, Rhodes's brother Frank, John Hays Hammond, George Farrar and Sir Percy Fitzpatrick; but the main supporters never agreed what form of government should replace the Kruger regime. Some were for a reformed republican government, while others wanted the Transvaal to become a British colony.

An early specific *Uitlander* grievance concerned being called out by the republican authorities to take part in commandos. The complaint reached Lord Ripon, the Liberal Colonial Secretary, who instructed Sir Henry Loch to make a personal courteous remonstrance to the Transvaal Government. While in Pretoria Loch discussed the general situation of the *Uitlanders* with Lionel Phillips, and went so far as to suggest that if they rose in rebellion help might be sent from outside. Loch returned to London to confer with Ripon and suggested possible intervention by the Bechuanaland Protectorate's police prior to the use of the British garrison in South Africa, which should, he said, be increased. The

[1] Others who stood out were: Samuel Marks; and A. Goerz and G. Albu, who operated on German capital.

Liberal Government, however, would not countenance this, and the general view was that Loch's proposal was extremely dangerous and would merely encourage the *Uitlanders* to make excessive demands.

Rhodes considered that old President Kruger was an obstacle to the federation of the South African states, and hoped the *Uitlanders* might assist in getting rid of him and his reactionary regime. He therefore embraced wholeheartedly the undertaking which Loch had been ordered to abandon. He even undertook himself to place a force on the western border of the Republic so as to give first aid should the *Uitlanders* rebel.

In June 1895 Lord Rosebery's Liberal Government resigned and the Unionists came into power. Lord Salisbury, the Prime Minister, gave great latitude in the formulation of colonial policy to his most exceptional Colonial Secretary Joseph Chamberlain. Chamberlain had started his political career as a Liberal; but in 1886 had led a secession from the party because, as an avowed imperialist, he could not support Gladstone's policy of Home Rule for Ireland. His appointment meant an increased intervention in South Africa and a more determined and persistent attempt at federation than had been made since the time of Carnarvon. Chamberlain welcomed Rhodes as an ally in bringing federation about.

Rhodes's plan, like Loch's, was based on a rising in the Rand, the placing of an armed force on the border, a raid, and finally the entry of the High Commissioner to settle matters when conditions were such that the Republican authorities were impotent. His first requirements were a base and an armed force. The former was provided in 1894, when the Chartered Company was permitted to take over the Gaberones strip to continue the railway from Mafeking to Bulawayo; the latter in 1895, when the whole Bechuanaland Protectorate was put in the care of the Company and its police thus made available for Rhodes's use. As in the Matabeleland invasion, Rhodes entrusted the coup to Dr Jameson. Also as in Matabeleland, Jameson chose an erstwhile professional to conduct the military operations:

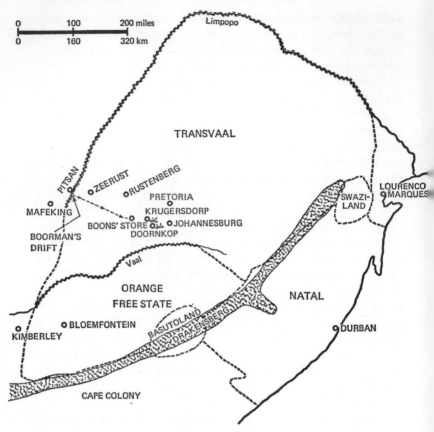

Map XII   The Jameson Raid

Colonel Sir John Willoughby, who had been commissioned
in the 'Blues' in 1880. By the 27 December 1895 Jameson,
Willoughby and 500 mounted police and volunteers were at
Pitsani, thirty miles north of Mafeking, ready to make their
180-mile ride to Johannesburg.

As the time set for the Rand revolution approached, the
members of the *Uitlander* Reform Committee of the National
Union became divided and confused. They quarrelled again
about whether they should attempt to set up a more tolerant
Afrikaner government or a new British one. They were so

172

undecided that it was soon evident that no proper rising would take place. Informed of this, both Chamberlain and Rhodes realized that there would be serious trouble if Jameson invaded without the pretext of a Rand revolution. Accordingly, Chamberlain had cables sent to Rhodes, threatening to revoke the charter of the British South Africa Company if Jameson moved; and Rhodes had telegrams sent to Jameson telling him to stay where he was. Jameson, however, was quite convinced that when the rebels heard he had crossed the border they would rise, even if they had not done so beforehand. In spite of further messages ordering a delay, he sent forward on 29 December, 1895, parties to cut the telegraph lines, and crossed the border at Boorman's Drift.

A string of five galvanized sheds containing bully beef, biscuit and forage for the horses had been set up as rest-stations along the route by a Rand Produce and Trading Syndicate, so-called to lull any suspicion on the part of the Boers. Under the same business disguise several hundred spare horses[1] had been stationed on a farm half-way to Johannesburg. It was an ingenious arrangement, but it did not work well. Too little time was spent at the stations for effective recuperation, and the remounts, which were coach-horses not really suitable for riding, proved difficult to catch.

The raiders soon lost the advantage of surprise. The northern telegraph line to Johannesburg from the neighbour-hood of Pitsani had not been cut, so that some Boer horsemen who discovered the raiders only had a thirty-mile ride to send back the news, and General Piet Joubert was able to dispatch mounted patrols to watch the columns advance while he organized his main forces to resist the invasion.

Fifty miles west of Johannesburg, at Boons' store, where one of the galvanized huts had been established, the raiders took their first prisoner in Lieutenant Sarel Eloff, Kruger's grandson. On arresting him they extracted a promise that he would remain at the store for two hours after they had ridden on. They were now in hilly country, and that night, in a skirmish with the encircling commandos, a policeman was wounded. By New Year's Day, 1896, with thirty miles to go,

[1] At Half-way House; to be used against Pretoria mainly.

173

many more Boers were hovering around. But they were unwilling to close in and fight as their artillery had not arrived. Kruger was keeping back the guns to deal with the surprise attack on the arsenal[1] at Pretoria, about which he had been warned.

Thirteen miles from Krugersdorp, on the last lap, the raiders were met by two cyclists sent with instructions from the Reform Committee in Johannesburg. The messages delivered were not very clear, but seemed to suggest that the best route was through Krugersdorp, where a force would be sent out to meet them. These directions proved unfortunate, for in a valley short of Krugersdorp the Boers had set up a formidable ambush. On a ridge ahead stood the Queen's mine, surrounded by earthworks, which served with little preparation as a fort, and on one side of the valley was cover in a farmhouse and on the other in some prospectors' trenches.

When the raiders boldly set out to attack the Boers in their prepared position they were met with heavy fire from three directions, which stopped them in their tracks. Willoughby turned the twelve-pounder and the Maxims on the enemy; but while the firing was in progress the Boers lay unscathed behind their dumps or in the trenches, so that not even the shrapnel from the twelve-pounder had much effect, and only some horses were killed. Next, Willoughby tried to storm the ridge again; but cross-fire, combined with fierce frontal fire, drove the raiders back.

When it became obvious that it was impossible to break through, Willoughby tried to discover a way round to the south to reach Johannesburg without passing through Krugersdorp. But he had the misfortune to consult a traitor guide who led them towards another ambush short of Doorn-kop, and after spending a night on the veld they found themselves surrounded. This time, the Boers had brought up artillery manned by members of the Transvaal State Artillery.

The raiders were exhausted, surrounded and heavily out-numbered, but they put up a fight until the Maxims jammed

[1] Situated in the camp of the Transvaal State Artillery, now the site of D.H.Q.

and the twelve-pounder ran out of ammunition. In spite of the protection of the farm buildings, Boer rifle fire was already causing a number of casualties, when the *Staats Artillerie* came into action. This was the end. A Hottentot woman's white apron was hoisted as a flag of surrender. From Doornkop Commandant (later General) Piet Cronje saw the white flag and afterwards received from Willoughby, on the behalf of Jameson, a message offering to surrender 'if a safe conduct out of the country was given to every member of the force'. Cronje was apt to follow his own line without reference to superiors and took it upon himself to reply to Willoughby without consulting the other two commandants present, with one of whom, Malan, he had had a tiff the day before. He said that, if the raiders would undertake to pay the expenses they had caused the South African Republic, and would give up their flag and lay down their arms, their lives would be spared. When Commandants Malan and Potgieter came up, they asked Cronje about the terms offered. When told, Malan became very angry. He said that commandants had no right to decide conditions. Only the Government could do that. The surrender must be unconditional. Potgieter agreed, and Cronje, after such a sharp reminder of his proper place, could only murmur, '*Goed, broeder.*'

Jameson and his officers were taken to Pretoria in carts and his men on horseback. That night, 2 January 1896, they were all in gaol, and no one was allowed to communicate with them. But they were well treated and there were no attempts at summary revenge. Casualties had been seventeen killed and fifty-four wounded. Cronje gave the Boer losses as four killed and three wounded.

On the news of Jameson's surrender, the High Commissioner Sir Hercules Robinson[1] left Cape Town for the Transvaal, not to preside over its incorporation with the rest of South Africa, as he had hoped, but to persuade the Johannesburg rebels to surrender to the Transvaal Government and get the best terms for them. Johannesburg was surrounded by 8,000 Boers, and President Kruger demanded its surrender unconditionally within twenty-four hours, stating

[1] Robinson had succeeded Loch in 1895.

that the lives of Jameson's men depended on compliance with the Government's terms. On this it surrendered. The Government granted an amnesty to all the rebels except the members of the Reform Committee. These were tried for high treason by a Transvaal court. The four principals – Lionel Phillips, John Hays Hammond, George Farrar and Frank Rhodes – were sentenced to death, but Kruger commuted the sentences to fines of £25,000 each. Other members were fined smaller sums. The commandants demanded the execution of Jameson and the other leaders of the raid. The wise old president, realizing the bad results likely to follow from such a course, decided instead to hand them over to the British Government for trial. First he had to convince his executive council, and then the commandants of the commandos assembled in Pretoria, who through the field-cornets would have to explain the reason for his action to the burghers. He struggled for four hours before he had his way with the commandants. 'Old Kruger is behaving splendidly,' wrote the Cape Secretary at this time. 'We have every reason to be grateful to the old man.'

On 14 January, after the pacification of Johannesburg and the handing over of the raider-prisoners to the Natal authorities, the High Commissioner left Pretoria. Jameson and five of his officers were later convicted and sentenced by a British court to fifteen months imprisonment. Rhodes, who accepted responsibility for the plot, resigned the prime ministership of Cape Colony, but retained his Cape parliamentary seat and contrived to preserve the charter of the British South Africa Company. At the time Chamberlain avoided exposure of any complicity, but when his papers became available they showed he had been involved. Yielding to pressure Chamberlain appointed a committee of inquiry, but as he was a member of it, he had little difficulty in preventing any probe into the raid from becoming too deep. The result was that its report castigated Rhodes and Jameson but exonerated Chamberlain and the officials of the Colonial Office.

The Raid had several important consequences. First it strengthened President Kruger's hold on his people, and

11　Emily Hobhouse

Boer artillerymen at Ladysmith, Natal

12   Paul Kruger in his coach leaving the Raadsaal at Pretoria under an escort of police and burghers (Coll. C. E. More)

Kruger addressing burghers from a railway coach at Newcastle, Natal, after the lifting of the siege of Ladysmith, 1900

enabled him to get elected for yet another five years, which included the Anglo–Boer War. Then the Orange Free State, which had sent a commando to the Vaal on the news of the raid, drew even closer, for although the Free State's customs union with the Cape remained, the state railways were taken out of Cape hands and placed into those of the Netherlands Company employed by the Transvaal. Also in the Cape, although W. P. Schreiner, J. X. Merriman and other British Liberals still co-operated with the Cape Afrikaners, the alliance between Rhodes's supporters and the *Bond* was broken up. Finally, because of growing unrest among the *Uitlanders*, the South African Republic began to arm for the coming struggle with Britain, which it now felt inevitable.

Among side results of the Raid were the rebellions in Matabeleland and Mashonaland. Jameson had taken many of the police away on the Raid, and the tribesmen made use of this opportunity to rise and murder the Whites. In the early days the native Karanga with their Rozwi overlords followed the instructions of a spirit, the Mlimo, after it had spoken to them through mediums in the form of witch-doctors who lived in caves scattered throughout the country. When the Mashona and Matabele came into the land as conquerors, they adopted this religion of the ancients in some measure, and in 1896 a medium of forceful character named Mkwati gained a large following. His reputation as a prophet and leader was further advanced when he made an advantageous marriage with the daughter of an important Rozwi chief, and he managed to confine the grievances of the Rozwi, Matabele and Mashona into a joint protest. Mkwati summoned the principal chiefs of the three tribes to his cave. They heard the disembodied voice of the Mlimo summoning them to kill every European living in the country; and thereupon agreed to try and do so.

The rebellion began in Matabeleland, when Europeans living at a distance from Bulawayo were set upon and murdered, men, women and children indiscriminately. Those who escaped slaughter in the country districts fled into Bulawayo for safety, and the town was put in a state of siege. Thanks to determined efforts, the Matabele were at first held, and then, after the garrison had been reinforced by 150 volunteers, the rebels were driven away. In three months the uprising in Matabeleland was as good as over. But then Mkwati triggered off a second rising in Mashonaland. This time the settlers were caught completely by surprise. They believed they had earned the gratitude of the Mashona for freeing them from Matabele raids. In any case, the Mashona were thought to be cowards. The saying had been, 'You only need a sjambok to take a Mashona kraal'. However, the Mashona rose and slaughtered the settlers in outlying districts as brutally as the Matabele had done. Although Salisbury was not besieged, other centres like Mazoe were. And they held out with difficulty. Eventually the rebels were subdued by an army of 2,000 Whites and several hundred native auxiliaries from the Cape under the energetic command of Colonels Plumer and Baden Powell. But it had been a terrible experience, and it made the White settlers of Rhodesia appreciate in their turn the terrors the Afrikaner people in the frontiers had faced for generations.

Chapter 11

The Uitlanders

Although the Reform Committee and the National Union had been destroyed by the failure of the Raid, they were soon replaced by the South African League operating in South Africa and the South Africa Association with branches throughout the Empire. Both supported, by political pressure and propaganda, a federation of the states of South Africa under the paramountcy of Britain, and the special function of the League was to help the *Uitlanders*[1] in their struggle for the franchise.

The compulsory withdrawal of the leaders after the Raid's failure had created a void which the League stepped in to fill, and it was assisted in instilling enthusiasm into the disgruntled *Uitlanders* by the *Star* and *Transvaal Leader* newspapers. The League had wider aims than the Union, for the Union had claimed to be loyal to the Afrikaner state and had sought the redress of grievances by appealing to the Republican authorities, and by fostering the growth among the Boers of a party sympathetic to their cause. The League addressed its appeals and remonstrances to the British Agent[2] in Pretoria for transmission to the Queen. Moreover, it asserted in the first article of its constitution an unalterable resolve to support the supremacy of Britain in South Africa; and the guiding principle of its propaganda was British intervention, with the ultimate aim of bringing

---

[1] The English-speaking Hollanders and the Germans generally supported the Transvaal Government.

[2] W. Conyngham Greene, formerly a British official at The Hague.

the Transvaal into union with the other territories of South Africa.

At this time the forceful Joseph Chamberlain was dominating the British Cabinet, and his views determined British colonial policy. Chamberlain upheld and furthered British interests wherever they were threatened and was prepared to extend the role of the state at home or abroad. Where British interests could be sustained by private enterprise without the Government having to make a substantial financial contribution or assume direct administrative responsibilities Chamberlain was content, but when private enterprise seemed incapable of doing this, he considered the Government should intervene. Thus, the Jameson Raid having shown that Rhodes on his own was unable to persuade the Transvaal to adopt a policy of co-operation with the other states, Chamberlain decided that the British Government must play a more direct role.

Chamberlain chose Sir Alfred Milner to succeed Sir Hercules Robinson as High Commissioner. Milner was an administrator of proven ability who had served with distinction under Cromer in Egypt. He believed in federation and gave support to the claims of the *Uitlanders* so as to help bring the Transvaal into a union with the other states under Britain. Although somewhat firmer and narrower in outlook, his views were close to Chamberlain's. Milner did not quickly come to the conclusion that war was the only way to consolidate British supremacy and achieve federation. He spent the first nine months in his post travelling around the country to make as many contacts as possible and to discover how he might achieve a peaceful solution. He learnt the *Taal* (Afrikaans) so as to speak to the Afrikaners in their own language and tried to persuade the Afrikaners of the Cape and the Orange Free State to get the Transvaalers to be more co-operative. Although the principal problem was the question of the relationship of the Whites in the Transvaal, there were also others. One concerned the position of the Coloureds who had gone to the Witwatersrand from the Cape. A number had assimilated Western civilization, and there were small building contractors and artisans among them. The pass-law

180

enacted by the *Volksraad* in 1896 made no distinction between Coloureds and raw natives, both groups having to wear a metal plate on their arm at all times. A number of Coloureds who would not wear the badge were arrested, and Milner decided to approach the Republican Government on this 'little matter'. The pressure he applied brought some result. The President gave a courteous reply and shortly afterwards persuaded the *Volksraad*, not without difficulty, to amend the pass-law so that Coloured persons carrying on a business or practising a skilled trade might, on payment, provide themselves with a certificate of exemption from wearing the badge.

Milner also tried to help the Transvaal's Asians, several thousands of whom had infiltrated into the republic from Natal during or shortly after the British interregnum, 1877–83. The immigrants were for the most part store-keepers and hawkers of fruit and vegetables. The Boers resented the Indian presence even more than that of the *Uitlanders*. To contain it they stopped further immigration and confined Indians to specific streets for residence and trade, both actions contrary to Article XIV of the London Convention by which they had agreed to allow free entry and movement to all British subjects except natives. As a result of Milner's protests the matter was referred to the arbitration of the Chief Justice of the Orange Free State who in April 1895 gave his award in favour of the South African Republic. The judgement was accepted, and this is understandable, 'bearing in mind the manner in which Chamberlain and Milner handled all Non-White questions',[1] for their aim was the extension and consolidation of British supremacy in South Africa, and they knew that too liberal an approach to the status of Non-Whites would offend the majority of the White colonists on whom they depended for support. For the same reason, Milner did nothing for the Transvaal's Bantu, who had no rights whatsoever. Although Milner considered that the Bantu were not being treated well, he adopted a policy of non-intervention. And so did Chamberlain. But as regards the dissatisfied section of the *Uitlanders*, Milner did try to establish that it was the Transvaal's duty under the

[1] J. S. Marais, *The Fall of Kruger's Republic.*

Conventions to give equal treatment to all White races, and a British responsibility to see that they did so. The Transvaal countered by pointing out that the word 'suzerainty' had been omitted in the London Convention. When it was claimed that the British had paramountcy, which was the same thing, the Transvaal Government questioned the interpretation of the articles and demanded full autonomy with no restriction to their state's freedom of action. However, in 1898, when J. C. Smuts was appointed State Attorney, some small concessions were made to meet the *Uitlanders'* grievances.

Jan Christiaan Smuts was an intellectual. Born in 1870 near Riebeeck West, fifty miles north-east of Cape Town, he had a brilliant student career, reading law at Stellenbosch and Christ's College, Cambridge; in 1895 he settled in Cape Town, and wrote articles for local newspapers while he waited for briefs. Initially he supported the Anglo–Afrikaner alliance in the Cape led by Rhodes. In 1898, after his appointment to office in the South African Republic, he set about tackling the administrative corruption and incompetence of which the *Uitlanders* complained; but he questioned the genuineness of their demand for political equality as is indicated when he wrote: 'On the W. W. Rand Cornwall miners who send all their earnings home every week and who have no other thought than to go home as soon as possible nevertheless shout for the franchise night after night with violent threats.' He agreed with President Kruger that to allow a free vote to the *Uitlanders* would destroy the character of the state, as would the unrestricted entry of more Whites, which was permitted under Article XIV of the London Convention which read: '. . . all persons, other than natives, conforming themselves to the laws of the Transvaal State will have full liberty with their families to enter, travel or reside in any part. . . .' In spite of pressure from outside, therefore, Smuts was as adamant against granting more concessions as the old President; and he agreed with him that it was their country[1] the British really wanted, and that they were using

[1] At the later Bloemfontein Conference President Kruger was to cry out emotionally, with tears in his eyes: 'It's my country, you want.'

the *Uitlanders'* grievances merely to achieve this end. It seemed to Smuts that the British wanted not only the gold but the country to complete their federal scheme and establish British supremacy in Southern Africa.

The crunch came in 1899 at the Bloemfontein Conference. Before the two sides met Milner had encouraged the League to step up its demand for reform. It responded vigorously by producing a petition with over 21,000 signatures calling for British intervention. Having forwarded the *Uitlanders'* petition, Milner followed it by a series of dispatches to Chamberlain, one of which was the famous 'helot' dispatch. It read:

'South Africa can prosper under two, three or six governments, but not under two absolutely conflicting social and political systems, perfect equality for the Dutch and British in the British colonies side by side with permanent subjection of British to Dutch in one of the republics.[1] . . . the case for intervention is overwhelming . . . the spectacle of thousands of British subjects kept permanently in the position of helots . . . calling vainly to Her Majesty's Government for redress, does steadily undermine the influence and reputation of Great Britain and the respect for the British Government within the Queen's dominions. A certain section of the press, not in the Transvaal only, preaches openly and constantly the doctrine of a Republic embracing all South Africa, and supports it by menacing references to the armaments of the Transvaal, its alliance with the Orange Free State and the active sympathy which in case of war it would receive from a section of Her Majesty's subjects. I regret to say that this doctrine, supported as it is by a ceaseless stream of indignant lies about the intentions of the British Government, is producing a great effect upon our Dutch fellow colonists . . . I can see nothing which will put a stop to this mischievous propaganda but some striking proof of the intention of Her Majesty's Government not to be ousted from its position in South Africa. And the first proof alike of its power and its justice would be to

[1] There was equality in the Orange Free State.

obtain for the *Uitlanders* of the Transvaal a fair share in the government of the country which owes everything to their exertions.'

Meanwhile, the Transvaal Government attempted unsuccessfully to settle the *Uitlander* problem by direct negotiation with the leaders of the mining industry; and the Cape Government offered its help. The Cape Prime Minister, W. P. Schreiner, proposed that the differences should be discussed at a meeting of the principals, and the Bloemfontein Conference between Milner and Kruger, supported by Smuts, was the result.

At the Conference Milner tried to confine the discussion to the franchise; he would not bring up any other points, although invited by Kruger to do so. Kruger believed that Milner was pressing for the franchise in order to extend British interests, and asked what he was prepared to concede if his requirements were met. It would be easier, Kruger said, to carry his *Volksraad* and burghers with him if he could show them some *quid pro quo*: 'I must tell them that something has been given in to me, if I give in to something.' Milner replied that he did not propose to make the franchise the subject of a Kaffir bargain, for the Uitlanders' request was reasonable and just. Kruger persisted in asking for a *quid pro quo*. He suggested the incorporation of Swaziland into his Republic or some offer of indemnity payable for the Jameson Raid. Milner was not willing to discuss either of these subjects; he brought the discussion back to the franchise; he demanded it immediately for those who had lived in the Republic for five years. Kruger explained that this would mean handing over his country to foreigners, and refused. Milner then pressed him to say what sort of franchise he was prepared to concede. After a discussion with his advisers, who included President Steyn of the Orange Free State, Kruger produced a franchise scheme which provided for a sliding scale varying from two to seven years for the full franchise, and including a vote for the President. *Uitlanders* who had settled in the Republic before 1890 could get the franchise after two years; those of two or more years standing, after five; the rest after seven years. They had to become naturalized citizens, but it was proposed to admit any who, had the necessary property qualifications, had not received a dishonouring sentence in the courts, could prove to have obeyed the laws, and had not been guilty of acts against the Government. Milner admitted that this was an advance on the existing position; but he disliked the restrictive clauses, particularly the ones concerning disloyalty. He also would not agree to the long periods of qualification still included, for he saw they would mean that no *Uitlanders* would be enfranchised at once. He stuck to his demand for a five years retrospective qualification which would ensure an instant enfranchisement of a large body of *Uitlanders*. As Kruger would make no more concessions, it appeared to be the end.

On 4 June 1899 Milner telegraphed to Chamberlain, saying the Conference seemed likely to fail. Chamberlain replied next day telling him not to give up too hastily; but before this message arrived, Milner had broken off his talks.

In August Smuts approached Milner and said that the Transvaal Government would grant the five-year franchise demanded provided the claim to suzerainty was dropped and the British refrained from further interference in the internal affairs of the Republic. Chamberlain rejected this offer on the advice of Milner, mainly because the restrictive clauses in the franchise still applied.

By that time it was evident that no European power would attempt to help the Transvaal. Kaiser Wilhelm II had aroused expectations of German support in January 1896 when he sent Kruger a telegram congratulating him on the capture of Jameson's men; but in August 1898 Germany left Britain a free hand in South Africa when an Anglo–German agreement provided for the partition of Portugal's South African possessions between Britain and Germany if, as was then expected, Portugal's financial difficulties made it impossible for her to retain them. In 1898, also, the Fashoda crisis had ended with France yielding to Britain on the upper Nile, which showed she was in no position to challenge Britain in South Africa, where in fact she had no interests or ambitions. Consequently, Chamberlain was able to persuade the British Cabinet to face the prospects of war with equanimity, though not with enthusiasm. Such troops as were in South Africa were sent towards the Transvaal frontier in north Natal, and an army corps was earmarked for dispatch. For several years before the Bloemfontein Conference the Transvaal had been arming, and when in October 1899 Kruger issued an ultimatum demanding that Britain should withdraw the provocative troops on the border, the Republic was in the stronger position militarily. Wishing to take advantage of this, when Britain did not answer the ultimatum and refused to withdraw her troops, Kruger gave leave for the invasion of Natal by his commandos. The war began on 11 October 1899. This time the Transvaal had the support of the Orange Free State.

Chapter 12

The Second Anglo–Boer War, 1899–1902

The Boer armies were mostly levies of burghers formed into commandos under elected leaders and composed of all males old enough to carry a gun. The commandos were drawn from electoral districts which had a commandant in charge of military matters and varied in numbers according to the size of the district and the scope of the operation. The Pretoria Commando, for example, had 3,000 names on its roll, yet the three commandos used to storm Majuba had numbered only thirty each. Electoral districts were divided into wards under field-cornets who were leaders in peace and war. Field-cornetcies were again divided into corporalships. A field-cornetcy was supposed to contain 150–200 men, and a corporalship nominally consisted of twenty-six. But there was no fixed rule, and a popular field-cornet or corporal might have twice as many men as an unpopular one, for a burgher could select which officer he wished to serve under, and could choose which commando to join, though he usually belonged to the one representing the town or district from which he came. To the field-cornet fell the tasks of mobilization, supply of ammunition, rations and forage, and the allotment of military tasks. Besides the commandos there were a few uniformed professional-type units. The foot police of the larger towns and the mounted police of the goldfields were combined to form a mounted force numbering about 1,400,[1] and there were also 400 men from the Swaziland police. 'Bullies in peace, but heroes in war', was how Conan

---

[1] They were known as ZARPS: Zuid-Afrikaansche Republiek Politie.

Doyle described these policemen. Another professional force wearing uniform was the Staats-Artillerie. This was initiated by President T. F. Burgers as the Battery Dingaan. In 1896, after the Jameson Raid, it was reorganized and renamed the Staats-Artillerie. Foreigners played a part in its training, but in the main it was a Boer force. The Orange Free State also had a small regular corps of artillery under the command of a German officer.[1]

In the Orange Free State President M. T. Steyn was the supreme military commander as well as the civic head of state, but in the Transvaal a commandant-general was elected by the burghers. This post was first held by General Piet Joubert and after his death in 1900 by General Louis Botha. The Transvaal was better equipped than the Orange Free State for the control of large formations. It boasted a war department of a civilian secretary and ten clerks, and had selected generals to command forces composed of several commandos.

There were some 2,000 European volunteers[2] fighting for the Boers besides the officers of the artillery. But this was more than compensated for by the help Britain got from the Empire. Thousands[3] of Australians, Canadians, and New Zealanders participated, and India sent non-combatants for the medical services and Ceylon a unit of European planters. Many from the Empire were of a type suitable for warfare on the veld. For example, the North-West Territories of Canada raised 1,000 expert horsemen and marksmen.[4] Another useful force was the Imperial Light Horse recruited from the *Uitlanders*.[5] Finally, there were British Colonial units recruited locally such as the Natal Mounted Volunteers, Kimberley Light Horse, Cape Police, Rimington's Guides, and many others. This generous support from the colonies was a

[1] Major F. W. R. Albrecht: he was to handle his little force with great skill.

[2] The Official History (Maurice) gives: Hollanders 320, Italians 75, Scandinavians 100, American–Irish and Irish 500, German 200, French 50, Russian 25, American 50, foreigners in commandos 800, Total 2,100.

[3] Australians 8,000, Canadians 3,000.

[4] Lord Strathcona's Horse.

[5] They left for Natal before hostilities began.

considerable comfort to Britain, for world opinion generally was on the side of the Afrikaners.

The South African Republic's preparations for war were thorough and complete, and no expense was spared in the provision of arms and ammunition. Vast numbers of rifles were bought in Europe, including enough Mauser rapid-firers to equip most of the Transvaalers and some Free Staters. The Boers' most noteworthy cannon were the ninety-four-pounder Creusot fortress guns or 'Long Toms', which, in spite of their size and weight, they moved around with great skill. At the other extreme in size was the little Vickers-Maxim pom-pom firing a string of one-pound shells – the effect of which was more of noise than of destructive power. The Boer artillery was equal in fire-power to the British, whose main weapon was the fifteen-pounder field gun. In numbers, the Boers were reckoned to have had up to 80,000 men under arms, and up to about 50,000 in the field, which was more than the British[1] at the start of the war.

Around Pretoria forts Klapperkop,[2] Schanskop, Wonderboompoort, and Daspoortrand were built on isolated hills, and another fort was built to protect Johannesburg. These works were to defend the two cities and prevent a possible repetition of such incidents as the Johannesburg riots of 1895–6 and the Jameson Raid. They were strong and powerful with bomb-proof casements and ammunition stores. They were supplied with electric power from a dynamo driven by a paraffin motor, and being linked by telephone were the first forts in the world to have a modern communication system at their disposal.

The Boers' survival had depended on looking after themselves in a country full of game and peopled by hostile savages. Their way of life, therefore, made them good soldiers. They showed this at Majuba by combining fire and movement to perfection. They were also good at using cover – at Krugersdorp they cleverly made use of earthworks and trenches to protect themselves against Jameson's shrapnel. In the matter of transport and supply, although their

---

[1] The British numbers went up eventually to nearly 200,000.
[2] Now the military museum of the South African Defence Force.

189

organization was weak, they still had the advantage, for with ox-wagons, mule-wagons and Cape carts they went farther and faster than the British transport officers could manage. Only on the railways was there parity of achievement. The Boer lived frugally in times of peace and was easily provided for in war. A small bag of rusks, a pocketful of biltong, a little coffee tied up in a bit of cloth would keep him for a week.

The Transvaalers advanced against Ladysmith in the east. and Mafeking and Kimberley in the west, and soon surrounded all three places; but for a whole month President Steyn's Free Staters wavered and waited before crossing the Orange River and making a third thrust southwards in the centre. The British plan had been to land an army corps in three parts at Cape Town, Port Elizabeth and East London, move up by railway and concentrate on the Orange, and then advance in strength north-east on the enemy capitals of Bloemfontein and Pretoria. The prior Boer offensive upset and retarded this plan, and the Commander-in-Chief, General Buller, directed the largest part of his corps to Durban to relieve Ladysmith, the second largest part to relieve Kimberley, and only what was left to delay the Free Staters advancing on Cape Town. Milner, alarmed at the defencelessness of the port, protested strongly, but Buller refused to leave the beleaguered towns to their fate; their capture, he said, would be too much of a blow to British prestige and too serious a loss of resources. For the Cape, Buller adopted 'holding tactics', which he entrusted to a small force under General Gatacre; to command in the west he chose Lord Methuen, while he himself took over in Natal.

In the second week of December 1899 – 'Black Week' as it came to be called – the British met with three serious defeats. At Stormberg on 9 December over 600 of Gatacre's men were captured; at Colenso on 15 December Buller's force was defeated when trying to break through to Ladysmith, losing ten guns and suffering over 1,000 casualties; and four days earlier, at Magersfontein on 11 December, Methuen was heavily defeated trying to penetrate a Boer defence line guarding the route to Kimberley.

Lord Methuen had brushed through two defence lines before he came up against the third one which had been carefully prepared at Magersfontein under the direction of General J. H. de la Rey[1] along a range of hills athwart the road and railway leading to Kimberley. Having crossed the Modder, Methuen planned to turn the enemy out of their position, but he unwisely gave his troops two weeks to recuperate from the previous battles, and this allowed de la Rey time to construct a line of trenches twelve miles long at the foot of the hills. These were made three to four feet deep and narrow enough to give protection from shrapnel; they were pushed forward 100 to 200 yards from the hills, and were well camouflaged so as to persuade the British gunners to waste their shells on the more obvious stone defence works on the hills behind. The wire farm fences were also used as additional protection. Thus de la Rey had provided defences well in advance of his time. Nor was that all. He sited the trenches so that he was able to use low trajectory fire which is so much more deadly than plunging fire from the top of hills.

To clear the Magersfontein complex, Methuen planned an extensive bombardment, a night march by the Highland Brigade, and finally a dawn attack on the dominating south-easterly hill. The bombardment appeared formidable and effective. According to one onlooker: 'The hail of shrapnel and the great volcano jets of red earth and ironstone boulders hurled fifty feet high by the bursting lyddite seemed to convert the whole hillside into an inferno of fire.' But the Boers were not in the stone defence works at which the British were aiming, and only three were wounded in the whole affair. The night march and dawn attack proved just as ineffectual. The brigade took so long over the march that by the time they were shaking out into open order in front of their objective it was already getting light. They could not see the Boers hidden in the well-camouflaged trenches ahead and were completely taken by surprise when a devastating volley

[1] Later, Cronje took over command.

191

met them. The brigade commander was killed instantly and many of the forward troops were shot down. Although elements of the rest of the force were brought up to protect the flanks of the Highlanders, some of whom stayed and faced the enemy throughout the day, Methuen did not call on the full strength of his force to rectify the situation. The Highlanders having been repulsed, he accepted defeat. He pulled back and put his troops into camp by the Modder river, and then waited for Lord Roberts to do the job for him.

Failure to relieve Kimberley and Ladysmith led to the appointment of Lord Roberts as Commander-in-Chief and Lord Kitchener as his Chief-of-Staff, and with the arrival in South Africa of these two great leaders the tide of war soon changed. Roberts decided to carry out the march on Bloemfontein and Pretoria originally planned, and set Kitchener the task of organizing a vast animal transport system so that they could leave the restricted routes provided by the railways and cut across country. His supplies assured, Roberts decided to abandon his railway line of communications, outflank the Magersfontein position and send his cavalry forward to relieve Kimberley.

The plan involved moving back from the Modder to Ramdam, near the scene of Methuen's early battles on the way to Kimberley, then turning and crossing the Riet, and finally advancing north again and seizing Klip Drift over the Modder, fifteen miles east of Magersfontein. With the Boer position outflanked, it was proposed to send the cavalry under General French in a dash to relieve Kimberley.

The cavalry were the first to quit the Modder River camp, and by leaving their tents standing they deceived the Boers. They reached Ramdam before Cronje was told they had moved. Even then he thought they were only staging a raid. But he sent down Christiaan de Wet with 450 men and two guns, and warned the burghers at Jacobsdal half-way between the Modder and Ramdam to keep on the alert.

After a brush with the Boers short of the drift, the cavalry crossed the Riet unmolested, for de Wet who was watching ready to pounce considered the cavalry column too formidable for his small force.[1] However, a body of Boers attacked as the cavalry passed Jacobsdal and were so aggressive that the horse artillery had to be brought into action to disperse them.

By the time the cavalry reached the Modder the heat and dust had taken their toll; a number of troopers had fallen behind, and several horses had dropped to the ground from exhaustion. However, the bulk of the brigade arrived in fighting condition and the small detachments of Free Staters who were camped around the drift, seeing they were no match for this mass of armed horsemen, galloped off. By late afternoon General French was able to report that Klip Drift was in his hands.

The main Boer force in the locality held a strong position on a line of hills a few miles north of the drift and completely blocked the route to Kimberley. However, there was a pass through the centre of the hills and French, having used his horse artillery to soften up the Boer position, sent his massed cavalry forward at this gap in a great charge. As the brigade thundered forward, the Boers opened up a tremendous fire but, protected from view by the dust they raised, few of the horsemen fell. On the cavalry's approach the Boers scattered. They mounted their ponies and fled in disarray; a few who were left were speared by the Lancers or taken prisoner. Meanwhile, Cronje's army was moving east to avoid being cut off from base, and French and his cavalry were across the route of the Boer army. But he did not turn aside and attack. Instead he took his cavalry straight on to relieve Kimberley.[2]

Before the main body reached Klip Drift, Cronje had passed across the British line of advance; but, slowed down by his cumbersome ox-wagons, he was not fast enough to escape Lord Roberts's force. First, French's cavalry returning from Kimberley got ahead of him, and then the main body moved eastwards and trapped his column under the banks of the Modder at Paardeberg. After a stout resistance the

---

[1] He let the infantry pass too, but played havoc with the supply train.
[2] One of the most grateful to be relieved was Cecil Rhodes.

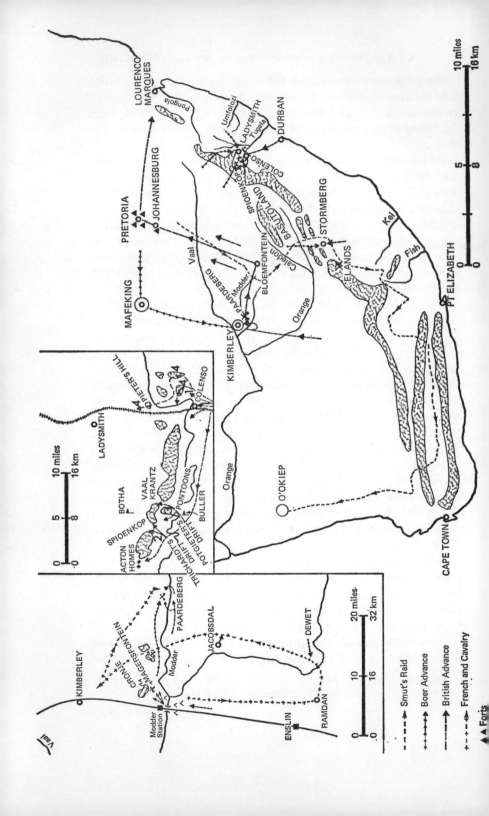

Boers were finally shelled into surrender. In February, on the nineteenth anniversary of Majuba, 4,000 gave themselves up.

Meanwhile, the Boer line beyond the Tugela, guarding the approaches to Ladysmith, was beginning to crumble. After the encirclement of Ladysmith, Louis Botha had taken over from Lucas Meyer as the leader on this front. He proved a great military commander, parrying in turn General Buller's attacks at Colenso, Spioenkop and Vaal Krantz. On Spioenkop the British suffered so severely that at nightfall the troops were withdrawn from the top; but the Boers had not realized the amount of punishment inflicted by their attacks and withdrew also. Many commandos in the centre of the line moved back in sympathy, and it seemed as if the Boer defences beyond the Tugela were on the point of collapse. On learning of the true situation at Spioenkop, Botha addressed his men, telling them of the shame that would be theirs if they deserted their posts in this hour of danger; and so eloquent was his appeal that the men in the neighbourhood of Spioenkop were soon filing back in the dark to reoccupy the hill. Botha spent the rest of the night riding from commando to commando exhorting and threatening until he persuaded the men to return along the whole line, thus averting a Boer disaster. However, when Buller attacked in force with massive artillery support a month later, at Colenso and Pieter's Hill, the Boer line began to give again. This time even Botha wavered, for he telegraphed to his superiors and suggested the siege of Ladysmith should be raised.

The bad news from Natal arrived at Boer headquarters at the same time as that of the surrender at Paardeberg. Nevertheless, the Boer leaders did not lose heart. Botha was ordered to stop where he was, and the staunch old Transvaal President left immediately for Natal. On arrival he exhorted his burghers to stand firm, saying:

'Worthy sirs and brethren, it seems to me as if your faith and that of your men has been replaced by unbelief. The moment that you cease to hold firm and fight in the name of the Lord, then you have unbelief in you; and the moment unbelief is present cowardice follows, and the moment you turn your backs on the enemy there remains no place for us to seek refuge, for in that case we should have ceased to trust in the Lord. No, no, my brethren; let it not be so, let it not be so. Has not the Lord hitherto given us double proof that he stands on our side? Wherever our burghers have stood fast, however hard the task, the Lord has beaten back the enemy . . .

Having endeavoured to restore the morale of his burghers in Natal, and having slowed down the retreat there, President Kruger set off to Bloemfontein to confer with President Steyn. They both agreed that Bloemfontein was so important that it must be held; but they could do little to achieve this as the British had already resumed their march. At Poplar Grove, fifty miles west of Bloemfontein, a run of koppies on either side of the Modder offered a possible line of resistance. But it did not hold. Lord Roberts sent forward his infantry in a series of attacks while his cavalry made a wide sweep to get in the Boers' rear. French's horses were by now half-starved and he made very slow progress; but it made no difference, for the Boers retreated in disorder without a fight. President Kruger was lucky to escape with the rest from the net of infantry and cavalry enmeshing them.

At Abrahamskraal, fifteen miles nearer Bloemfontein, the President, de Wet and de la Rey, who had joined with 1,000 Zarps, tried very hard to stop the rout. An eye-witness records that the old President at this moment seemed almost frantic: 'He lifted his heavy stick against the fugitives whom no one seemed able to check; and even ordered the Zarps to shoot anyone who attempted to flee.' It was of no avail. The police would not shoot, and a mass of horses and wagons went off in a cloud of dust towards Bloemfontein. The town contained many English and moderate Afrikaners opposed to the war. Without any encouragement in the capital, the disheartened burghers did not stop; they trekked out north, and their leaders departed by train after them. They managed to get away just before one of General French's patrols cut the railway. On 13 March 1900, Lord Roberts made his formal entry at the head of his cavalry who had served him so well in the operations since leaving the Modder River camp. The troops were tattered, hungry and tired, but their eyes shone at the sight of gardens, solid buildings, and women, and the promise of the pleasures of urban life. Nor was their reception a usual one for a force entering an enemy capital. Quite the contrary. The streets were decorated and the crowds cheered.

After pausing for seven weeks in Bloemfontein,[1] largely because of a serious outbreak of enteric among the troops, Lord Roberts resumed his march to the north. Nothing could now stop the triumphant British, who relieved Mafeking, occupied Johannesburg and Pretoria, shepherded the Transvaal forces eastwards down the railway leading to Portuguese East Africa and Lourenço Marques. From that port President Kruger went to France in the Dutch warship *Gelderland* to seek help for his nation in its desperate need; and Vice-President Schalk Burger replaced him in South Africa for the rest of the war. Meanwhile, President Steyn, with an escort of 250 men and the gold reserves, had set off on a circuitous route back to the Free State. Steyn had been loth to start the war, but was as tenacious in continuing as the Vice-President of the Transvaal. In fact, although both governments had been dislodged from their capitals they still retained authority. In Lord Roberts's view, however, the war was over, and in October he left for England, leaving Lord Kitchener to deal with the guerrilla operations which followed.

The commandos still at large in the field proved difficult to find and disperse. The most elusive commandant was Christiaan de Wet, and the British columns had little success at catching him. In December 1900 he was with his men near Bethulie[2] in the extreme south of the Orange Free State, intent on raiding Cape Colony. Kitchener called in columns from far and wide and well-nigh surrounded him. De Wet

---

[1] Lord Roberts had contemplated staying only a few days to reorganize.
[2] J. B. M. Hertzog was with his commando at Bethulie also, but managed to elude the British more easily.

escaped south. With difficulty he got across the rain-swollen Caledon River only to be stopped by British troops on the Orange. Not wanting to take refuge in Basutoland, he fought his way back across the Caledon, and then made north towards Thaba Nchu. Here another British column barred his way. Again it seemed that de Wet must be caught; but there was a gap in the British line, and he led his men towards it at the gallop. Although shells and bullets came at them from all sides, the dust and their speed were protection, and they escaped with only one man wounded.

In the early months of 1901 Lord Kitchener introduced new tactics to counter the raids. He began the prodigious task of setting up continuous lines of barbed-wire across the open veld, with manned posts at intervals. The posts were blockhouses with interior and exterior walls of corrugated iron, the space being packed with stones to stop bullets. At more strategic points beside railway bridges and drifts they were built of stone, two-storeyed, and topped with a corrugated-iron roof against the sun. Little garrisons of half a dozen men were left stocked up in the blockhouses, their task being to stop by cross-fire any Boer raiders trying to cross the fences. The first lines of the blockhouses were widely spaced across the veld and there was little chance of stopping raiding parties who waited until dark before cutting their way through unseen. However, the spacing was progressively reduced to – one mile, half a mile, and finally in parts of the Cape to 200 yards. Besides the blockhouses and barbed-wire there were other important ways used to limit the range and effectiveness of the Boer raiders. As they were based on their home farms and returned to them for supplies, the British burned the farms and removed the stock of those still continuing the fight. As a corollary to farm burning came camps for the dependants of Boers out on commando. Women and children could not be left in their destroyed homes to starve or be set upon by natives, and out of humanity Kitchener organized centres where they could be cared for. Unhappily the British Army was not qualified to organize such camps. They became insanitary and were swept by diseases – pneumonia, measles, and enteric fever – which killed thousands, mainly children. This naturally increased the odium under which Britain lay in world opinion.

Reports of the terrible conditions under which the Boer women and children were living in the camps reached Emily Hobhouse, the niece of Lord Hobhouse, an important figure in the Liberal Party. Emily Hobhouse was a woman of wide sympathies. Five years earlier she had gone off as a missionary to work among the iron miners in Minnesota. With the mines closed her work there ended and she had returned to England. When she realized the hardships the South African women and children were undergoing her heart was touched. She first organized a distress fund, and then left for South Africa with the money raised, intent to do all she could for the poor sufferers. She was permitted to visit a camp at Bloemfontein, where she found 2,000 women and children living in tents and sleeping on the ground under army blankets. The camp's water supply was tainted and typhoid was taking a heavy toll. Emily Hobhouse had fought typhoid in the United States. 'Boil all water,' she ordered. And then set about seeing that the apathetic Boer womenfolk obeyed her instructions, and kept everything as clean as possible as well. By insisting on the women helping themselves – one group took buckets of earth and dammed a freshwater stream to get pure water – and by bullying the authorities to provide necessities, she brought about a more reasonable existence for the inhabitants of the camp. Because of her splendid work in the camps she became an Orange Free State heroine. She is buried beside the imposing monument to the women and children who died in the camps, which was erected in the grounds of the war museum outside Bloemfontein. Emily Hobhouse was of course not the only one to care. In July 1901, after much agitation in *The Times* and other newspapers, a Ladies Commission of five was appointed by the British Government and sent out to South Africa to report on the camps. As a result conditions in these camps slowly improved and the appalling death-roll was reduced.

Kitchener's drastic methods eventually brought results. In July 1901 Piet de Wet and his men were surrounded, and a little later Ben Viljoen's commando was taken; but Christiaan de Wet evaded capture. At this stage Commandant Vilonel[1] was co-operating with the British and was trying to persuade the 9,000 or so still in the field to give themselves up.

While this was happening in the north Jan Smuts was making his epic raid into Cape Colony. 'The adventures of this handful of resolute men led by General Smuts', says the *Times History*, 'forms one of the most interesting episodes of the guerrilla war.' Before he left the Transvaal Smuts exhorted his men to do great deeds. The enemy, he said, was resolved upon the extermination of the Afrikaner race. To resist this he was leading them into the Cape Colony. Terrible privations awaited them and many would not see their native country again; but theirs was a just cause and one for which they should be willing to give their lives. If any shrank from the dangers ahead, let them say so and depart to his own place.

Smuts then led them on a 300-mile trek from the Transvaal through the Orange Free State. Before entering Cape Colony he was joined by Deneys Reitz,[2] and at Eland's Rivers Poort soon afterwards had a lively brush with the British. On emerging from a valley and entering open country, a farmer rushed out from a house beside the road to warn them of English cavalry ahead. Soon afterwards, as they were passing through a fringe of trees they almost rode into fifteen or twenty troopers cantering towards them. Leaping from their horses, they opened fire. They emptied several saddles, and the rest of the troopers hurriedly made their way back to camp. Smuts's men surrounded the camp. Then, having exchanged fire with the defenders, and picked off a number who were unwise enough to expose themselves, they charged. After a brief encounter, in which the Boers got the best of it, the English surrendered. Then the commandos began ransacking the camp, watched from afar by a small relieving force which dared not intervene. Smuts's men found all they needed in the shape of fresh horses, rifles, clothing,

[1] Two Boer generals and about 1,500 Boers called National Scouts were assisting the British.

[2] Author of *Commando*, a best-seller.

saddlery, boots and ammunition. In the fight only one of Smuts's men was killed and six wounded, whereas thirty troopers were killed and many more wounded.

After this engagement Smuts trekked south-westwards and came within twenty miles of Cape Town, threatening the port. However, the close-knit, newly-constructed defence lines were strong enough to deter the raiders and he was soon pushed off in a northerly direction, clear of the farthest blockhouse line. He then withdrew across the wastes of south-west Africa and laid siege to the rich copper-mining centre at O'okiep. While it was being stoutly defended by the miners and some British troops, his escapade ended, for he was called away under British safe conduct to take part in the peace talks.

The peace negotiations proceeded better than had been feared, considering that neither side was united in its views of what was required. At first, Milner was adamant that there should be no negotiated settlement. The Boers, he said, should surrender unconditionally and return to their colonial status. Kitchener, however, was prepared to end hostilities by negotiation. On the other side, some Transvaal military leaders were willing to negotiate, whereas none of the Free State leaders would do so without a guarantee of independence in advance. There followed long drawn out discussions between the Afrikaners themselves at Klerksdorp; between representatives of the Afrikaners and Milner and Kitchener in Pretoria; between the representatives of the Afrikaners at an assembly of the people at Vereeniging; between the Afrikaners and British again; another session of the assembly of the people at Vereeniging, and finally the signing at Pretoria. The Treaty of Vereeniging, as it came to be called, brought the Republics back to colonial status for a time, but promised them eventual self-government; it ensured that natives in the Republics were excluded from political participation, and it safeguarded the Dutch language. It seemed at the time to be a civilized and liberal settlement of a bitter struggle.

Chapter 13

Union

Gigantic problems faced Milner after the war. A quarter of a million people from the ill-famed refugee camps had to be returned to their former farms in a devastated country, along with many thousands of prisoners who had been sent to St Helena, India, Ceylon and the British West Indies. The existing railways had been run down during hostilities and needed re-equipping, and the construction of new railway lines and new roads was necessary to link up isolated country districts with industrial areas. Finally the mines had to get into full production.

The task of repairing the ravages of war in the conquered territories was entrusted to a coterie of gifted young men from Oxford University who came to be known as 'Milner's Kindergarten'. These proved capable administrators. Under Milner's lead they instigated scientific farming projects and forestry and irrigation schemes, set in motion the building of new roads and railways, and made imperial grants of money to individuals deserving compensation and governments willing to sponsor economic developments. Under their supervision, the rehabilitation of the country was carried through with efficiency and skill.

The mines initially enjoyed a post-war boom, but by 1903 a shortage of labour was affecting productivity. Milner had come to an arrangement with the Portuguese authorities whereby the mines were permitted to recruit workers in Mozambique in exchange for favourable rates on the Delagoa Bay railway line; but Non-Whites from Mozambique as from elsewhere seemed reluctant to come and work in the mines. In the gold mining industry alone there was a shortage of 130,000 unskilled workers. In desperation Milner introduced immigrant indentured short-term Chinese labour. This brought the required results, for productivity immediately improved, but it turned out to be a political bombshell. Attacked by the Liberal Party in England as a new form of slavery, it was instrumental in causing the fall of the Unionist Government in 1906.

Milner's efforts at political and social reconstruction were less successful than his work on rehabilitation. He wanted to anglicize the country by large-scale British immigration and by restricting the use of the Dutch language. In neither direction did he make much headway. No mass immigration took place. In spite of the encouragements fewer than 5,000 British settlers – men, women and children – were established on the land under his subsidized schemes. In 1911 Afrikaners still continued to form well over fifty per cent of the White population of South Africa. As before the war, they were much more numerous than people of British descent in the Orange River Colony and the Cape Colony, and were about as numerous in the Transvaal. Only in Natal was there a clear majority of British in the White population. As to language, thanks to the efforts of Free Stater General J. B. M. Hertzog, lawyer and war hero, and monetary assistance[1] from Holland to the Dutch Reformed Church schools, the equality of Dutch with English was preserved.

Milner abolished the harsher provisions of the pass-laws, and improved the working and living conditions of Non-White mineworkers. He was responsible for the appointment of a Native Affairs Commission which extended the territories available for Bantu settlement, and he established Bantu political constituencies with White members to represent Non-Whites. But he was in agreement with the prevailing opinion in South Africa concerning the place of Non-Whites in society. He is recorded as saying: 'One of the strongest arguments why the White man must rule is because that is the only possible means of raising the black man, not to our

[1] The Christian National Education Movement appeal.

level of civilization – which it is doubtful whether he would attain – but to a much higher level than that which he at present occupies.'[1]

The first development among Afrikaners after the war was a cultural revival in which the schoolmasters and the *predikants* of the Dutch Reformed Church played a vital part. Schools using the Dutch language were founded so as to give the children an alternative to the government schools where English was the sole medium of instruction, and then came the introduction and greater use in instruction of the vernacular or the *Taal* which is Afrikaans. Not all Afrikaners welcomed this, nor the assertion that Afrikaans, instead of High Dutch, should be the official language because it was spoken by the original White inhabitants. But Lord Selborne, who became High Commissioner in 1905, was tolerant towards the growing use of the *Taal* in place of Dutch because it was not a written language and had practically no literature. 'Consequently,' he said, 'although in my opinion the *Taal* will be a language of affection and patriotism in South Africa for centuries to come, from the political point of view there is no reason for any jealousy between English and the Taal.' In fact he was wrong. Afrikaans soon developed into a literary language. Through the influence of writers and journalists like Gustave Preller, and poets like Eugène Marais, Jan Celliers, J. D. du Toit and others, not only did it help to produce an individual Afrikaner national consciousness and culture, and to provide an impetus to the idea of nationalism, but eventually it superseded Dutch. In 1925 it became the second official language in the Union alongside English and with equal rights.

The developing resurgence of Afrikaner national feeling was strengthened by the emotions engendered by the funeral of Paul Kruger in Pretoria on 16 December 1904, and in January 1905, the first post-war Afrikaner party came into being in the Transvaal with the formation of *Het Volk* by Generals L. Botha, J. C. Smuts and J. H. de la Rey. In the Orange River Colony there were also signs of Afrikaner

[1] Milner Papers.

political awakening; after a series of meetings at Bloemfontein in July 1905 the *Orangia Unie* was established by General Hertzog, supported by General Christiaan de Wet and Abraham Fischer.

In December 1905 the new Liberal Government under Sir Henry Campbell-Bannerman adopted a conciliatory attitude to the Afrikaners of the two conquered territories. The outgoing government had been intending to offer them representative constitutions, but Campbell-Bannerman went further and suggested the full self-government which Article 7 of the Vereeniging Treaty had promised 'as soon as circumstances allowed'.

In view of the repeated representations that the British Government had made to President Kruger before the war about the treatment of natives in the Transvaal, and the fact that little had been done for them since they had been under British rule, it was suggested that some concessions might be sought before responsible government was restored. In weighing the pros and cons it then became obvious to the Liberal Government that no solid body of European opinion outside the Cape supported any extension of political rights to Non-Whites. In Natal, franchise requirements had been made so severe that only Whites participated. In the Transvaal and Orange River Colony, the English-speaking sections of the community had the same view on the position of Non-Whites as the Afrikaners. As Lord Selborne wrote: 'However democratic Whites in South Africa may be in respect of each other, there is nothing in the world less democratic than the attitude of the White working-men towards every Black of any position or extraction.' The Liberals in England who were most concerned for the welfare of the Non-White subjects of the Crown were also apt to be the most emphatic pro-Boers and revolted by the 'methods of barbarism'[1] used by their predecessors in conducting the war. Although they respected the argument that the Imperial Government had an obligation to hold the balance between White settlers and indigenous peoples in colonial societies, it seemed to most of them that the events of the previous decade up to 1907 had

[1] Farm burning and concentration camps particularly.

created a still greater obligation to make amends to the Afrikaners. They realized that if they tried to provide votes for the Non-Whites both the White communities, British and Afrikaner, would be outraged and that the attempt at appeasement between the two White sections would then fail. Consequently, they persuaded themselves that the Ver-eeniging Treaty bound them to launch the former republics into responsible government with only White electorates, although the treaty would have allowed them to include the Coloureds and Asians. They eventually decided to grant self-government to both the Afrikaner states, and letters patent were issued promulgating responsible government in the Transvaal in December 1906 and in the Orange River Colony in June 1907.

The new leaders in the Transvaal, Botha and Smuts, evolved for their *Het Volk* party a policy of general conciliation. First, the Afrikaners were to be reconciled one to another. In 1901 a corps of National Scouts had been formed composed of Boers who were prepared to try to persuade their fellows to finish what seemed to them a hopeless struggle and bring to an end the misery dependants were suffering in the refugee camps. About 1,500 National Scouts were active in the Transvaal and Orange Free State. These Afrikaners and the so-called 'hand-uppers', who surrendered before the start of guerrilla operations, were despised and hated by the 'bitter-enders' who had continued the struggle. Greatly to their credit, Botha and Smuts partly managed to persuade brother to forgive brother for making different decisions during the war. Then the majority of the Afrikaners and the settlers of British descent in the Transvaal were brought together by the plea that as their fates were interlocked, their welfare depended on a capacity to co-operate. Finally, an attempt was made to get all the White peoples of South Africa to forget the past, bury the hatchet and seek good relations with Great Britain.

Understandably this conciliation policy was not popular. Many could not forget the war. Afrikaners steeped in the doctrine propounded by the *predikants* that Afrikanerdom was an organic unit with a divine mission feared that a policy of conciliation and co-operation might cause it to be overwhelmed by British culture and financial strength. In the Transvaal these critics did not constitute such an immediate threat as in the Orange River Colony where the Afrikaners had so great an electoral majority that the *Orangia Unie* did not need the support of English-speakers. The two most influential men in the colony were M. T. Steyn, the former President, who had found it impossible to take part in the Peace of Vereeniging and resigned for reasons of ill-health, and General Hertzog, the lawyer and war hero, who was Minister of Education. Both Steyn and Hertzog were critical of the conciliation policy and, when Smuts steered an education act through the Transvaal parliament that stopped short of placing the Dutch language on a footing of equality with English in the schools, and Botha attended the 1907 colonial conference in London and made speeches extolling the British Empire, they began to suspect that both Botha and Smuts had become disloyal to the Afrikaner cause. They were relieved to find, however, that the two leaders of *Het Volk* were in agreement with them on the native question. Indeed, in their attitude to Non-Whites Botha and Smuts were typical Afrikaners. They believed that in a plural society like South Africa political equality was undesirable because Non-Whites were not capable of using political power wisely.

The grant of self-government to the Afrikaner states was the first step towards a union of all the states of South Africa. Initially union was promoted by Lord Selborne and Milner's young administrators, most of whom had remained when their leader left. To the British leaders unification was desirable, not only because it would bring economic advantage, but also because it would produce the overall British supremacy for which the war had been fought. The first architect of union was Lionel Curtis of Milner's Kindergarten, who resigned from his post as Assistant Colonial Secretary to the Transvaal in order to prepare a weighty memorandum outlining the advantages to the states of coming together. He stressed particularly the economic advantages of co-operation and the value of having a single native policy.

There was friction at this time between the states over customs duties and railway rates. The Cape Colony and Natal required high duties and rates to bring in revenue, while the Transvaal and the Orange River Colony was less dependent on these dues because of the former's income from taxable profits on mining operations and the latter's receipts from supplying food to her wealthier neighbour. The result was that Natal and the Cape Colony wanted to raise the charges, and the other two states wished to lower them in the interest of their consumers of imported goods. The issue was complicated because Milner had agreed earlier that in return for permission to recruit labourers for the mines from Portuguese Mozambique, he would allow the duties and rates on goods from Lourenço Marques to Johannesburg to be lower than those from the colonial ports. Because Lourenço Marques was closest to the Witwatersrand it appropriated what was considered by the others to be an unfair share of the trade.

Renewed conflicts with natives in Natal was another reason for Whites coming to see that some form of political union was desirable. During the Second Anglo–Boer War the natives had been quiescent. In the Transvaal, the Pedi and Tswana warriors had attacked Afrikaners sporadically, but elsewhere the natives had for the most part respected the instructions given them by both sides not to intervene in the White man's quarrel. In Natal, in 1906, new troubles had made the White community feel insecure. The administrators were so few and far between that they had to rely on influence rather than force to exert authority, and there was no leader with a forceful personality like Shepstone of old to help keep the natives content. In 1905, faced with labour and financial problems, the Natal parliament enacted a poll tax of one pound on all unmarried Zulu adult males, with the dual purpose of persuading the men to go out to work and of providing revenue. The imposition of this tax coming as it did soon after the census of 1904 which had been regarded with suspicion by tribesmen, caused the resentment smouldering among them to erupt into violence. In the early months of 1906 sporadic murders and disturbances in many parts of Natal led to the proclamation of martial law and the mobilization of the militia. The unrest developed into open revolt when Bambata, a minor chief of the Greytown district, defied the local magistrate and raised his followers in rebellion. In the ensuing battle with the militia at Mome Gorge, Bambata and thousands of his warriors were killed for the loss of some thirty militiamen. This rebellion was thus soon over; but when unrest and violence continued the Natal Government became convinced that Dinizulu, head of the Zulu royal house and descendant of Shaka, must be behind the disturbances. Dinizulu had been in trouble with the British authorities before, but had been reinstated as paramount over part of Zululand with reduced authority. In December 1907 he gave himself up and was committed to trial. Defended by W. P. Schreiner, a former Prime Minister of the Cape Colony, he was acquitted on the more serious charges, but was found guilty of harbouring rebels and sentenced to a fine and five years' imprisonment, a penalty that was considered severe by the authorities in Britain.

Relations between Indians and Whites were also strained after the war. In the Transvaal the Indians had been hopeful that the restrictive laws which had been the subject of unsuccessful arbitration before the war would be lifted now the state was under the British control. In 1906 they found a champion in the barrister M. K. Gandhi, who was successful in getting the Colonial Secretary to disallow a registration ordinance. However, one of the first acts of Botha's new government was to pass a law introducing finger-print registration to control the influx of Indians. Gandhi had founded a Natal Indian Congress on the lines of Congress Party of India and he used this organization to launch a massive passive-resistance campaign against the measure. The Government countered this by imprisoning many Indians, but further campaigns followed against other such unpopular measures as the invalidation of Indian-style marriages, the tax on the unindentured, and the law prohibiting the movement of Indians between Natal and the Transvaal.

There appears to have been no political co-operation between the Zulus and Indians, but both series of troubles showed the dangers inherent in the separate states having no common policy towards the Non-White peoples.

Some of the arguments put forward by the British authorities to support union appealed also to the Afrikaners. Union had always been the declared objective of the *Afrikaner Bond* in the Cape Colony, and even some Republicans had also looked forward to the day when the four states would be joined. Before the war it had been beyond the bounds of practical politics because the Republicans had not wanted to lose their independence, but now they saw in it a chance of limiting Imperial interference. The economic arguments for union and the ones relating to the advantage of a joint native policy were as cogent for the Afrikaner as for the British colonists. But Lional Curtis's memorandum met with a cool reception all the same. In the Cape parliament J. X. Merriman's opposition party, supported by the *Bond*, were put off when they saw Jameson's ruling Progressives were so keen, and Botha and Smuts mistrusted the idea because it seemed to have such strong Imperial support. Eight months later the situation had changed. The Cape rebels had regained the vote they lost immediately after the war, and with their support Merriman had replaced Jameson as Prime Minister of Cape Colony. Anti-imperialists now had control of three of the four self-governing colonies and unification might be achieved under anti-imperialist direction. Botha and Smuts were encountering an isolation sentiment in the Transvaal *platteland*, where conservative Afrikaners were proposing that their state should go its own way and turn its back on the impoverished colonies; but supporting unification themselves, they decided it would be best to call a meeting of delegates from all the colonies to consider the issue.

An inter-colonial conference[1] to consider Transvaal's notice

[1] During the same period military conferences were held to obtain uniformity and co-operation. These discussions included Rhodesia.

to quit the customs union had already been fixed for May 1908, and after the railway and customs agreements had been patched up, it was agreed that the four colonial parliaments should appoint delegates to a National Convention to prepare a draft constitution for a united South Africa. There were thirty delegates: twelve from the Cape Colony, eight from the Transvaal, and five each from Natal and the Orange River Colony. Fourteen were Afrikaners and sixteen of British origin. The Convention sat behind closed doors in Durban and Cape Town under the chairmanship of Sir Henry de Villiers, Chief Justice of the Cape Colony. Finally, the delegates unanimously signed a report, which included a draft constitution, and presented it to the colonial parliaments for their consideration.

The main points at issue were: equal rights, proportional representation, equality of the English and Dutch languages, the admission of Rhodesia and the High Commission territories, and the Non-White franchise of the Cape Colony.

Equal rights meant that each member of the new Union parliament should represent as nearly as possible the same number of people, though all the voters at this time were males. This gave an advantage to the British element in the Transvaal, since many there did not have families. The Transvaal election of 1907 had shown that the Afrikaners were still capable of winning elections without the assistance of loaded constituencies, and to demonstrate the sincerity of their conciliation policy the Transvaal delegates decided initially to agree to the British demand for equal rights. On Smut's advice they also committed themselves to proportional representation which had been put forward by the British. However, after much discussion first proportional representation was abandoned, and then the British, influenced by the Progressives of the Cape, conceded a loading in favour of rural constituencies. It was agreed that divisions with widely scattered population could have up to thirty per cent fewer voters than urban divisions. This concession was to play an important part in allowing the Nationalist Party to come to power in 1948.

Following compassionate speeches by extreme Afrikaner

nationalists[1] demanding that English and Dutch should be official languages of the Union usable in parliament and the law courts, and that all civil servants should know both languages, resolutions were passed unanimously adopting most of their demands.

It was assumed that when the Union got over its teething troubles it would absorb the other British territories of South Africa. The three Rhodesian delegates who attended the conference asked that their country might be left to build up numerical strength under the shelter of Company Rule – and to satisfy themselves that the Union was not going to fall under Afrikaner domination. This was allowed, but included in the constitution of the Union was a provision empowering the Monarch to issue an Order-in- Council incorporating territories administered by the Company into the Union.

The future of Basutoland, Bechuanaland and Swaziland was not so easily settled. After much discussion, following a suggestion by Lord Selborne, it was agreed that the British Government should be empowered to transfer the territories to the Union at some unspecified date, subject to conditions to be set out in the Constitution for the protection of the African inhabitants. The chiefs have never been willing to be placed under the control of White South Africans and in spite of demands for the incorporation of the territories into the Union, and later into the Republic, the British Government has never consented to hand them over. Recently they have been granted independence. As regards the Non-White franchise, the position was left as it was before Union, with only the Cape Colony allowing any degree of Non-White participation.

It took some time to turn the recommendations from the Convention into the South Africa Act of Union. But by 31 May 1910 every legal point had been cleared and the Act came into force. It united the territories occupied by White people in a British Dominion under a government led by Botha and Smuts which believed in Anglo–Afrikaner conciliation, and in co-operation with the other members of

[1] Hertzog and Steyn.

the British Empire. Political unity was achieved in 1910; and military unity was achieved in 1912 by the passing of the South Africa Defence Act and the subsequent abolition of the colonial forces and the departure of the Imperial troops from South African soil.

Chapter 14

Botha, 1910–19

When the Union came into being four parliamentary parties emerged: the South African Party comprising the *Het Volk* movement and the *Orangia Unie*; the Unionist Party made up of the British Colonies' Progressive parties; the Labour party of general White content; and the Independents. The South African Party had sixty-seven seats to the Unionist thirty-nine and was by far the largest.[1] Led by General L. Botha, who became Prime Minister, it included General J. H. de la Rey, ex-President M. J. Steyn and J. X. Merriman, former prime minister of the Cape. General Smuts became Minister of the Interior and General J. B. M. Hertzog, Minister of Justice. To begin with there was a degree of unity, but this came to an end when General Hertzog and his followers questioned the Government's conciliation policy. Hertzog first opened the rift by declaring that in his view the British leaders were not loyal to South Africa because of their British connection. He called them 'foreign fortune hunters'. Naming Sir Thomas Smartt, the leader of the Unionists, as a prime example, he said that with some exceptions they were loyal to the British Empire rather than to their adopted country. Next, Hertzog made a special issue of the language question. The matter came to a head when a Unionist member introduced a motion which alleged the incompatibility of the Orange Free State's education policy with the principles of freedom and equality of opportunity embodied in the constitution of the Union. Fanatical for

[1] Labour 4, Independents 11.

what he believed to be true language equality, Hertzog had made it compulsory in the Free State for English-speaking children to learn Dutch and Afrikaner children to learn English. The Afrikaners accepted the measure, but many English-speaking parents could not understand why their children should learn Dutch. Although it applied in the Free State only, this act – and the man responsible for it – was attacked from all parts of the country. Botha avoided making a stand by appointing a select committee to investigate the matter and make recommendations. The committee of which Hertzog was a member found that there was no true language equality in any of the four provinces except the Orange Free State; but the majority nevertheless did not approve of Hertzog's compulsory bilingualism. The committee recommended that parents in the Free State, as elsewhere, should be allowed to choose the language medium for their children. To this Hertzog eventually unwillingly agreed.

In the eyes of Botha and his cabinet Hertzog seemed to be stirring up racial hatred at a time when they were striving to bridge the gap between Afrikaans and English-speaking South Africans by steering a middle course, and they came to the conclusion that he was too much of a trouble-maker to be retained as a minister. Botha asked Hertzog to resign, and when he refused Botha tendered his own resignation. The same day Botha was asked by the Governor-General to form a new cabinet. This time he omitted Hertzog.

An important measure passed by Botha's Government was the *Natives Land Act* of 1913. This introduced territorial segregation of the Non-White peoples. The African National Congress which had been founded in 1912 to look after the interests of the Bantu opposed the measure, not because of the segregation but because of the upheaval of the native families involved. It was so concerned about the restrictions and hardships such a major rearrangement would bring that it sent a delegation to the Union government to ask for the act to be repealed. It also sent to London a deputation of five members including J. L. Dube, its first chairman, and Dr Rubusana, the first native member of the Cape parliament, to urge the British Government to annul the act. Both requests were refused; the *Natives Land Act* came into force, and large areas were allotted for exclusive native settlement. Although this alienation of land to natives was never popular with the White population, over the years the areas have been greatly extended, and the Act may be said to be the genesis of the present 'Homeland' policy of the Republic.

Botha's Government was determined to stem the flow of Indians into South Africa and in 1913 an Immigration Act was passed that made their further entry impossible. The Indians were already complaining about rigid restrictions and, led by the lawyer Gandhi and officials of the Indian Congress Party, 10,000 staged a great march of protest from Natal into the Transvaal which they had been forbidden to enter. Many were arrested, but this early passive resistance movement brought the redress of at least some of their grievances, for the *Indian Relief Act* which followed in 1914 abolished the three-pound tax on Indians in Natal, recognized the validity of Indian-style marriages and facilitated the entry of the wives of Indians into South Africa.

The most serious troubles of the period stemmed from the dissatisfaction of sections of the White population, both Afrikaner and British. There were disputes between the workers and mine-owners which made it necessary for the Government to intervene. In June 1913 the workers struck at the Kleinfontein mine over working conditions and the recognition of their trade union. The strike spread throughout the Witwatersrand and riots followed. Since the police could not control the situation, and the South African army was still in the process of being organized such British troops as were still in the country were called in. Clashes between strikers and troops occurred, and the strikers showed their resentment by setting fire to the Johannesburg railway station and the offices of *The Star*, mouthpiece of the mineowners. When the strike appeared to be getting out of control Botha and Smuts went to Johannesburg to negotiate with the miners. Discussions took place in the Carlton Hotel while a turbulent crowd gathered in the street outside. Botha and Smuts realized they were powerless and were obliged to accede to the miners' demands for an investigation of their grievances. This victory made other workers believe that further strikes could be profitable. Led by extremists, one of them a Hollander who was leader of the Railway Workers' Union, another strike broke out in January 1914, which immediately assumed far worse proportions than the first. It started among railwaymen in Pretoria, spread to other railway centres, and then to the gold-mines on the Witwatersrand. This time the Government was determined not to yield to the demands of the strikers. General Smuts mobilized units of the new Union Defence Force[1] which had been created in the second half of 1913 and sent them into Johannesburg under his old comrade-in-arms, General J. H. de la Rey. The strikers were completely overawed by the strength of de la Rey's force and immediately capitulated. But Smuts was not content to let the matter rest there. He took the law into his own hands and deported nine of the ringleaders without trial. This autocratic move evoked much criticism, but it certainly helped to quell the workers' urge to strike. Not until 1922 did friction occur again.

On 4 August 1914, when Great Britain declared war on Germany, the entire British Empire, including South Africa, was at war as well. To help the British war effort the South African Government agreed to attack German South-West Africa. A number of Afrikaners not only opposed this but considered it an opportunity to throw off the British yoke and declare an independent republic. In the House of Assembly Botha's war policy, although opposed by Hertzog, was approved by ninety-two votes to twelve; but this did not reflect popular opinion. Afrikaner leaders like Christiaan de Wet, de la Rey, and serving officers like Brigadier-General C. F. Beyers,[2] Colonel Manie Maritz and Major Kemp were not only opposed to the war policy but willing first to protest and later to take up arms against the Government to thwart it.

De la Rey, after much soul searching, turned against

---

[1] Forerunner of the present S.A. Defence Force.
[2] Commandant-General of the Active Citizen Force.

Botha and, encouraged by Beyers, decided to urge Afrikaners to stage a protest against the war policy. On 15 September the two of them set out after nightfall for the western Transvaal. According to what Beyers said later, it was their intention to address people in the towns, urging opposition to the Government's planned attack on South-West Africa. It happened that the police had been alerted that night to prevent the escape from Johannesburg of some dangerous criminals known as the Forster gang. When the occupants of de la Rey's car disobeyed an order to stop, it was fired at. A bullet aimed at a back tyre hit the hard road, ricocheted, and struck and killed de la Rey. A groundless story was put around that the shooting was a deliberate act of the Government, but Botha and Smuts denied this hotly. Smuts said, 'We were almost brothers, before the war, during the war, after the war. De la Rey has departed this life under tragic circumstances without a stain on his character.'

De la Rey's death did not put an end to opposition to the war policy, which increased when rumours circulated that the Government was going to call up civilians to serve in the campaign against the Germans. In October 1914 Colonel Maritz, who was commander of an armed force at Upington, rebelled and joined the Germans with a number of his men. He promoted himself General, proclaimed the independence of South Africa, declared war on England and sent an ultimatum to the Government to say that he would invade the Union next day unless safe-conducts were provided for Hertzog, Beyers and de Wet to come and confer with him. The Government met this challenge by declaring martial law and calling up men to be ready to deal with what seemed to be a threat of rebellion supported by the Germans. It also made public Maritz's ultimatum, an act which brought a strong protest from Hertzog because it made him appear in collusion with Maritz – when he seems to have been still sitting on the fence. Beyers and de Wet, meanwhile, responded by raising commandos in the Transvaal and Free State respectively: Bergers to demonstrate and thereby compel the Government to change its policy; de Wet according to his own pronouncements, to procure arms from Maritz, to trek to Pretoria, to pull down the British flag and proclaim a free South African Republic. In spite of this, Botha and his Cabinet continued to try to re-establish the authority of the state by persuasion. Their inaction brought complaints, including a furious letter from J. X. Merriman, now a member of the Senate, which read:

'What I wanted to express was the feeling of myself and a good many others, Dutch as well as English, that this palavering with avowed rebels has gone altogether too far. Just look at the facts. On 26 October de Wet at the head of a band of ragamuffins, collected, not on the spur of the moment, but by a carefully prepared plot, destroys the railway, inflicting severe loss and damage on public property. On the 28th, having in the interval stolen (commandeered!) arms and property he appears at Reitz, makes a ridiculous and seditious harangue, damages public property, seizes private goods and proclaims that he is in rebellion. All this time, palavering is going on. You are sending his avowed confederate to him, and above all you are giving him plenty of time to increase his forces and to unite them with other bands of malcontents. Decent respectable farmers are living in error of having their stock stolen by these ruffians . . . All this time you are parleying with the ringleader. Is there no law? Are the crimes of robbery, sedition, and public violence merely venial eccentricities when committed by a certain section of the community? . . .

I feel most strongly that unless this malady is extirpated, not smoothed over, and the authors, aiders and abettors soundly punished, there will be little respect for the law in the future and that the condition of South Africa will be that of Mexico or Peru.'

In spite of Merriman's pleas, the parleying went on; Botha sent a message to ex-President Steyn saying 'a word from you would go far'. He wanted Steyn to condemn the rebellion publicly and appeal to the men in the commandos to return to their homes. But this Steyn declared himself unable to do in such simple terms: he said he did not find it hard to reprobate treason and condemn the action of Maritz and de Wet; but he equally felt called upon to condemn the Government's plans for the invasion of South-West Africa. In a second appeal, Botha told Steyn that the danger was so near that the ex-President had a responsibility to keep silent no longer, but to use his influence with Beyers and de Wet to avoid bloodshed. Steyn once again declined to commit himself publicly, but this time he did agree to get in touch with the rebellious generals and to discuss the disbandment of their forces upon terms agreed with the Government.

It proved impossible to get the generals to visit Bloemfontein, for General C. F. Beyers would not go without de Wet and Kemp, and these two refused. Instead, Steyn's son acted as an intermediary and for a space of nearly three weeks passed to and fro between Bloemfontein, Pretoria and the rebel camps presenting the Government's terms and taking back the generals' replies. The Government said it would consider freedom from punishment for all who laid down their arms and that only volunteers would be called upon to fight the Germans in South-West Africa; but the rebellious leaders would not agree to these terms. Thereupon, Botha began military operations against them.

De Wet's son had already been killed in a skirmish with Government troops when on 12 November de Wet's men were heavily defeated by a force led by Colonel (later General) J. L. van Deventer at Mushroom Valley, south of Winburg. De Wet managed to escape, but on 2 December he was captured on a farm in the Kuruman district of British Bechuanaland while on his way to join Maritz. Six days later Beyers was trapped near the Vaal River which was then in flood. His horse was shot, and as he tried to swim to safety on a fresh one he was pulled down by his heavy coat and drowned. By this time Kemp and his men were also being hotly pursued. They succeeded in getting across the Kalahari Desert and joining the Germans, who re-equipped the little force. Later Kemp and Maritz attacked and dispersed a Government force at Nous and then advanced against the military base at Upington from where Maritz had started off on his adventure. The attack was beaten off, Kemp was compelled to surrender, and Maritz fled to Portuguese

Angola and from there sought refuge in Portugal. Near Pretoria a rebel commando was still fighting on, led by Jopie Fourie, one who had helped suppress the Jameson raiders. After a fierce struggle in which twelve Government soldiers were killed, and as many rebels, Fourie was captured by his cousin, Colonel Pretorius. Unlike the other rebel leaders, Fourie had defected without first resigning his commission or even changing his uniform. Because of this, and the unnecessary casualties he caused, he was tried by court martial, sentenced to death and executed. Smuts confirmed the sentence and afterwards said that he could not otherwise have faced the parents of those who had lost their lives through Fourie's actions. But the affair led to a storm of criticism of Smuts and his methods, and made Fourie an Afrikaner hero.

So ended the 1914–15 rebellion. It had been a struggle entirely between Afrikaners, for Botha, anxious to avoid involving the English, had used only Afrikaans-speaking soldiers, mainly Active Citizen Force members, to fight the rebels. There had been surprisingly few casualties: 190 among the rebels and 132 in the Government forces. Of nearly 12,000 rebels only 281 were summoned to appear in court. Those convicted were imprisoned, the maximum term being seven years, or fined, the maximum sum being £2,000. Before the end of 1916 all those gaoled had been released, so that with the exception of Jopie Fourie the Government treated the rebels fairly leniently. But despite this, bitterness remained, and Botha and Smuts were considered by a section of Afrikaners to have acted like henchmen of Britain.

As soon as the rebellion had been quelled, Botha raised a force of 43,000 and prepared to attack the German colony, which could muster only about 9,000 for its defence. Botha took command. In February 1915 he landed at Walvis Bay preparatory to advancing inland on Windhoek, and at the same time a three-pronged attack was launched from the south under Smuts, with the forceful J. L. van Deventer in command of one of the columns. The Germans were no match for the larger South African forces ably led by Botha, who showed himself just as skilful as he had been against Buller on the Tugela in 1899. By the end of April the whole area south of Windhoek had been occupied by Smuts's forces. In May Botha entered an undefended Windhoek and then marched north in pursuit of the retreating Germans. In July they surrendered. Botha's terms were remarkably generous: the regular other-ranks were interned but the officers, reservists and volunteers were released on parole and allowed to return to their farms or settle where they wished. The campaign had been concluded speedily at small expense with only 113 South Africans killed. It was a military triumph which earned Botha and his able lieutenant Smuts the heartfelt thanks of the British Government.

With the Unionists in support, the Government now decided to give further help to the British war effort. A small number of volunteers were sent to fight in Europe, and 19,000 volunteers were dispatched to reinforce Imperial and Belgian troops attacking German East Africa (Tanganyika). By the end of 1915 the British forces had achieved very little, for General von Lettow-Vorbeck, the German commander, had proved himself to be a leader of superb resolution and skill. He took up a strong position in the mountains in the north of the German colony, and from there repulsed with heavy loss a more numerous British force which had attempted a seaborne landing at Tanga on the coast, and routed a force assembled at Jassini farther up the coast.

In February 1916 General Smuts was appointed to command the British forces in East Africa. These consisted of Indians, East Africans, West Africans, British, Rhodesians and South Africans, a real polyglot army. Smuts's plan of attack on von Lettow-Vorbeck's northern stronghold was a general advance from several directions in co-ordination with British and Belgian forces advancing from the area of Lake Tanganyika in the west. First he started several probing attacks on the line of hills stretching from Mount Kilimanjaro south-eastwards towards the Indian Ocean. Then his main attack was made across the Kenya border on Taveta, in the gap between the hills and the volcano. But he also sent van Deventer and the cavalry sweeping round the north and west sides of Kilimanjaro to try and cut off the German forces if they retreated from their positions. To begin with, Smuts's campaign went well. The important area of irrigated agricultural land near the volcano was taken, and the enemy was driven south towards the railway line running westwards from Dar-es-Salaam to Lake Tanganyika. After this initial success, however, although Smuts showed himself to be a forceful leader, difficulties arising from the climate and the terrain slowed up the allied advance and caused many casualties from disease. Von Lettow-Vorbeck, ably served by Askaris for transport, escaped encirclement and established himself in another strong hill position in the Uluguru Mountains, a hundred miles west of Dar-es-Salaam. Eventually, to avoid being cut off, he slipped across the frontier into Portuguese Mozambique in the south. Content to let the future of German East Africa depend on the result of the war in Europe, he maintained only a guerrilla campaign throughout 1918 until shortly after the Armistice. With an original force of 5,000, mainly Askaris, Von Lettow-Vorbeck had occupied the attention of up to 130,000 troops for several years, which was no mean feat.

Although the East African campaign was not as successful as that in South-West Africa, Smuts is usually considered to have conducted the operations well. After the first phase in the northern mountains, Smuts replaced the British commanders by South African leaders of his own choice. He enforced new vigour into the assaults on Von Lettow-Vorbeck's northern stronghold and proved himself a superb leader, if not a great tactician. Three South African battalions took part and seem to have fought well. In a letter to his wife describing the attack on the rich lands in the area around Kilimanjaro, he speaks of the force engaged being fifty-fifty Afrikaner and British, and 'all of them fought splendidly'. He also remarked how sad he felt at the casualties his 'little Afrikaners' suffered.

A number of volunteers also served in France and Belgium on the Western Front, and it was here that South Africans won renown during the Somme Offensive from 15–20 July 1916, when the South African Brigade was given the task of capturing Delville Wood beyond Longueval, in the centre of the front eight miles east of Albert. 'Once inside the wood the South Africans made a feint of retiring – a ruse which was entirely successful. Then they dashed forward with fixed bayonets. They took the wood once, were counter-attacked and took it again.'[1] For this gallant and successful operation they received great praise, but their losses had been severe: only 780 officers and men survived out of the 3,150 who had entered the fight.

Before the end in German East Africa, Smuts was recalled to join the Imperial War Cabinet in London. During the rest of the war he played an important part in the conduct of Allied operations. Highly regarded by Lloyd George and his British colleagues, his help was sought on a number of matters. By stressing the experience of South Africa he advised De Valera to seek Dominion Status for Ireland before claiming a republican status, and thereby assisted in the difficult political reconstruction of that country after the war. He played an important part in the reorganization of the air services and has sometimes been called the father of the British Air Force. He also helped draft the clauses embodied in the Covenant of the League of Nations.

In December 1918 Botha joined Smuts in London, and at the beginning of 1919 they went to Versailles to represent South Africa at the peace talks. Along with representatives of the other self-governing countries of the British Empire, they demanded and were accorded the privilege of signing the peace treaties in their country's right – an acknowledgement, they believed, of the accepted independent status of South Africa. In the distribution of German possessions, South-West Africa was awarded to South Africa as a mandate to be administered under the supervision of the League of Nations, so their successful campaign had not been fought in vain. However, it is said that they had also hoped to receive the port of Lourenço Marques in exchange with Portugal for a port in German East Africa. This did not materialize.

* * * * *

[1] *Manchester Guardian*, 20 July 1916.

13 A rare picture of President Kruger
(Coll. C. E. More)

Adderley Street, Cape Town, at the turn of the century

14   The Cabinet of General Louis Botha, first Premier of the Union of South Africa, as it was constituted in 1911.
Front (*l. to r.*): Dr C. O'Grady Gubbins, J. W. Sauer, General Louis Botha (Prime Minister), A. Fischer and Colonel G. Leuchars
Back (*l. to r.*): General J. C. Smuts, K.C., Sir David de Villiers Graaff, Advocate H. Burton, K.C., H. C. Hull, General J. B. M. Hertzog and F. S. Malan

General Botha in 1914 (Radio Times Hulton Picture Library)

Two other delegations from South Africa visited Versailles in 1919. The first came from the African National Congress and asked the assembly to bring about a change in South Africa's native policy. Lloyd George, who was the only one to grant an interview, pointed out that since 1910 South Africa had been a self-governing country and neither the British Government nor any other could interfere in its internal affairs. The other deputation was led by General Hertzog. Inspired by the declaration of President Wilson that all countries had the right to self-determination, it demanded that the independence of the Transvaal and Orange Free State should be restored. President Wilson refused to see them, and Lloyd George, having listened to their pleas, refused to take any action. He said the settlements of 1902 and 1910 had been freely negotiated with the whole of the South African people and it was impossible to alter them because of a demand from a section.

The South African Party was to pay a considerable price for its support of the British war effort. Many of its followers joined Hertzog's group both in the war years and immediately afterwards, and there was an upsurge of his brand of Afrikaner nationalism. The first mouthpiece of Hertzog's National Party was *Die Burger*, which started publication in Cape Town in 1915, and in this period Afrikaner poets like Jan Celliers, Eugène Marais and Louis Leipoldt started to write in Afrikaans, thereby bringing it into wider use. Although the South African Party maintained its parliamentary majority in the 1915 election by gaining 54 seats to the Unionists 40 and the National Party's 26, with Labour having 4 seats and Independents 6, in 1920 it was topped by the National Party, which had 44 seats to their 41; this time the Unionists had 21 seats and the Independents 3, but the Labour Party increased their share to 21. By 1920 Botha was dead[1] and his mantle had fallen on the shoulders of his friend and confidant Smuts. The policies for which Botha had worked so hard in what he saw as the interests of both the White races of South Africa were now under fierce

---

[1] Botha died on 27 August 1919.

attack from Hertzog and his followers; but Smuts still endeavoured to encourage co-operation with Britain and also between a section of the Afrikaners and British South Africans; and he continued to do so during the twenty-eight years during which he was engaged in active politics.

Chapter 15

Smuts and Hertzog

In the March 1920 election the South African Party won 41 seats, the Nationalists 44, the Unionists 25, the Labour Party 21 and the Independents 3. To acquire allies in order to get a workable majority, Smuts began negotiating with the Nationalists. However, Smuts's views on South Africa's relations with Britain were so radically different from those of Hertzog and his followers that nothing came of this attempt at *rapprochement*. Smuts then turned to the Unionists. With them he had more success, for negotiations led to their merger with the South African Party in November 1920. This political blood transfusion strengthened Smuts's party considerably, but to try to improve his position still further he went to the polls again on 8 February 1921, eleven months after the previous election. This time there were no three-cornered urban contests and so the South African Party captured many urban seats from Labour. The final result was, the South African Party 79, the National Party 45, and the Labour Party 9, so Smuts was once again firmly in control. He rewarded his new colleagues by including three of them in his cabinet, and the transformation of the South African Party was complete. Hertzog, who had been a minister in 1912, was now leader of the opposition, while Sir Thomas Smartt, opposition leader in 1912, held a cabinet post.

Like Botha's government before and during the war, Smuts's had to deal during its term of office with several serious revolts.

In 1921 and 1923 Smuts was at variance with Indian leaders at the Imperial Conferences. In 1917 he had been unwise enough to state that a recent act, stopping Indian immigration, would make it easier to do justice to the Indians already in the country. Seizing on this, Srinivasa Sastri moved a resolution at the 1921 conference claiming for Indians in the Dominions, including South Africa, 'all the rights of citizenship'. The Prime Ministers, except Smuts, received the resolution sympathetically. Smuts rejected it. He reminded Sastri that the Smuts–Gandhi agreement contained no reference to the franchise. Gandhi, he said, had known South Africa too well to raise that thorny issue. White South Africans were an entrenched minority in the black mass of the population. Inequality was their constitutional and political bedrock. 'If they gave equal political rights to the Indians they would have to give them to the Natives. No South African government which accepted Sastri's resolution would last a fortnight.'

On 9 May 1922 H. G. Mackeurtan, representing a Natal constituency, moved a resolution in the House of Assembly requesting the Government to introduce legislation for the compulsory segregation of Asiatics. He considered himself a moderate man, he said, because he did not take up the popular cry for shipping all the Indians back to India; segregation was the middle course between compulsory repatriation and leaving things as they were. Sir Abe Bailey, the member for Krugersdorp in the Transvaal, was not content with a middle course. Krugersdorp had started the anti-Indian drive by launching a successful legal action and by founding the South Africans' League, a propagandist association which within a few months had vigorous branches in the Transvaal and Natal. The League enumerated many complaints against the Indians. It said they sent money out of the country; their habits were insanitary; they depreciated the value of property; their standard of living was low; their methods of competition were unscrupulous; they closed important avenues to White employment; they produced nothing and consumed Indian rather than South African products; they were, in fact, unassimilable and a bad influence on the natives. Sir Abe Bailey did not believe there was any room for Indians in South Africa, and moved an amendment calling on the Government to increase its efforts to ensure the departure of Asiatics from the Union. This did not go far enough for the next speaker, J. J. Byron. He demanded compulsory repatriation at once of all the Indians. J. X. Merriman, however, was more tolerant. He reminded the House of the repeated warnings he and others had given the country against bringing in the Indians, and against keeping them after they had served their indentures. Having brought them in, he considered it was only right to treat them in a humane and reasonable way. Summing up, Smuts deprecated most of these proposals, which he said were not beneficial for South Africa and would cause offence throughout the British Empire. However, at a conference at Pietermaritzburg later, he announced that his government would introduce new segregationist legislation.

Smuts's policy with regard to the natives is clearly set out in a speech he made in May 1917 at the Imperial Institute in London, in which he said:

'We have realized that political ideas which apply to our White civilization largely do not apply to the administration of Native affairs . . . and so a practice has grown up in South Africa of creating parallel institutions – giving the Natives their own separate institutions on parallel lines with institutions for Whites. It may be that on those parallel lines we may yet be able to solve a problem which may otherwise be insoluble. . . . Instead of mixing up Black and White in the old haphazard way, which instead of lifting up the Black degraded the White, we are now trying to lay down a policy of keeping them apart as much as possible in our institutions. In land ownership, settlement and forms of government we are trying to keep them apart, and in that way laying down in outline a general policy which it may take a hundred years to work out, but which in the end may be the solution of our Native problem. Thus in South Africa you will have in the long run large areas cultivated by Blacks and governed by Blacks, where they

229

will look after themselves in all their forms of living and development, while in suitable parts you will have your White communities which will govern themselves separately according to the accepted European principles. The Blacks will, of course be free to go and to work in the White areas, but as far as possible the White and Black areas will be separate, and such that each community will be satisfied and develop according to its own proper lines.

This doctrine of parallel institutions and separate development was of long standing. It had been tried by Cecil Rhodes when the old Cape Colony gave local institutions to the natives in the Glen Grey reserve. Later it was applied in the Transkeian territories. In 1903 Milner chose Sir Godfrey Lagden as Chairman of a South African Native Affairs commission. Two years later, in 1905, this commission recommended the separation of Black South Africans from White South Africans both as occupiers of land and as voters. The report of the Lagden Commission was destined to survive as the main blueprint of Native policy in South Africa. In the framing of the Act of Union it was assumed that the enlarged state would become responsible for the British protectorates of Basutoland, Bechuanaland and Swaziland, and in an appendix to the treaty Lord Selborne laid down that native territories in South Africa should be governed apart from the parliamentary institutions and on different lines, so as to achieve the principle of native self-government. Although the protectorates were never incorporated in the Union, they became the model for the administration and development of other areas of compact native settlement, which were already within the state's boundaries.

In 1913 Botha's Government increased the amount of land available for exclusive native settlement in accordance with another recommendation of the Lagden Commission, but the complete separation of the natives as occupiers of land and as voters proved difficult at the start because in the Act of Union there were clauses which stated that in the Cape Province natives had unrestricted freedom of land purchase in order to qualify as voters. To Hertzog that part of the Act of Union was an outrageous blot. There was one way, he maintained, of getting rid of it, to abolish the Cape's franchise for natives. Because that franchise had been entrenched in the constitution of the Union, the constitution would have to be amended as soon as the requisite two-thirds majority could be achieved. That would finally settle the land question, and at the same time solve the franchise question, which in Hertzog's view was the more fundamental. Like the Lagden Commission, Hertzog believed that the Whites and the Blacks should not only live in separate areas but also vote on separate rolls, otherwise the day would surely come, he said, when Black voters on the common roll would outnumber White. That would mean the end of White civilization in South Africa. Smuts had also once told Merriman that he did not believe in politics for natives; but he and Merriman had nevertheless subsequently worked out the compromise which enabled the Cape's joint franchise to co-exist with the all-White franchises of the former republics. In practice, therefore, Smuts was more tolerant than Hertzog. All the same, as will be seen, he dealt firmly with natives who broke the law.

The *Natives Land Act* of 1913 made it illegal to purchase land in White areas and also ordered the eviction of 'squatters' who settled there. To balance this, White people might not purchase or occupy land in Black areas. Though apparently equitable, the measure proved unworkable, for there was not enough land available for the evicted natives.

The clause relating to 'squatters' led to the Bulhoek affair of 1921. By the early 1920s Bantu separatist churches or sectarian movements could be numbered in scores and one such was the Israelite Church. The Israelites' leader had sinister visions of a forthcoming forcible removal of the Whites from their country, and impressed by his pronouncements large numbers of natives came and 'squatted' at Bulhoek, north of East London, where he had established his church. The 'squatters' made themselves a nuisance to the local natives and White farmers, and when ordered to leave they refused to do so. When 800 police and soldiers moved in to force them to depart, they resisted, and 163 Israelites

231

were shot dead in the encounter with the authority's forces before they were removed. This seemed very severe treatment, and Smuts – who was responsible – was severely criticized for the way he had allowed the incident to be dealt with.

In 1922 a somewhat similar affair occurred in South-West Africa when a Hottentot tribe in the south of the mandated territory refused to hand in arms, pay their taxes, or deliver wayward members of their tribe for trial. The administrator of South-West Africa took a very serious view of this revolt. With Smuts's permission he marched against the Hottentots with a force of 370 men supported by aircraft from Pretoria. It proved a most unequal contest, for within a matter of days the revolt was crushed, and while the Government force lost only two men, a hundred of the Hottentots were killed. The Opposition made the most of this incident by pointing out how merciless Smuts was, and the evil reputation he had for shedding blood unnecessarily.

However, the main crisis of Smuts's first ministry was the great strike and revolt among the workers in the Witwatersrand in 1922. Owing to an economic depression, a fall in the price of gold, and a subsequent decrease in gold production, a proposal was made that in order to save costs there should be a higher proportion of cheaper native workers employed and the remaining White workers should have their wages cut. The White workers objected strongly to this. In January they went on strike and marched in protest through Johannesburg. In February a council of action was formed of five extremists, who ordered the formation of worker commandos. These commandos subsequently clashed with the police, and started robbing, burning and killing natives and opponents. Meanwhile, the strikers' council declared they intended to overthrow the Government and form a red or syndicalist workers' republic. By March the situation in Johannesburg had become so serious that Smuts, who up till then had been content 'to let things develop', declared martial law. Detachments of the army, supported by the air force, entered Johannesburg, and fierce fighting took place at various points, while the aircraft bombed the strikers. On 14 March, after a bombardment of the building which housed the strikers' headquarters at Benoni, the red flag on the building was lowered and resistance ended. Two of the council who were in the building chose to commit suicide rather than surrender, but the rest gave themselves up, and the bulk of the strikers agreed to return to work. During the revolt 153 people died. Eighteen of those responsible for the murders of policeman, natives and opponents were brought to trial and sentenced to death, though only four were executed. It was a total defeat for the miners. All previous engagements were cancelled, more natives were engaged, many White workers were dismissed and those retained had their wages cut. On the other hand the outcome was also disastrous for Smuts and his Government. Smuts was criticized in the House of Assembly by Opposition leaders for the severity with which he had put down the revolt. The miners, seething with resentment against the Government, ranged themselves solidly on the side of the Opposition Labour and Nationalist parties, and these made use of the opportunity to join forces against the South African Party at the next election. This saw returned 63 Nationalists, 53 from the South African Party, 18 from the Labour Party and 1 Independent. When the result was declared, Smuts, who had been Prime Minister for five years resigned, and the Governor-General asked Hertzog to form a government.

Hertzog's chief assistants were Tielman Roos, the leader of the Transvaal branch of the National Party, Dr D. F. Malan, the leader of the Cape branch, who became Deputy Prime Minister, and N. C. Havenga from the Free State. But he included the Labour Party leader Colonel F. H. P. Creswell and another English-speaking member of the Labour Party in his Cabinet; and Creswell as Minister of Labour quickly introduced legislation to protect White urban workers against competition from the Non-Whites.

The Nationalist victory in 1924 meant full government support for the Afrikaans language and culture movement. As Minister of the Interior, Dr D. F. Malan did much to promote Afrikaans in the civil service where English still

233

predominated, and in 1925 he piloted the act through parliament which replaced Dutch by Afrikaans as one of South Africa's two official languages. The Nationalists' main policy was to loosen the British connection with South Africa, and Hertzog's first aim was to change the country's status from one of subordination to Britain to one of complete sovereign independence. Out of regard for Creswell, Hertzog permitted the presence of monarchists in the party; and he promised, while the coalition with Labour lasted, that he would not alter the existing constitutional relationship of South Africa to the British Crown. But he was determined to sever as soon as practicable every other link. At the Imperial Conference in London in 1926, Hertzog had an opportunity to achieve something concerning the status of South Africa. All questions concerning relations within the British Empire were referred to a committee, headed by Lord Balfour. In this committee Hertzog demanded a clear statement concerning the status of the British Dominions. At first this move was opposed, but in the end the members of the committee agreed to draw up a definition. Its wording presented problems, for Hertzog resisted the inclusion of terms like 'common citizenship', which he considered gave an impression of one superstate rather than several of equal status. In the end Lord Balfour produced his now famous declaration which said that the Dominions were 'autonomous Communities within the British Empire, equal in status, in no way subordinate one to another in any aspect of their domestic or external affairs, though united by a common allegiance to the Crown, and freely associated as members of the British Commonwealth of Nations'. The independent status of the Dominions having been recognized in 1926, the Imperial Conferences of 1929 and 1930, and finally the Statute of Westminster of 1931, removed any other traditional practices which individual countries might consider to infringe their independence, like, for instance, the right of appeal to the Privy Council in London.

Having won the recognition of their country's independence within the British Commonwealth, the Nationalists next sought their own distinctive flag, and in the 1926 parliamentary session a bill concerning a flag was introduced. This immediately caused a bitter dispute. While at one extreme there were those who wanted nothing but the Union Jack, at the other were people like Malan who wanted a flag with no British symbols on it at all. This dispute split the Labour Party and was eventually one of the factors which led to the break-up of the coalition, but to start with Creswell supported the Nationalists. However, both he and Roos realized that a compromise was necessary, and they urged the Prime Minister to delay the passing of the 'flag' bill for another year. When in 1927 the bill was again laid before parliament, Hertzog suggested they might have van Riebeeck's flag with the Union Jack, the *Vierkleur* and the Free State flag in miniature on a shield. Smuts then proposed that all these four should be combined on the main flag. However, after a good deal of argument, during which Malan resigned temporarily because he had not been consulted, a completely different solution was found. It was finally agreed that South Africa should have two flags. One was the national flag, consisting of three horizontal stripes of orange, white and blue with miniature versions of the Union Jack and the two republican flags on the middle white stripe. The other was the Union Jack, which could not be flown alone but only together with the national flag on certain specified places, such as the Houses of Parliament and the more important government buildings. The new national flag and the Union Jack were flown together for the first time in South Africa on 31 May 1928.

From 1924 to 1929 the economy had been flourishing, but from then on South Africa began increasingly to feel the effects of the world economic depression. The price of wool and gold fell sharply, and in almost all spheres of economic activity there were marked recessions. On 20 September 1931 Britain announced that she had left the gold standard, and in the same year she formed a National Government of all parties to pilot the country through the depression. Many in South Africa considered that their country should follow Britain's example in both respects, but some economists thought it was to South Africa's advantage to remain on the gold standard. Hertzog did not like the idea of following blindly in Britain's footsteps for fear that it would give the impression that South Africa was not truly independent; he therefore acted in accordance with the views of those who advised remaining on the gold standard.

Capitalists now began to send large sums of money out of the country, believing that South Africa would eventually abandon the gold standard and that their money was safer outside until she did; because of this, the already precarious economic condition deteriorated still further. Great pressure to leave the gold standard was now put on the Government from all sides. In parliament Smuts likened the country to a wounded man bleeding to death; unless action was taken soon to stem the outflow of money, he said, South Africa was doomed. Eventually, Tielman Roos made a speech supporting Smuts's demand for the country to leave the gold standard, and sensing this now to be the view of the majority in the country, Hertzog at last took action. Within fourteen days of Roos's speech the Minister of Finance, Havenga, announced that South Africa had left the gold standard. The effects of this step were felt immediately. The price of gold and gold mining shares started to climb, and money began pouring back from overseas. Nor was that all. Roos had also suggested that a coalition government should be formed on the lines of the one in Britain. The Labour Party had been split on the flag question and Hertzog's majority was in peril. He therefore began negotiations with Smuts regarding a coalition. In this he was supported by Havenga but strongly opposed by Malan. Despite this opposition, negotiations were continued and by 15 March 1933 an agreement was reached between the Nationalist Party and Smuts's South African Party. In the general election the two coalition parties were returned with an overwhelming majority, and all was set fair for Hertzog's second ministry. It was to last until the outbreak of the Second World War in 1939.

The formation of the Coalition Government offered an opportunity for the introduction of an agreed body of legislation affecting Non-Whites. In 1936 parliament passed the

Natives Representation Act, which removed the Cape Bantu from the White voters' roll, and as compensation gave them the right to elect three White members to the Union parliament and two to the Cape provincial council. It also set up a Natives Representative Council to act as a sounding-board and platform for African opinion, and under the earlier Natives Trust and Land Act allotted more land for exclusive native occupation so that segregation could be extended. Hertzog's policy towards the Coloureds was one of economic and social segregation combined with parliamentary integration; but so many of his followers were determined to achieve the ultimate parliamentary segregation of Coloureds that he was unable to proceed with his proposed legislation to extend the parliamentary status held by the Coloureds in the Cape to the other provinces.

The conflict among Afrikaner nationalists between supporters and opponents of fusion with the South African Party had been bitter. When parliament met in 1935 Malan and eighteen of his followers sat on the opposition benches, and in 1938 his small Purified National Party contested the election with Hertzog's and Smuts's United Party. On this occasion Malan did not do well. He won only twenty-seven seats to the United Party's 111. But the advent of the Purified National Party in 1938 coincided with a remarkable revival of Afrikaner patriotism in the country, and this was to bring many Afrikaners into Malan's camp.

From the early days of the Union there had developed an exclusively Afrikaner conception of South African nationhood. This was encouraged by the formation of the *Afrikaner Broederbond* in 1918. The *Broederbond* was a secret society dedicated to the service of the Afrikaner Volk, and it recognized no other nation in South Africa. It classed the British as late-comers with a divided loyalty and no just claim to equality unless they were willing to cast off all their outside ties. It considered that the loyalty of the Bantu was to Africa as a whole, and they had no right to claim the areas occupied by Whites because they had arrived after the Whites in South Africa. It reckoned the few yellow-skinned peoples as a sub-species and insignificant. Only concerning the Coloureds

237

did it have some doubts. Over the years from 1918 the *Broederbond* developed into a formidable group whose members, all in situations of influence, formed a network of cells and branches in every province except Natal; and through its influence on the *Federasie van Afrikaanse Kultuurvereniging* (F.A.K.) the cultural life of a number of Afrikaners soon bore the stamp of the *Broederbond*.

Hertzog and Smuts denounced the *Broederbond* as a sinister secret society provoking national disunity. Hertzog turned on both the society and Malan's Purified National Party. He described in detail the *Broederbond*'s organization: its local cells, its techniques of devolution and interlocking directorates, its penetration of the civil service and the teaching profession. Its aims, he insisted, were not merely cultural but essentially political. Its ambition was to rule South Africa. In support of that assertion he cited names, dates, facts and figures culled from the *Broederbond*'s secret records. The *Broederbond* and the Purified National Party, he said in effect, were the two opposite sides of the same penny: the *Broederbond* was the Party in action underground; the Party was the *Broederbond* pursuing its aims in public. Later, Smuts declared that the *Broederbond* was a political body, membership of which would be treated as a contravention of the law. He said that no *Broeder* would be permitted to hold a post in the civil service. When, however, Hertzog named D. F. Malan as a member of the *Broederbond*, Malan admitted membership, not apologetically but with pride, and retaliated by claiming that Hertzog like Smuts, was an enemy of the Afrikaner nation.

A new upsurge of Afrikaner nationalism in 1938 stemmed from the centenary celebrations of the Great Trek, when many Afrikaners and a number of British throughout South Africa paid homage to the Voortrekkers. The foundation stone of a splendid monument was laid on a hill outside Pretoria and symbolic ox-wagon treks were organized from the four corners of the country. There was a wave of patriotism. The heroic struggles of the Voortrekkers were re-enacted, people wore Voortrekker clothes, and children were christened in the shadows of ox-wagons. From the celebrations there developed an ox-wagon cult and the formation of yet another patriotic society, the 'ox-wagon society' or *Ossewa Brandwag*. This started as a cultural group but developed into a political party. It became aggressive and strong-arm in its methods, and was to cause considerable trouble to the Government of the day during the Second World War.

The rising spirit of Afrikaner nationalism had its influence on Hertzog, and as a result he announced that the Afrikaner nationalist's *Die Stem Van Suid-Afrika* would be the state's anthem instead of the British national anthem and that the new flag would replace the Union Jack which would in future be flown only on special occasions. This growing anti-British mood, which had already led to the break-away of Malan and his followers, now caused a rift in the Union party and was to end the Coalition when the Second World War began in 1939.

Hertzog maintained that Hitler's war affected only the European powers, and that South Africa should keep out of it, but Smuts was determined to enter the war as an ally of Britain. In the Cabinet five members supported Hertzog and six supported Smuts, so it was decided to put the issue to a free vote of the House of Assembly. The debate there continued in a tense atmosphere. Hertzog was supported by all of Malan's followers and most of his own, but Smuts was backed by sufficient members from diverse parties to secure the verdict by eighty votes to sixty-seven. That same evening Hertzog asked the Governor-General to dissolve parliament. When this was refused, he resigned, Smuts was then asked to form a cabinet and agreed to do so.

Smuts united those who wished to enter the war in a coalition government, and then threw all his amazing energy into the South African war effort. He was determined that his country should contribute her share. He organized industry to produce weapons of war and ammunition; he set up training establishments which produced a stream of splendid South African airmen; he offered facilities in South Africa to train British pilots; and he dispatched his country's

239

soldiers as volunteers to fight alongside British and Indian troops in East and North Africa.

The 1st South African Division under General George Brink played an important part in the campaign in East Africa and the occupation of Addis Ababa. South Africans also distinguished themselves under General O'Connor in the Desert in December 1940, when they helped defeat the Italians at Sidi Barrani, and followed the enemy up as they retreated westwards, taking many prisoners. The second siege of Tobruk, however, was a serious blow to South African prestige. In June 1942 the British were forced by Rommel to retreat from Gazala to Tobruk and beyond, and General Klopper and the 2nd South African Division with some British and Indian troops were left to defend the port. Auchinleck had decided that in the event of another attack by Rommel he would not try to hold Tobruk, as the Royal Navy had found it difficult to keep supplied. Because of this its defences were allowed to fall into bad repair. But at the first siege the fame of Tobruk had gone round the world. It would be too much of a blow to English pride to let it go. Although now quite unsafe, Churchill ordered it at the last moment to be held at all costs. In the fateful battles of Gazala which followed, however, Tobruk had to be surrendered with 25,000 men, over 10,000 of whom were South Africans. This was a great blow to the allies in general and to South Africa in particular, but the latter's contribution to the war effort did not end on such a depressing note. South Africans played an important part along with British, Australians, New Zealanders and Indians in the great offensive launched by General Montgomery at El Alamein in October 1942, and in the subsequent long advance westwards and the defeat of the *Afrika Korps* under Rommel's successor. The South Africans also fought with success in Italy.

During the Second World War, although there was no repetition of the 1914 rebellion, there were bitter internal political quarrels. An early agreement between Hertzog's and Malan's supporters produced the *Herenigde* Party under Hertzog. But his leadership was soon attacked because he

15   Field Marshal Jan Smuts

General J. B. M. Hertzog (South
African Embassy, London)

Dr Daniel Malan (Radio Times
Hulton Picture Library)

16 J. G. Strijdom
(South African Embassy, London)

Dr H. F. Verwoerd
(South African Embassy, London)

Advocate B. J. Vorster (South African Embassy, London)

was not considered sufficiently enthusiastic about Afrikaner nationalism and allowed non-republicans to belong to the party. At the Orange Free State congress of the new party the extent of the opposition to Hertzog's leadership became clear. When two draft constitutions, one from Hertzog and one from the council, were voted on, Hertzog's draft was rejected by a large majority. Hertzog considered this to be a motion of no confidence in his leadership and resigned. He also resigned as a Member of Parliament and withdrew from public life. Two years later, on 21 November 1942, he died.

Hertzog's departure left Afrikaners divided into five parts: Smuts's followers, a small group under N. C. Havenga who had previously followed Hertzog and now called themselves the *Afrikaner Party*, the rest of the *Herenigde Party* under Malan, a small body of Hitler-type National Socialists, the Greyshirts, and the *Ossewa-Brandwag*, so anti-Government that they were willing to attempt to sabotage the war effort. It was a divided Opposition that faced the 1943 election, which Smuts's United Party could in any case approach with confidence as the war was starting to turn in the favour of the Allies. It was not surprising, therefore, that the United Party won 105 seats to the Opposition's forty-three, and Smuts was able to continue in office. Despite irritating shortages of imported commodities, the war years were a period of economic prosperity for South Africa, during which there occurred a noteworthy development of industry. With the nation's economy in a fairly sound state, Smuts's Government was able at the end of hostilities to tackle the ever important question of race relations. In 1946 an act was introduced which gave the Indians the franchise but at the same time withdrew their previous right to possess fixed property. This act pleased no one: the Opposition were horrified at the clauses which gave Indians the vote; the Indian Government broke off trade relations because of the discriminatory property clauses.

Smuts also had no success when he sought the approval of the United Nations to incorporate South-West Africa into the Union. He was not allowed to do so and brought on himself a bitter attack from India and other member states because of South Africa's racial policies. This was particularly harmful to the United Party, which was the most tolerant towards Bantu aspirations. Criticism from outside had the effect of making the Whites more attached to segregation policies, because they realized that if the elimination of colour bars found elsewhere in the world was brought about in South Africa there would be a real threat to their survival. Latching on to this mood for a stricter attitude to Non-Whites, most of the opposition parties came together under the leadership of Malan and launched a combined attack on Smuts, whom they set out to show was a waverer on race relations and a henchman of the British Empire, quite unsuitable as a leader of the Afrikaner nation.

Few people in South Africa expected a change of government in 1948. The prestige of the United Party had increased because of the successful outcome of the war, and it was also fortunate in having a leader of world-wide reputation. When Smuts spoke the world listened attentively. In Britain and the United States he was particularly highly esteemed. Of all the statesmen in the Dominions he alone was admitted to the War Cabinet. To him was given the task of writing the preamble setting out the nature of the United Nations Organization. No other South African had ever risen to such heights of international fame, yet there were many Afrikaners who did not want him to continue as leader because they did not share his views on colour and thought he was neglecting South Africa.

It is difficult, however, to determine what Smuts's views on colour were at this time. Twenty years earlier he had believed in separate development; but he had always been inclined 'to let matters develop' rather than apply regimentation. For example, he had been loth to remove the Cape Bantu from the White voters' roll, and he did not wish to take the vote away from the Cape Coloureds. By 1948 he was beginning to be affected by his conscience because he could not match the humanitarian views he expressed before the world at the United Nations with the policies he was applying in his own country. Some part of his dilemma is revealed in a letter he wrote to M. C. Gillett in November 1946, after the South African Government had been accused by the Indian Government of denying justice to 300,000 South Africans of Indian descent:

'Colour queers my poor pitch everywhere. But South Africans cannot understand. Colour bars are to them a divine order of things. But I sometimes wonder what our position in years to come will be when the whole world will be against us. And yet there is much to be said for the South African point of view who fear getting submerged in Black Africa. I can watch the feeling in my own family which is as good as the purest gold. It is a sound instinct of self preservation where the self is so good and not mere selfishness.'

By 1948, however, it is clear that he no longer believed that the policy of segregation would keep the Whites from being swamped, for he writes:

'Attempts, as you know, have been made to get round this fear (of being swamped) by the policy commonly called "segregation" – the policy of keeping Europeans and Africans completely apart for their self-preservation. . . . The high expectation of that policy has been sadly disappointed. How can it be otherwise? The whole trend in this country and throughout Africa has been in the opposite direction. The whole movement of development here on this continent has been for closer contacts to be established between the various races and the various sections of the community. . . . Isolation has gone and segregation has fallen on evil days too. But there are other phenomena springing out of these conditions . . . a revolutionary change is taking place among the Native peoples of Africa through the movement from the country to the towns – the movement from the old Reserves in the Native areas to the big European centres of population. Segregation tried to stop it. It has, however, not stopped it in the least. The process has been accelerated. You might as well try to sweep the ocean back with a broom.'

To the Afrikaner Nationalists the view expressed above

was a council of despair and was sufficient to turn the majority of Afrikaners against Smuts. Malan, the leader of the *Herenigde* Party, and Havenga, the leader of the Afrikaner Party, succeeded in reaching an agreement, and the colour question was the crux of their attack on Smuts's United Party. The White minority knew that racial integration must inevitably cause them to lose their dominant position, so the separate development which Malan and his allies promised to apply determinedly appealed to them, and turned them away from the United Party – which they felt was being led by a waverer – towards the confident New Nationalists' Party under the supremely confident Malan. On 26 May the nation voted. The result was a victory for the Malan–Havenga coalition which acquired a majority of five over the United Party, the Labour Party and the White representatives of the Natives. A bitterly disillusioned Smuts resigned as prime minister and Malan formed a cabinet. Like Hertzog, Smuts was only to enjoy a few years of retirement. In September 1950 he died, just four months after he had celebrated his eightieth birthday and 3,000 people had lined the streets of Johannesburg in his honour.

Chapter 16

Apartheid

Since 1948 the National Party has governed South Africa with steadily increasing majorities over the United Party, and no other party has gained more than a few seats. Taking this to mean support from the White population for their segregation policies, Malan and his successors as prime ministers, Strijdom, Verwoerd and Vorster, felt justified in putting into effect fully their party's separate development plans. But the application proved very difficult, and brought a storm of abuse from the world outside, strong criticism from South African liberals, and resistance and riots in the country among the Non-Whites.

The National Party's apartheid policies were both negative and positive. On the negative side they formalized and legalized the degree of social separation already customary. In 1949 the *Prohibition of Mixed Marriages Act* made marriages between Whites and Non-Whites illegal – though there had never been more than 100 per year compared with 25,000 White marriages. There followed in 1950 the *Immorality Amendment Act* which prohibited extra-marital sexual relations between Whites and all Non-Whites, including Coloureds and Indians. The next step, also in 1950, was the introduction of fuller residential apartheid through the *Group Areas Act*. Residential apartheid between Whites and Bantu[1] was a

[1] In 1939 the members of the Native Representative Council requested the government to use the word 'African' rather than 'Native'. Smuts permitted this, but his successors reverted to 'Native' for official usage until it was superseded by the language-group term 'Bantu' used by the Nationalists in their apartheid legislation. As they dislike the term 'Bantu', South African liberals

long established South African custom, but the areas for Coloureds and Indians had so far not been marked out, and this act, considered by some Afrikaners as the corner-stone of apartheid, demarcated separate residential areas for all the various racial groups. Next to appear on the Statute Book in 1953 was the *Reservation of Separate Amenities Act* which made apartheid compulsory in all public places where provision could reasonably be made for separate amenities. This law stated that when the owner or person in charge of any property, whether a park, a train, a swimming bath, offices or anything else, provided separate conveniences for the various races, it would be a punishable offence to transgress such separations. Apartheid in public places was not new because there had been separate buses, separate railway coaches, separate benches in public parks and separate bathing facilities on beaches for the different races long before 1948. The innovation was that what had previously been left to custom had now become incorporated in written laws. Residential apartheid was further enforced through two laws which were closely related to the *Group Areas Act* above: the *Resettlement of Natives Act* of 1954, which resulted in 100,000 Bantus being removed from squatter camps in the western suburbs of Johannesburg and resettled in the residential area of Meadowlands, and the *Natives Urban Areas Amendment Act* of 1955, which became known as the 'Locations in the Sky Act' because it ended the large-scale accommodation of Non-White servants on the top floors of buildings. The *Bantu Education Act* of 1953 placed all the Bantu education which formerly had been mainly in the hands of subsidized churches and mission societies under the control of the state; and the *Separate Universities Act* of 1959 prohibited the open universities of Witwatersrand and Cape Town from admitting any more Non-Whites, and provided separate universities for the Bantu, for the Indians and for the Coloureds.

Most of these laws were negative and prohibitory, enforcing traditional separation, but apartheid also had a positive

---

use the term 'African'. The term 'Kaffir,' which is considered derogatory, has not been used for many years.

aspect of giving Non-Whites their own homelands, townships or locations where they possessed political rights such as Whites enjoyed in their parts. This had been started in 1913 when, by the *Natives Land Act*, Botha's Government had increased the amount of land available for exclusive native settlement. Later Smuts and Hertzog had provided more land. But in 1948, following a report by P. O. Sauer, this policy was developed systematically. The party commission under the chairmanship of Sauer produced recommendations in time for the 1948 general election, and it also put into currency the word 'apartheid' to describe the National Party's segregation policy. Their report rejected any suppressing or exploiting of the Non-Whites by the Whites. 'National policy,' it said, 'must be so designed that it will advance the ideal of ultimate complete separation on a natural basis.' It considered that to avoid the swamping of towns and the disruption of the peaceful life of inhabitants, Bantus should be put in separate residential areas, and that in future they would legally count as visitors while serving in White areas. The report also envisaged separate townships or locations for Indians and Coloureds.

So much for theory. In 1950 Professor F. R. Tomlinson was appointed to investigate the practical steps needed to put Sauer's plans for the future of the separated races into effect. The Tomlinson report was very thorough; it contained a million words and sixty-six maps. Its main suggestion was that the 264 existing scattered Bantu areas should be consolidated into a small number of 'homelands' for the principal races, Xhosa, Zulu, Venda, Tswana and the like. These 'homelands' were eventually to become miniature states each with its own government, but linked together in a sort of Black commonwealth, and possibly including later the erstwhile British protectorates of Swaziland, Basutoland and Bechuanaland.

The first implementation of the ideas of the Tomlinson report came when the *Bantu Authorities Act* of 1951 abolished the old Native Representative Council and gave new powers to headmen and chiefs. Though criticized as representing a revival of tribalism, the act allowed for mergers between different tribes and provided for Bantu authorities who would be responsible for larger regions and ultimately for whole territories administered under Bantu laws and customs. Similar arrangements in line with Sauer's recommendations were to be made for Bantu self-government in townships on the outskirts of cities. Next, the *Promotion of Self-Government Act* of 1959 reduced the many reserves to eight large units and appointed a commissioner to head each one with instructions to guide his region towards self-government. The granting of political rights to the Bantu made native representatives in parliament unnecessary and under the 1959 act they were withdrawn. Self-government under the 'homelands' policy was achieved by the Xhosa in the Transkei in 1960, by the Ovambo in South-West Africa, by the people of the Ciskei in the eastern part of Cape Province in 1968, and by the Zulus in Zululand and the Venda in the north-east of the Transvaal in 1971.

The most contentious of the Apartheid measures was the one which removed the 38,000 Cape Coloured voters from the ordinary White voters' roll and placed them on a separate Coloured voters' roll, allowing them to return their own representatives to Parliament. The trouble for the Nationalist authorities was that Coloured voting rights on the general roll had been entrenched in the Act of Union of 1910 and this could not be altered except by a two-thirds majority of both houses of parliament. When an act to remove the Coloureds was passed by a straight majority and the Supreme Court accepted it, the opposition referred it to the Appeal Court which declared it invalid. The matter was temporarily shelved, but when Johannes Gerhardus Strijdom replaced Malan as Prime Minister he took it up again. Strijdom was perhaps the least tolerant of South Africa's Prime Ministers, and with fiery determination he set about forcing the act through. He achieved this eventually by first passing a *Senate Act*, which increased the number of senators from forty-eight to eighty-nine, next by changing the form of the Senate so that the National Party could hold seventy-seven out of the eighty-nine seats; and finally by increasing the number of judges to hear constitutional cases in the Appeals

Court from five to eleven. By these means he managed in 1956 to get the act removing the Coloureds from the common roll on to the statute book. He gave them instead four White representatives.

There has been continuous criticism of South Africa's apartheid policies at the United Nations Organization, especially by representatives of the emergent states of Black Africa. Even before the National Party came to power various countries had complained of South Africa's discriminatory attitude towards the Non-Whites within its borders. Opportunity for criticism specifically arose when South-West Africa – over which the United Nations claimed trusteeship rights – came under discussion; and also when India was protesting against the treatment of the Indians in South Africa. South Africa's racial policy is also directly attacked on the grounds that it is a threat to world peace. Opposition within the country among the Whites has, however, been limited.

After the loss of the 1948 election the United Party, which embraced most of the liberals, began to decline steadily. Smuts, who at the insistence of his followers remained as leader until his death in 1950, was unable to offer any constructive solution to South Africa's race problems and had nothing to counter Malan's apartheid policy. His successor, J. G. N. Strauss, met at once with opposition to his leadership and made even less headway. When he was replaced by Sir de Villiers Graaff in 1956, this did not halt the decline in the fortunes of the United Party, for at every successive election they continued to lose ground. A new Progressive Party, backed by the rich magnate Harry Oppenheimer, was established in 1959 but was short-lived. It had at the start eleven members of parliament who had seceded from the United Party, but only one of these was left after the 1961 election. Because of the failure of the parliamentary Opposition to make any real impact, resistance to the Afrikaner nationalists was taken up for a time by unofficial organizations such as the War Veterans Torch Commando, and the Women's Defence of the Constitution League – known as the Black Sash because of the ladies' habit of wearing black sashes during silent public protest demonstrations. The formation of the Torch Commando, numbering at its height 250,000, was a reaction against the Government's plans to remove the Cape Coloureds from the common voters' roll. It organized torchlight protest processions, meetings and petitions. It also combined with the United Party and Labour Party to fight the 1953 general election; but after defeat it began to splinter, mainly because its members disagreed over the tactics to be employed for the future. The Black Sash movement was founded to challenge the country's conscience over the packing of the Senate and the Appeal Court to take the Coloureds off the common roll. It operated on a smaller scale and depended for its impact on silent protest in public places; but it nevertheless lasted much longer than the Torch Commando.

Organization of Non-Whites to seek their rights began with the formation of the Natal Indian Congress by Mohandas Gandhi in 1894. Gandhi's organization launched the first civil disobedience campaigns in the Transvaal during the 1906–8 period, and further campaigns in 1913.

In the decade after Union, African nationalism developed considerably. In 1912 the South African National Congress was formed – this was renamed the African National Congress in 1923. To begin with, the activities of the African National Congress took the form of petitions and deputations. As has been mentioned, a deputation visited Versailles in 1919 and was seen by Lloyd George. But the Congress soon started to practise the same type of civil disobedience as the Indians. In 1919 the Rand and Johannesburg branches decided to throw away their passes and court arrest. After many had been arrested and brought to trial, a mass of other protesters gathered outside one of the court-houses and were only dispersed after mounted police had charged repeatedly.

Also in 1919, the Industrial and Commercial Union was formed in Cape Town by Clements Kadalia in association with a White socialist; this group included both Coloured and Bantu workers. In 1928, at the height of its power, it had about half a million members, but it lost ground when the authorities took action, and also when disputes arose between its communist members and its more conservative leaders.

The Communist Party proper was founded in 1921. It soon took over control of several Bantu trades unions, and it formed them into a Non-White trades union federation. At first the Federation attempted to improve the economic and political position of its members by lawful means, but later encouraged strike action which led to disturbances and violence. The Communist Party drew off the more militant members from the Industrial and Commercial Union and from the African National Congress, and this led to the decline of the former institution. In 1930 the Communist Party instructed protesters to burn their passes on Dingaan's Day,[1] 16 December. The only effective response was in Durban, where the demonstrators clashed with the police; in the ensuing conflict the local organizer and three others were killed. The Party continued to encourage rioting and disturbances over many years, with the result that in 1950 the Government passed the *Suppression of Communism Act* which banned the Communist Party and excluded Communists from the trades unions. In 1956 the Government even went so far as to close the Russian Consulate, having come to the conclusion that Soviet officials were giving money and other assistance to the Communist agitators who were disrupting industry.

Meanwhile, the African National Congress was still organizing demonstrations against the apartheid laws. On 1 May 1951, it called on all Bantus to stay away from work; and in clashes with police trying to protect non-strikers from intimidation, eighteen Bantu were killed. Undeterred, Congress leaders wrote a letter to the Prime Minister threatening to stage more demonstrations unless six particularly obnoxious apartheid laws were repealed. Dr Malan rejected the ultimatum and told the leaders they would bear the consequences if they encouraged the Bantu to violate the laws. There followed a massive resistance campaign during which some 8,000 Bantus infringed the pass laws by entering railway

[1] The Day of the Covenant.

coaches and waiting rooms reserved for Whites, and ignoring curfews and other restrictions. When the offenders were arrested they offered no resistance; they refused to pay fines and elected to serve prison sentences. Less passive demonstrations followed, during which there was rioting involving murder and arson, so the Government passed in 1953 the *Public Safety Act* and *Criminal Law Amendment Act* which gave the authorities more control over offenders. A meeting was held at Kliptown near Johannesburg on 26 June 1955, which was attended by 3,000 delegates from the African National Congress, the Coloured Peoples Organization, the Indian Congress and the Council of Democrats, the last being a White leftist organization. Using their new powers under the Public Safety Act, the police soon closed this congress of the Non-Whites, but not before the delegates had adopted a freedom charter demanding a socialist democracy for South Africa and equal rights for all races.

Considering that the trouble was due to a few loquacious agitators and that the silent majority was generally content, the authorities in 1956 arrested 156 leaders, White and Non-White, on charges of high treason. Among them were: Albert Luthuli, President of the African National Congress; Dr G. M. Naiker, President of the Indian Congress; and L. B. Lee-Warden, a native representative in parliament. There followed the famous South African Treason Trial which soon hit the headlines of the world's newspapers. The men were charged with inciting people to violence and preparing to overthrow the Government by violent revolution. Although most of the accused were discharged after nine months, the case against twenty-nine dragged on for years. The offenders attracted much sympathy in the world outside, and a large sum of money was collected in Britain to help pay their legal costs.

In spite of the severe measures taken by the authorities, resistance and rioting continued. In 1959, under the leadership of Robert Sobukwe, some members of the African National Congress who considered the association too passive broke away and formed the more militant Pan African Congress. The Pan Africanists chose their name because they looked to the newly independent nations of Africa for inspiration and help. Where the African National Congress dreamt of a multi-racial society in South Africa, the Pan Africanists' plan was for a Black South Africa. In 1959, under its direction, rioting broke out throughout the country, the most serious incidents occurring at Windhoek in South-West Africa, where twelve rioters were killed in clashes with the authorities, and at Cato Manor near Durban, where the protestors stormed a police-station and killed nine constables. Early in 1960 the Pan African Congress advised its followers to present themselves at the nearest police-station and to court arrest by handing in their passes. If the campaign was successful, the factories and farms would be without labour, and the courts and gaols would overflow. One such demonstration was staged at Sharpeville, a Bantu location of 15,000 people thirty miles south of Johannesburg, which provides labour for the industries of near-by Vereeniging. Vereeniging's previous claim to fame was as a site of the peace conference in 1902 ending the Anglo–Boer War. Its wide streets and square lay-out give it the appearance of a prairie town, but it is a factory city with its own power-station, steel works and industries, in addition to neighbouring coalmines.

The call for action was for 21 March, but things began happening a few days earlier. The sergeant in charge of the police detachment at Sharpeville was not slow to notice the mounting tension within the location. He reported to the captain at Vereeniging police-station, who went out to Sharpeville and was shown a number of pass-books that had been defaced and discarded. This was an angry omen, for throwing away his pass-book precluded a Bantu from getting work. Two days later there were more ominous signs. Reports came in that groups of several hundred men were roaming the location. The Vereeniging police captain now assembled ten White and twenty-seven Non-White policemen and took them over to Sharpeville, where he found at the police-station a number of Negroes who were complaining of having been assaulted by the roaming bands, and of having their pass-books seized. In an attempt to stop further intimidation, the captain led off his men in search of the marauders. He met one band of young Bantu, some armed with sticks and some not, and coming to the conclusion that those without weapons were being detained by the others, he ordered his constables to disarm and disperse the group, which after a scuffle they succeeded in doing. Continuing his patrol, the captain encountered another band, but when two shots were fired into the ground in front of them, they scattered. About two in the morning more Negroes were found holding a meeting. This gathering was broken up by a series of baton charges. In the course of the whole night fifteen parties were encountered and dispersed.

There was little sleep for anyone in Sharpeville on Sunday night, and before dawn on Monday 21 March a crowd started to gather near where the buses waited at the entrance to the location, with the intention of stopping any workers who proposed going to their jobs in Vereeniging. The police estimated that there were about 7,000 people involved in stopping the buses leaving, and they sent a request to Vereeniging for some tear-gas bombs to try to disperse them. Later, when the crowd began to move in on the police guarding the entrance to Sharpeville five bombs were fired and the people fell back about thirty yards. In the crowd were a band of some 600 young stalwarts who began to taunt the police, blowing whistles, crying 'Afrika,' and shouting the Pan African slogan '*Izwe Lethu*' which means 'Our Land'. At this stage small police reinforcements arrived in some Saracen armoured cars, along with the head of the Rand security branch, and Colonel Pienaer of the uniformed police who took over command.

The whole police force, which numbered about 150, now withdrew into the compound of Sharpeville's police-station, where it was separated from the enormous crowd of protesters by a five-foot wire-mesh fence. The air force had been alerted to help the surrounded policemen, and just before noon, when the crowd was estimated at 15,000, planes dived with screaming engines in an endeavour to frighten the people away. It had little effect. A few shook their fists at the Sabre jets, or threw their hats in the air in defiance. No one fled.

The mob, armed with axes, iron bars and knives, then closed in and launched an attack on the defenders of the police-station with volleys of stones and half-bricks. These missiles injured several constables but at this stage the defenders did not retaliate. Next, three Bantu who managed to climb the fence were seized and taken inside the police-station. This appeared to enrage the rioters for they surged forward almost flattening the mesh of the fence. Three shots were now heard in the crowd and one policeman, mindful of the fate of his comrades at Cato Manor, opened fire without being ordered to do so. Immediately fifty others along the western side opened fire in sympathy, pouring, according to an official report, 476 bullets into the crowd. This ended the riot, but 69 were killed and 180 were wounded, including some women and children, and in a matter of seconds, as is always the case on such occasions, a nation's good name was jeopardized.

On the same day very serious riots broke out in Langa, a Bantu township near Cape Town, and a procession of 30,000 moved right into the centre of the city. There were strikes too in a number of other towns, and all in all it was the most serious crisis of its type that South Africa had yet experienced.

The Government was now under Dr Hendrik Verwoerd, a cleverer man than Strijdom but just as determined, and who like so many Nationalist leaders had been a member of the *Broederbond*. Verwoerd immediately declared a state of emergency in eighty districts. He mobilized units of the Active Citizens' Force, piloted through parliament the *Unlawful Organization Act*, which made it possible to ban the African National Congress and Pan African Congress as unlawful organizations, and ordered the mass arrest of the instigators of the demonstrations. These Government measures, combined with the drastic action of the police at Sharpeville, had effect: within a short space of time all traces of resistance and violence disappeared. The state of emergency was ended a few months later on 31 August 1960.

. . . . . .

Law and order having been re-established, Dr Verwoerd next turned his attention to a matter close to his heart, the establishment of a republic in South Africa. In September 1960 he appealed to both Afrikaans-speaking and English-speaking voters in a personal letter written in their respective languages. He argued that as long as there was no republic it would be impossible for the two White races to unite because the English-speakers had a divided loyalty between South Africa and Britain whose monarch they shared. He ended with a warning that unless they said 'yes' to a republic they would risk being driven out as others like them had been driven out recently from one state after another in Africa. Events in the Congo reinforced Verwoerd's cogent appeal, and when it came to a referendum to decide the matter, the majority of Whites came to the conclusion that a republic would be to their advantage. But only just. In October, when the votes were counted, it was found that 850,458 had voted in favour and 775,878 against.

As India had been allowed to become a republic and stay within the Commonwealth it was hoped that South Africa might be granted the same privilege. It was not, however, to be. Almost all the countries of the Commonwealth so strongly disapproved of South Africa's racial policies and were so critical of them that Dr Verwoerd withdrew the application for South Africa to remain in the Commonwealth after becoming a republic. This decision appears also to have been endorsed by the majority of Whites, for both at the general election of October 1961, after the country had been declared a republic, and in the subsequent election in 1966 the Nationalists increased their vote and gained more seats.

After the assassination of Dr Verwoerd on 6 September 1966, his place was taken by Advocate John Vorster. As Prime Minister Mr Vorster has shown himself just as dedicated as his three predecessors to the principle of separate development for the different races of South Africa. In spite of continued abuse from the emergent Afro–Asian nations and others, the policy of leading the different Bantu national units towards independence in the areas of their traditional

Homelands has been extended. In these Homelands, enlarged by appropriation of additional land from what had been considered White regions, many Bantu nations have begun attempting to modify traditional systems of government to enable them to cope with their own self-rule under modern conditions.

This policy of separate development in the Homelands reached its first milestone in December 1963 when the Xhosa of the Transkei were granted self-government. A general election to establish the Legislative Assembly of the Transkei – South Africa's first Bantu parliament – was held during the previous month on the basis of universal adult suffrage. Some 800,000 Xhosa voters in the Transkei and other parts of South Africa went to the polls. The civil administration of the Transkei was transferred to its citizens a few days before the 1963 election. At that stage the Civil Service establishment consisted of 2,476 posts, 1,900 of which were then filled by Transkeian citizens. This number has since been substantially increased and it is envisaged that all these posts will eventually be occupied by Transkeian citizens. In 1971 the Transkei Government consisted of 4,150 permanent officials of whom only 350 were White officials seconded from the South African Government. The constitution of the Transkei provides that, at this stage, forty-five members of the Legislative Assembly be elected and the remaining sixty-four seats be allotted to chiefs and paramount chiefs, who are key figures of the apex of the traditional government system of the Bantu. In terms of the constitution, the Transkei has its own flag, which is flown throughout the territory alongside the flag of the Republic. The Xhosa also have their own national anthem, *Nkosi Sikelel' i Afrika*. Xhosa, English and Afrikaans are the official languages of the Transkei but Seshoeshoe is also used for administrative purposes. The constitution has created a Transkei citizenship which is extended to Bantu domiciled in the Transkei, and to all Xhosa who live and work outside the Transkei and have no other homeland.

At the first session in 1964, the Transkei Assembly elected a Cabinet consisting of a Chief Minister and five Ministers.

R   257

Legislative power is vested in the Legislative Assembly, subject to the approval of the State President of the Republic of South Africa. The legislative power of the Assembly and executive responsibility of the Cabinet are substantial. The former is empowered to legislate for all affairs of State, with the exception, as yet, of defence, foreign affairs, immigration and certain aspects of transport, security and finance, which for the time being remain the prerogative of the South African Government. But the latter consults the Government of the Transkei if legislation in these spheres also affects the Transkei. The Transkei has six Departments of State: Finance; Agriculture and Forestry; Education; Interior; Roads and Works; Justice (with control over all lower courts in the territory). The administrative heads of these departments at present continue to be White civil servants of the South African Government seconded to the new Government. They remain on the payroll of the South African Government but are responsible only to the Transkei Cabinet. The aim is that the Transkei Civil Service will eventually consist of Transkeian citizens only.

In 1968 the Ciskei (whose people are also Xhosa-speaking) and the Tswana Territorial Authorities were established, followed by the Lebowa (North Sotho), Machangana (Tsonga-Shangaan), Venda and South Sotho Territorial Authorities in 1969 and the Zulu Territorial Authority in 1970. During 1971 and 1972 these authorities were granted increased powers in terms of the *Bantu Homelands Constitution Act* 1971. They now all have a Legislative Assembly. In 1972 the Transkei and Ciskei sought to join together in one large Bantu state.

Executive power in the Homelands is vested in an Executive Council. These Councils, each headed by a Chief Councillor, consist of six members, except in the case of the South Sotho, where there are only four. Each of these Councillors is responsible for the administration of a Department. A civil service has been established in each instance, staffed by citizens of the respective homelands. White officials will serve the homeland governments on secondment until trained Bantu citizens are able to take over all duties.

258

Also in terms of the policy of separate development of the different races a Coloured Persons Representative Council of the Republic of South Africa has been established. It consists of forty elected and twenty nominated members of the Coloured community. The first general election was held in 1969, prior to which 637,920 Coloured voters were registered. The Council has legislative powers and its Executive, consisting of five members, is responsible on behalf of the Coloured community for the management of finance, education, community welfare, pensions and local government in rural areas and settlements. The Administration of Coloured Affairs has approximately 20,000 administrative and professional posts for Coloureds.

Finally, for the Indians there is the South African Indian Council, a statutory body which consists of twenty-five representatives of Indian communities in the Transvaal, Natal and the Cape Province. Several fields of activity – such as education, agriculture, commerce, industry, social welfare and local government – are represented. The Indian Council advises the Government on all matters that affect the economic, social, cultural, educational and political interests of the Indian population and serves as a channel of communication between the Government and the Indian population. The all-Indian town of Verulam, north of Durban, was the first to run its own civic affairs under a town board, and in 1972 Isipingo, with a population of 10,000 south of Durban, became the second.

Chapter 17

Conclusion: Place Names

Since becoming a Republic South Africa has prospered. Agriculture, mining and industry have flourished, and the country has become the richest on the African continent. The Nationalist Governments which have been continuously in power since 1948 have firmly established law and order and thereby prevented the massacres and military take-overs suffered by many of the emergent African states. Because of this, and the good results economically which have followed, the three prime ministers of the period, Malan, Strijdom and Verwoerd, have been placed in esteem by their supporters alongside national heroes like Piet Retief, Andries Pretorius, Paul Kruger, Louis Botha and Jan Smuts. It has been a long established South African custom to name places after the great ones of the past, and the services of the three prime ministers have been recorded in similar fashion by attaching their names to particularly important institutions, appropriate to their great contribution to the country.

The extent to which South Africa's place-names have been derived from the names of its historic citizens must be unique in the world, and even a few of them afford a significant recapitulation of South African history as described in this book. The Portuguese Saldanha, who is reckoned as the first man to have climbed Table Mountain, is represented in the bay sixty miles north of Cape Town. Jan van Riebeeck is commemorated in Riebeeck West,[1] near where Smuts was born – and Riebeeck Kasteel, both close together some fifty

[1] Riebeeck East is near Grahamstown.

miles[1] north-east of Cape Town. Stellenbosch, twenty-five miles east of Cape Town, recalls Simon van der Stel, and Swellendam, 130 miles east, was named after the Governor from 1739–51, Hendrik Swellengrebel and his wife, whose maiden name was Ten Damme. Tulbagh township, near the Riebeecks, represents the energetic Governor who developed gardens at the Cape, planted chestnut trees and established a library. Plettenberg Bay, half-way to Port Elizabeth on the 'Garden Route', is named after Governor Baron van Plettenberg, who was liked even by the rebellious burghers, who planted a beacon to mark the north-east corner of the province, and who came to an agreement with the Xhosa that the Fish River should constitute the eastern frontier. Also relating to the Company period, Graaff-Reinet, 140 miles north of Port Elizabeth, recalls C. J. van de Graaff, Governor from 1785–91.

After the short occupation of the Cape by the British it was handed back into the charge of the Batavian Republic in 1802, and Commissioner-General Jacob Abraham Uitenhage de Mist, who spent some time reorganizing the administration, gave one of his first names to the new settlement of Uitenhage, near the later Port Elizabeth.

The governors and other distinguished persons in the second period of British rule from 1806 are well represented in place names. The frontier posts of Cradock and Grahamstown are called after Lieut-General Sir John Francis Cradock, who started close settlement on the frontier, and Colonel Graham, who carried out the successful campaign which drove the Xhosa back across the Fish. Somerset East, between these two frontier posts, and Somerset West near Cape Town commemorate Lieut-General Lord Charles Henry Somerset, who continued Cradock's close settlement policy with his 1820 Settlers scheme. Both Sir Benjamin D'Urban and Sir Harry Smith were popular and successful governors. D'Urban's name replaced Port Natal and Smith gave his through his wife to Ladysmith in Natal and Ladismith east of Cape Town. This idea of incorporating the wife's name – already begun in Company days – now became fashionable. The

[1] To convert miles to kilometres multiply by 1·6.

extended Fort Frederick on Algoa Bay was called Port Elizabeth after the deceased wife of acting Governor Sir Rufane Shaw Donkin; the township of Lady Grey, 170 miles north of East London, commemorates indirectly the academic-minded[1] Sir George Grey; and Lady Frere, eighty miles south of Lady Grey, recalls the instigator of the Zulu War, Sir Bartle Frere. However, the bombastic General Sir Garnet Wolseley is represented in his own right by a township plainly named Wolseley, near the Riebeecks and Tulbagh.

Natal records the early Voortrekker presence with Pietermaritzburg, named after Piet Retief and Gerrit Maritz, and Weenen (Weeping) on Bushmans River, where in 1838 Dingaan's impis slaughtered the settlers in their camps. Just south of Ladysmith, where two battles were fought in the Second Anglo–Boer War, is Colenso, named after the fiery Natal prelate, and eighty miles south of Durban is Port Shepstone, named after the well-liked and successful native administrator. Just outside the area, half-way between Johannesburg and Durban, lies Warden, recalling the energetic British officer who demarcated Basutoland and for a period maintained law and order among the various claimants to the area west of Moshesh's kingdom.

As might be expected, the Transvaal is studded with placenames recalling the Voortrekker and Afrikaner great ones. In the Soutpansberg in the north is the township of Louis Trichardt,[2] and half-way between it and Pretoria lies Potgietersrust. On the way from here to the Kruger Game Reserve is Burgersfort, recalling the Rev. Thomas François Burgers, President of the South African Republic from 1872–7. Near Johannesburg are Krugersdorp and Meyerton, the latter commemorating Lucas Johannes Meyer, President of the *Nieuwe Republiek*[3] from 1884–5 and the general of the Second Anglo–Boer War from whom Louis Botha took over command on the Tugela front.

The Orange Free State, following fashion, has Ladybrand,

---

[1] He founded Grey College, Bloemfontein.
[2] After Trigardt (Tregardt).
[3] page 132.

eighty miles east of Bloemfontein named after the wife of its distinguished President J. H. Brand who, in his twenty-five years term from 1866–91, turned his country into what was considered a model state. M. T. Steyn, who was President during the Second Anglo–Boer War, is represented by Steynrus and Petrus Steyn, both lying about half-way between Bloemfontein and Pretoria on different routes. Further west are Hertzogville and Bothaville, the latter south of the Vaal, although Botha was more closely associated with the Transvaal. Dewetsdorp, forty miles south-east of Bloemfontein, recalls the greatest Free State war hero, of whom there is also a splendid and much admired equestrian statue outside the Fourth Raadsal.

In the vicinity of Cape Town two highways leading east are called Voortrekker and Settlers Way respectively, and Cape Town's airport is named after D. F. Malan, the instigator of separate development for the different races of South Africa when he became Prime Minister and leader of the Nationalists in parliament in 1948. Rhodes has an impressive monument at *Groote Schuur* and his house there has become an official residence, while a section of a road leading south is called Milner.

The environs of Johannesburg are rich in historical references. Two great parallel highways leading north towards Pretoria are named Louis Botha and Jan Smuts respectively, and where the latter road is met by another its continuation is called Verwoerd. The name of Hendrik Verwoerd, the creator of the Republic, has also been chosen for the great drainage complex and dam on the Orange River, and Advocate Strijdom, the successor to Malan as Prime Minister, is commemorated by the J. G. Strijdom Dam on the Pongola 100 miles east of Vryheid in the north-east. To the east of Johannesburg on the way to Jan Smuts airport are found an interesting mixture of historic references. Seven miles from the town centre is a disappointingly small section of a minor road called Churchill. Some two miles east of the centre are Kitchener and Roberts Avenues, leading parallel towards the airport. Finally, in the south near Crown Mines golf course is a short stretch of road called Alamein to commemorate

263

the gallant contribution of South African arms to the Allied victory in the Desert in the Second World War.

The above represent only a fraction of the mass of place-names used in South Africa to commemorate their great men and to record the history of European achievement; but with the creation of the Homelands new Bantu names of similar significance are appearing, and soon, perhaps, a complete history will be indicated by the place-names of the country.

Appendixes

A GEOGRAPHY AND PEOPLE

South Africa consists of a great tilted plateau with its eastern edge
formed by the Drakensberg. From the long line of these mountains
there is a gradual slope westwards for a thousand miles towards the
Atlantic, and a steep scarp slope leads down to the narrow lowlands
of Natal. In the hilly area between Cape Town and Port Elizabeth
are the two narrow plateaux of the Great Karroo and the Little
Karroo.

The Orange River and its tributary the Vaal flow westwards across
the southern part of the plateau. The Vaal separates the two former
Afrikaner Republics and the Orange forms the border between the
southern one and the Cape Province. A number of short rivers flow
down the scarp slope of the Drakensberg eastwards, the most important
being the Tugela which, with its tributaries the Buffalo and Blood,
separates Zululand from Natal, and the Umfolozi, whose basin forms
the heart of Zululand. Farther north, the Limpopo forms a natural
boundary in its upper reaches between the Transvaal and Rhodesia,
and in its lower reaches between the Transvaal and Portuguese East
Africa or Mozambique. Encircling South Africa and Rhodesia in the
north is the Zambezi, with the Victoria Falls in the west, between
Rhodesia and Zambia. The plateau and mountain groups of Rhodesia
lie on the watershed between the Zambezi and the Limpopo, with
tributaries flowing from central Rhodesia north and south towards
the two great rivers.

The value of South Africa agriculturally depends on the rainfall,
which is adequate in the east but scanty in the west. The mean annual
rainfall of Durban is forty inches and of Port Nolloth only two inches –
even less away from the coast. This is due to the prevailing south-
easterlies, bringing rain towards the Natal lowlands, and the plateau
to the west of the Drakensberg being in a rain shadow of growing
intensity westwards. The area around Cape Town lies in the path of
the north-westerlies during the winter in the Southern Hemisphere

265

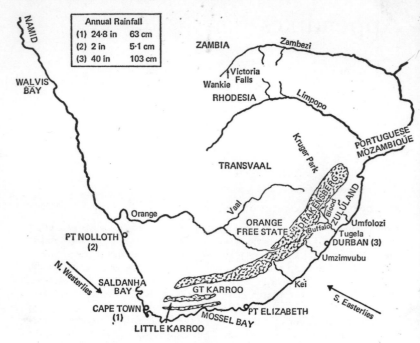

Map XIV   Main Geographical Features

and has a mean annual rainfall of 24·8 inches,[1] with a maximum in June of 4·4 inches.

In spite of periods of drought there was sufficient natural vegetation over much of the country to support directly or indirectly animals like lions, rhinocerous, giraffes and elephants, as well as large herds of game, in which the eland appears long dominant, judging by its frequent appearance in the rock paintings of the Bushmen. Most of these animals are now restricted to the great game reserves like the Kruger National Park in the north-east of the Transvaal and the Wankie Reserve in the west of Rhodesia. The country in its natural state was also able to support scattered bands of yellow-skinned peoples,[2] and the more fertile eastern lowlands attracted Negroes from the north, who arrived in the area in the seventeenth century about the same time as the first Whites. The Europeans first lived at and around the ports, but later a large number settled inland in the areas where diamonds and gold were present in the old rocks of the plateau.

[1] c.f. London, 24·5 inches.
[2] Bushmen and Hottentots.

The People
According to the population census of May 1970 the nations of the
Republic consist of:

Zulu (1971)*	4,026,058	Whites	3,751,328
Xhosa (1963)*	3,930,087	(Afrikaans speakers	60%:
Tswana (1972)*	1,719,367	English speakers	40%)
N. Sotho†	1,600,000	Coloureds	2,018,453
S. Sotho†	1,420,000	(Mixed blood, Hottentots,	
Tsonga†	731,000	Bushmen, Malays)	
Venda (1971)*	357,919	Asians	620,436
S. Ndebele	230,000	(predominantly Indian)	
N. Ndebele	180,000		
Other Bantu	314,000		

* with a self-governing Bantu homeland
† with a specific Territorial Authority area, advancing to internal self-
government

B PRE-HISTORY

The Earlier Stone Age
On the evidence of fossil remains, the earliest men of South Africa had
Neanderthal brow-ridges and were about four feet high and lightly
built. The remains discovered indicate that there were two main types,
the more robust seemingly vegetarian, and the other omniverous.
Small, erect and not particularly fleet of foot, they do not appear at
first to have possessed weapons. From the food-getting point of view,
no special equipment would have been needed by the vegetarian,[1]
whose fossil skull shows massive teeth and jaws for grinding. The
omniverous[2] early man could well have satisfied himself with easily
taken game like fledgelings, rodents and lizards and added to this food
supply when necessary by scavenging in the wake of large animal
predators such as lions. On occasion, they both may very well have
picked up and thrown stones, a habit observed among various non-
human primates.[3]

Most authorities agree that the early men of South Africa were
tool-users of a sort, while the evidence that they were tool-makers is
inconclusive. At the Taung and Sterkfontein sites in the Transvaal
near the present town of Krugersdorp, in deposits of the Early Pleisto-
cene period of up to two million years ago, no utilized stones or tooth,
horn or bone artifacts have been noted; on the other hand, in later
breccia at the same site, remains of these early men occur in association
with stone tools. Remains, dated at the earlier period, have also been
found along with large quantities of animal remains at Makapansgat

[1] *Australopithecus robustus.*
[2] *Australopithecus africanus.*
[3] See the works of A. H. Schultz.

in the Transvaal, indicating that the early men were able to kill such creatures in some manner or other. Then, the Swartkrans site, also in the Transvaal, though dated later at between a half and one and a half million years ago, has yielded yet another early form of man, living contemporaneously with the other two at a time when stone tools were being made.

On the evidence, R. A. Dart believes that the early men were tool-makers; but R. J. Mason has argued that stone culture in South Africa belongs to the second half (Acheulian Culture Stage) of the Earlier Stone Age rather than to the first half. He considers that the crude hand-axe makers of indigenous or immigrant origin existed only in South Africa from 500,000 years ago until 40,000 years ago.

Numerous Acheulian sites of the second half of the Earlier Stone Age have been investigated in South Africa, and these show that during this period man was fairly widespread, and using not only hand-axes, but also hammers and flaking tools. The nature of the small flaking tools suggests a range of specialized work on skins, sinews and wood, so that it is not unreasonable to infer the use also of organic materials by hunter-gatherers in South Africa in the second half of the Earlier Stone Age.

The Middle Stone Age
First Intermediate Period (Fauresmith, Orange Free State and W. Transvaal).
Middle Stone Age proper.
Second Intermediate Period (Howieson's Poort).

At the end of Earlier Stone Age, after the Acheulian culture stage, came the 1st Intermediate Period of Fauresmith culture stage during which there was a reduction in size of stone tools, and more sophisticated forms and improved working edges were developed. This stage was the forerunner of the developments of the Middle Stone Age during which stones were properly hafted to form effective knives and spears, as well as to provide tools for digging pit-fall traps. Judging by the extensive spread of Middle Stone Age sites, man was very widely distributed in South Africa by the end of the Fauresmith period.

However, only a dozen Middle Stone Age sites have been examined, and these not very fully. From the evidence in stratified deposits and such radio-carbon dating as has been carried out at Mwulu's Cave, the Cave of Hearths in the Transvaal, and Florisbad in the Orange Free State, the tentative dating is of an early stage of the Middle Stone Age, that is some 37,000 years ago when improvements were limited. Technical developments which have been attributed to the Middle Stone Age include the introduction of finely struck triangular points and squat triangular deeply notched flakes, an improvement in scrapers, and the advent of adze blades, possibly used for woodworking. One wooden implement – probably part of a throwing-stick – has been found at Florisbad, and it may therefore be inferred, with even more certainty than for the Early Stone Age, that wood was employed for a variety of purposes in the Middle Stone Age. The character of some of the heads referred to above indicates that the art of hafting with natural mastics was well known at least by the middle of the period, and probably earlier. A number of human skulls and skeletons which were discovered have now been placed in the Second Intermediate or Howieson's Poort culture stage which followed the Middle Stone Age proper. These conform essentially to a *homo sapiens* type, and some may be ancestral to the indigenous population present in South Africa when the first Europeans arrived there.

The Later Stone Age and the Iron Age
The study of the archaeological remains of the Later Stone Age has produced evidence of two major culture groups in South Africa. These are the so-called Wilton and Smithfield. The first has been divided into a pre-pottery Wilton and a Pottery Wilton. The Smithfield has been sub-divided on the basis largely of the size of scrapers and implements into as many as five groups; but it is impossible from the limited field evidence available to place them in time. The peoples of the Later Stone Age appear as simple hunter-gatherers, for no remains of domestic animals have been discovered in their sites. Except for certain similarities between their pottery and pottery from sites in East Africa, there is no evidence that they came from the north-east. In fact, following also negative results from recent anthropological studies, this migration concept of the yellow-skinned peoples has been largely discounted.

When the first Europeans arrived in AD 1652, the yellow-skinned hunter-gatherers, who came to be called Bushmen, were ignorant of the processes of metal working. The Iron Age is therefore generally considered to have come to the present Cape Province through the impact of the Negro Bantu-speakers. Moving down into the area from the north, these may also have been responsible for teaching some of the yellow-skinned folk how to make use of domestic animals. A study of the rock-paintings done by Bushmen suggests how this may have happened. Rock-paintings and engravings are widespread south of the Zambezi. A number in Rhodesia and the south-west Cape depict long-tailed sheep; but there are very few showing cattle, which are strictly limited to Natal, Basutoland and eastern Cape Province. This implies that it was the cattle-owning Bantu-speakers who moved in numbers down the east coast who were responsible for providing the subjects for these paintings. On this slender evidence the cattle encountered by the earliest European explorers may have been introduced to their yellow-skinned owners by the cattle-owning immigrant Bantu. The yellow-skinned peoples who formed themselves into bands to practise pastoralism came to be known as Hottentots. One group, the Nama, also seem to have acquired the art of metal working from the invaders. This is further confirmation that, as mentioned before, the introduction of Iron Age cultures to the Cape was due to the influx of the Negro Bantu-speakers.

The amount of research that has been carried out on Iron Age sites in South Africa is extremely small. Radiocarbon dating has been done in only a few cases, and there is a shortage of recording and publication. A beast burial dated AD 1055 in a pit containing iron has been investigated at Bambandyanalo in northern Transvaal, and almost half the human burials there are accompanied by evidence of metal work. Also, ten other pits, considered to be some of the earliest features on the site, contain iron. The Iron Age occupations on Mapungubwe Hill, in the same area as Bambandyanalo, have been given the dates AD 1370 and AD 1410.

Work on the Uitkomst and Buispoort sites have shown that the cultures there have associations with those of the stone-village builders. The ruins of these villages were noticed and recorded by the missionary Dr Robert Moffatt when he was travelling from Kuruman to visit Mzilikazi, King of the Matabele, at his kraal near present-day Pretoria. Ruins of these villages are widespread in the Transvaal and Orange Free State and resemble the stone-built villages of Rhodesia dated from the eleventh century. The Sotho builders in stone may have been early members of the Venda tribe which by tradition is said to have reached its present situation in the northern Transvaal from somewhere to the north-east. This is further substantiated by the resemblance of Venda pottery to pottery in a cemetery at the south end of Lake Nyasa. Other than stone-building the only significant Uitkomst and Buispoort culture that has been noted is a special type of nicked-rim pottery.

To sum up, it seems that archaeological evidence confirms the historical evidence of Portuguese and Dutch reports that Bantu-speakers had moved down along the east coast lowlands as far as about the River Kei by the seventeenth century. Recent radiocarbon dating in the Transvaal suggests that Negro Bantu-speakers brought and practised Iron Age cultures in Swaziland and the northern Transvaal several centuries earlier. Finally, it is possible that ancestors of certain groups of the present Sotho[1] people may have been responsible for the Uitkomst culture from AD 1060 to 1650 in western Transvaal, and that some of the Bantu now present in the Transvaal and Orange Free State may be descendants of the well-organized metal-working inhabitants and builders of the old stone-villages.

[1] The western branch of Bantu-speakers, which can be clearly distinguished linguistically from the Nguni eastern branch which includes the Xhosa and Zulu.

C THE AFRIKAANS LANGUAGE[1]

Jan van Riebeeck and his companions brought with them to the Cape in 1652 the language and dialects of seventeenth-century Holland, so that the language spoken first in South Africa was a mixture derived from the dialects of Zeeland, Utrecht, North Holland and South Holland, from where most of the early Company servants came. To this Netherlandish were added bit by bit words and phrases from Creole or Malay–Portuguese, which was the *lingua franca* of seaports and spoken between master and eastern slave at the Cape. Other factors which helped to change seventeenth-century Dutch into Afrikaans were the addition of local terms taken from the language of the Bushmen and Hottentots, and modifications brought by the Huguenot settlers and German immigrants. Later, further contributions were made by English and Bantu.

Afrikaans is a simplified form of Dutch, more appropriate to an African setting. Its supple idiom, packed with African influences and rich in poetic imagery, makes it a splendid spoken language; and this for a time it remained, the *Nederlands* or High Dutch used in the Bible being the language written and read.

In 1875 there began in the Cape Province a movement to transform Afrikaans from a spoken into a literary language. The early enthusiasts formed themselves into what they called the Society of True Afrikaners, at the head of which was a *predikant* of the Dutch Reformed Church, the Rev. S. J. du Toit. Under his direction the first Afrikaans journal, *Di Patriot*, was produced and a campaign begun for the translation of the Bible into Afrikaans. The paper was published about the time of the formation of the patriotic Afrikaner Bond under Jan Hofmeyr and came to be used for propaganda purposes to further the Afrikaner cause. After defeat in the Second Anglo–Boer War, the Boers saw their language as a means of helping to re-establish their identity as a people. At this time an unexpected first flowering of Afrikaans poets raised the status of the language. There was Jan Celliers, who away in Europe began to write very feelingly about his country and his people; there was Eugène Marais, whose poem *Winternag* is perhaps the finest in the Afrikaans language; and also Totius, the pen-name of J. D. du Toit, son of the first editor of *Di Patriot*. Although many of their poems concerned the war and the tribulations that followed, they used folk and national themes as well and were in fact lyrical writers with a wide range. Apart from establishing a wonderful poetic foundation for Afrikaans literature, these early poets showed that what had for long been only a spoken language had now become a written language of great beauty. Later, Alan Paton in the glossary of *Cry, the Beloved*

---

[1] Based on a lecture by Roy Macnab, a South African English writer, to the Royal Society of Arts in 1957.

Country, aptly described Afrikaans as 'a beautiful version of the language of Holland'.

A further advance in status came in 1914 when Afrikaans was recognized next to English as a medium of instruction in schools; in 1916 it replaced Dutch in the Dutch Reformed Churches, and in 1925 it became with English an official language of South Africa. But 1934 was the really big date in its development. In that year there were landed in South Africa by the British and Foreign Bible Society the first consignment of the Afrikaans Bible, a triumph for the language, and one in which Totius had the lion's share as translator, thus realizing the early hopes of his father S. J. du Toit.

In the 1920s romantic novels in Afrikaans were being written, and stories of animal life by Sangiro and the Hobson brothers, the latter being English South Africans who preferred to use Afrikaans to convey what they felt about the fauna of the veld. In the period preceding the Second World War there was a further flowering of poets. For example, W. E. G. Louw and Van Wyk Louw, the latter producing a major work in *Raka* which examines the conflict between animal and spiritual forces in the context of an African tribe; and also Uys Krige, I. D. du Plessis, Elisabeth Eybers, and a little later the youngest of the poets emerging in the thirties and early forties D. J. Opperman. Opperman is a strongly intellectual poet, not afraid to tackle enormous themes. He uses a modern style which in imagery reflects South African urban life with its symbols of scientific and industrial advancement.

Afrikaans is now highly valued. English-speaking South Africans know it and use it, and there are many thousands of books written in the language, including as well as political and cultural works a wide range in the field of history, science and technology. Afrikaans has thus arrived and is playing a full part in making the South African of all races[1] articulate.

The beauty of Afrikaans for descriptive purposes is shown in Commandant Ploeger's 'Foreword' to this book. The 'Foreword', which in its rightful place appears as an English translation somewhat curtailed, is given below in its original Afrikaans.

'N WOORD VOORAF

Wie aan die suidpunt van Afrika staan en op 'n sonnige of 'n newelagtige dag naby die Kaap die Goeie Hoop die eindelose spel van die golwe bewonder en die skuim van die branders op die harde rotsmassa sien vervlieg in ontelbare waterdeeltjies, dink onwillekeurig aan die twee oseane wat mekaar in hierdie omgewing, naby die eeue-ou halfwegstasie tussen Oos en Wes, ontmoet.

Skepe wat naby hierdie baken of in die verte in oostelike of westelike rigting, met hul eindbestemmings in die gedagtes van die gesagvoer-

[1] Afrikaans is the mother-tongue of about sixty per cent of the Whites, and ninety per cent of the Coloureds. More Asians speak English than Afrikaans. Many Bantu can speak English or Afrikaans or both.

ders, verbygaan, vorm die skakels tussen die mensdom wat ons aarde bevolk.

Ons staan hier op die grens van wêrelde, met aan ons voete een van die belangrikste skeepvaartroetes van die wêreld.

En dan, by 'n ander geleentheid, nou meer as 'n duisend kilometer van dieselfde Kaap die Goeie Hoop verwyder, sien ons die son oor die bosveldbome in 'n betowerende kleureprag ondergaan.

Ons is nog steeds in dieselfde land, Suid-Afrika, waar, in Johannesburg en Kaapstad, die steeds hoër wordende geboue mekaar verdring.

In die Westelike Provinsie, naby Kaapstad, herinner die sierlike Kaaps-Hollandse gewels ons aan die sewentiende en agtiende eeuse koloniste; op pad van Transvaal na die sub-tropiese Natal staan, as klein stippels in die landskap, die tradisionele Bantoe-huisies, verskillend gebou ooreenkomstig eeue-ou boukundige, dikwels kunssinnige tradisies van bepaalde stamme.

Of staan naby die oop myn te Kimberley, daar waar koorsagtig gesoek is om die bodem sy rykdomme te ontruk.

Mynhope aan die Witwatersrand getuig van die steeds voortgaande en nie verminderende dors na goud.

In die Vrystaatse vlaktes waai die stofwolke op wanneer die boer met sy trekker of sy osse vore deur die vrugbare aarde sny.

Soms word die vlaktes van Suid-Afrika geteister deur genadelose droogtes, dan weer sorg hulle op 'n bykans ongekende wyse vir 'n oorvloed van voedsel vir mens en dier, opdat almal sal lewe.

En na 'n dag van gewoel en gewerskaf word die stede 'n see van lig; op die platteland, agter die vensters van 'n eensame boerewoning, brand 'n kers. Die Bantoes sit rondom 'n vuurtjie die gebeurtenisse van die dag bespreek of staar stil-stil in die vlamme van houtstompe.

In die verte weerklink die gefluit van 'n trein in die nag, motors met sterk, deurdringende koplampe soek 'n pad deur die nagtelike duister, terwyl hoog in die lug 'n vliegtuig voortspoed.

Na 'n byna ondraaglike somerdag dreun die weer en begin, na 'n onheilspellende stilte, die stormwind opsteek. Die hemel verander in 'n opwindende spel van geluid en lig. Dan val die seënende reën of die verwoestende hael. . . .

In die winter waai dieselfde wind deur verdorde gras en huiwerende bossies, terwyl mens en dier wag vir die lewebringende lente, die vervulling van 'n belofte, soos 'n reënboog na 'n storm. . . .

Dit is kortliks, Suid-Afrika, 'n land van teenstellings, 'n land wat 'n mens moet leer ken om lief te hê, maar dan – na 'n jarelange verblyf – nooit of te nimmer met 'n ander land wil of sal verruil nie.

Want Suid-Afrika gryp die mens aan, Suid-Afrika met sy wel en wee oefen 'n bomenslike aantrekkingskrag op die mens uit.

Een van die grootste en sterkste aantrekkingskragte is en bly die geheimsinnigheid van Suid-Afrika. Enersyds is Suid-Afrika 'n deel van die wêrelddeel waarvan dit geografies en etnologies, om slegs 'n paar aspekte te noem, 'n onverbreeklike deel is. Andersyds is dit 'n deel van die Weste, van Europa, van Amerika, van westerse tegniek en jeugdige energie wat soms, as gevolg van sy betreklike jeugdigheid, in oormoedigheid oorslaan en dan tereg of ten onregte dié bedagsaamheid mis wat ouer samelewings kenmerk.

Die geheimsinnigheid van Afrika! Ja, wanneer die mens terugsien, is die bekende, op skrif gestelde verlede ruim drie eeue oud, terwyl die oorgelewerde geskiedenis miskien 'n paar eeue verder teruggaan.

En agter hierdie, taamlik resente beginpunte in die verlede van die bewoners van die land wat ons tans Suid-Afrika noem, lê die voorbeelde van ouer drange om aspekte van die lewe van elke dag op rotswande in kleur vas te lê.

En nog verder lê die bodemvondste in die vorm van klipwerktuie, versteende oorblyfsels in rotsformasies, oorblyfsels van mens en dier, stil getuies van geologiese prosesse uit die oertyd. . . .

Oor al hierdie verskynsels en gebeurtenisse, waarvan die hedendaagse mens slegs hier en daar sluier gelig het, vertel 'n skrywer wat nie alleen daarna gestrewe het om sy deur inspanning eie aanskouing en oordenking verworwe kennis ten toon te sprei nie maar gelyktydig die gawe besit om sy lesers te boei.

Hy begin sy belangrike verhaal oor Suid-Afrika in die newels van die verlede en voer ons geleidelik verder tot dié tydperk waarin ons, letterlik gesproke, geleidelik meer grond onder die voete kry.

Hy voer ons van die ryk van gissings en teorieë na die tydperk waaromtrent die student van die verlede oor meer feitelike gegewens beskik. Hy lei die leser deur stormagtige en vreedsame tye, deur periodes van rus en ontstuimigheid, deur tye van vooruitgang en teenspoed en terugslae, steeds verder langs die pad van Suid-Afrika.

Hierdie pad is soms met dorings en dan weer met rose besaai. Dan weer was dieselfde pad vol rotsblokke en versperrings, het belange gebots en bloed gevloei. . . .

Maar niks kon Suid-Afrika stuit nie. Die wiel van die geskiedenis het verder gedraai, net soos die wiele van die Voortrekkerwaens wat, tydelike teenslae ten spyt, 'n nuwe bestemming gesoek en gevind het.

Altyd is daar weer iets nuuts uit Suid-Afrika verneem. Berigte van skouspelagtige gebeurtenisse het oor die lengte en breedte van die wêreld gegaan.

Dan weer het alle geluide in Suid-Afrika weer verstom en het die wêreld sy aandag op ander lande en volke, ander samelewings, toegespits.

274

In die jongste tyd staan Suid-Afrika weereens in die middelpunt van belangstelling. Hierdie belangstelling spruit gedeeltelik voort uit spesifieke probleme, eiesoortig aan Suid-Afrika, terwyl andersyds die hedendaagse ontwikkeling van Suid-Afrika as 'n nywerheidsland die aandag van die wêreld trek.

Die dekolonisasieproses wat die aandag van die wêreld op Afrika toegespits het, die opkoms van nuwe state, die geleidelik ontplooiende staatkundige, politieke en ideologiese verhoudings in die vroeëre «donker» Afrika, trek aanhoudend die belangstelling van vriend en vyand.

Dan is daar die belangrikheid van die seeroetes om die Kaap die Goeie Hoop, die verhouding tussen die Republiek van Suid-Afrika en sy buurstate, die pogings wat Suid-Afrika aanwend om sy binnelandse vraagstukke tot 'n bevredigende oplossing te bring en ander aspekte wat die aandag en belangstelling, nie alleen van alle Suid-Afrikaners nie, maar ook van die buiteland volkome regverdig.

Wie die geskiedenis van 'n land, met ander woorde sy eie verlede, nie ken nie, sal nie in staat wees om die hede te verstaan nie. Hy sal geen insig in dié soms verborge, soms duidelik waarneembare kragte en dryfvere hê nie wat tot die hedendaagse toestande en verhoudings gelei het.

Om, met bostaande in gedagte, 'n duidelike beeld daar te stel, was ongetwyfeld een van die dryfvere van 'n skrywer wat hom, op meer as een besondere terrein, in Suid-Afrika en die Suid-Afrikaanse geskiedenis verdiep het.

Vir die poging wat die skrywer aangewend het om die vrugte van sy studie, sy oordenkings en sy beskouings op skrif te stel, verdien maj. John Selby ongetwyfeld die dank van almal wat sy werk ter hand sal neem.

Ten slotte ook 'n woord van dank aan die uitgewer, die onmisbare skakel tussen die skrywer en die leser.

Mag die vrugte van hul heelhartige samewerking in alle opsigte tot die gewenste doel lei, naamlik om 'n groot aantal belangstellendes met die verhaal van Suid-Afrika te laat kennis maak opdat hul kennis verryk word oor 'n onderwerp wat beslis die moeite werd is om noukeurig bestudeer en geken te word.

Pretoria, Julie 1972.

Bibliography

Archives
State Archives (Pretoria)
Cape Archives (Cape Town)
Natal Archives (Pietermaritz-
burg)

Orange Free State Archives
(Bloemfontein)
Public Record Office (London)
Ministry of Defence Library
(London)

Collections
Cory Library (Grahamstown)
Killie Campbell Collection
(Durban)

Strange Collection (Africana
Museum, Johannesburg)

Papers
Colenso (Durban)
Merriman (Cape Town)
Shepstone (Durban)

Kitchener (P.R.O.)
White (India Office Library)
Wolseley (Hove Public Library)

Published Books
Agar-Hamilton, J. A. I. and Turner, L. C. F. *Crisis in the Desert
May–July 1942* (Cape Town 1952); *The Sidi Rezeg Battles 1941*
(Cape Town 1957)
Agar-Hamilton, J. A. I. *The Native Policy of the Voortrekkers, 1836–1858*
(Cape Town – n.d. London 1937)
Amery, L. S. (ed.) *The Times History of the War in South Africa*,
7 vols (London 1900–09)
Arbousset, T. and Daumas, F. *Narrative of the Exploratory Tour of the
N.E. of the Colony of the Cape of Good Hope* (Paris 1852)
Arnot, D. and Orpen, F. H. S. *The Land Question of Griqualand West*
(Cape Town 1875)
Arthur, George (ed.) *The Letters of Lord and Lady Wolseley, 1870–1911*
(London 1922)
Axelson, Eric *Portuguese in South East Africa 1600–1700* (Johannes-
burg 1960)

Ayliff, J. and Whiteside, J. *History of the Abambo (Fingos)* (Butterworth, Cape Province 1912)

Bain, A. G. *Journals of Andrew Bain*, ed. M. H. Lister (Cape Town 1949)

Baines, T. *Journal of Residence in Africa 1842–53*, vol. ii, ed. R. F. Kennedy (Cape Town 1964)

Ballinger, R. B. *South Africa and the United Nations* (Johannesburg 1963)

Barrow, J. *An Account of Travels into the Interior of Southern Africa*, 2 vols (London 1801)

Becker, P. *Hill of Destiny (Moshesh)* (London 1969); *Path of Blood (Mzilikazi)* (London 1962); *The Rule of Fear (Dingane)* (London 1964)

Bengough, H. M. *Memoirs of a Soldier's Life* (London 1913)

Binns, C. T. *The Life and Death of Cetshwayo* (London 1960); *Dinuzulu: The Last Zulu King* (London 1963)

Bird, J. *The Annals of Natal 1495–1845*, 2 vols (Pietermaritzburg 1888)

Böeseken, A. J. *Nederlandsche commissarissen aan de Kaap 1657–1700* (The Hague, 1938)

Brown, J. A. *A Gathering of Eagles: The Campaigns of the South African Air Force in Italian East Africa* (Cape Town, Johannesburg, London 1970)

Bryant, A. T. *The History of the Zulu and Neighbouring Tribes* (Cape Town 1964); *A Zulu-English Dictionary* (Mariannhill 1905); *Olden Times in Zululand and Natal* (London 1929); *The Zulu People* (Pietermaritzburg 1949)

Bullock, C. *The Mashona and Matabele* (Cape Town 1950)

Burchell, W. J. *Travels in the Interior of South Africa 1822*, ed. I. Schapera (London 1953)

Campbell, C. T. *British South Africa* (London 1897)

Campbell, J. *Travels in South Africa 1813* (London 1815); *The Second Journey 1820*, 2 vols (London 1822)

Campbell, W. B. *The South African Frontier 1865–1885* (Year Book 1959)

Casalis, E. *My Life in Basutoland* (London 1889)

Chapman, J. *Travels in the Interior of South Africa*, 2 vols (London 1868)

Chase, J. St. C. *The Natal Papers* (South Africa, 1843)

Clements, W. H. *The Glamour and Tragedy of the Zulu War* (London 1936)

Cloete, H. *The Great Boer Trek* (London 1900)

Collins, W. W. *Free States* (South Africa 1907)

Colvin, I. *The Life of Jameson*, 2 vols (London 1922)

Cory, G. E. *The Rise of South Africa*, 5 vols (London 1910–1919)

Coupland, R. *Zulu Battle Piece: Isandhlwana* (London 1948)

Davenport, T. R. H. *The Afrikaner Bond* (Cape Town 1966)

De Kiewiet, C. W. *A History of South Africa* (Oxford 1941); *British Colonial Policy and the South African Republic* (London 1929)

De Mist, J. A. (ed. Gie, S. F. N.) *The Memorandum of Commissary J. A. de Mist* (Cape Town 1920)

Doughty, O. *Early Diamond Days* (London 1963)

Dower, W. *The Early Annals of Kokstad and Griqualand East* (Port Elizabeth 1902)

Duncan, P. *Sotho Laws and Customs* (Cape Town 1960)

Dunn, J. *Cetshwayo and the Three Generals* (Durban 1886)

Du Plessis, I. D. *A History of the Christian Missions in South Africa* (London 1911)

Du Toit, J. D. *Ds. S. J. du Toit in Weg en Werk* (Paarl 1917)

Du Toit, S. J. (*et al.*) *Die Geskiedenis van Ons Land in die Taal van Ons Volk* (Paarl 1876)

Ellenberger, D. F. *A Century of Mission Work in Basutoland* (South Africa 1938)

Ellenberger, D. F. and Macgregor, J. C. *History of the Basutos* (London 1912)

Elmslie, W. A. *Amongst the Wild Ngoni* (Edinburgh 1899)

Engelbrecht, S. P. *Thomas François Burgers A Biography* (Pretoria–Cape Town 1946)

Eybers, G. W. (ed.) *Select Constitutional Documents Illustrating South African History 1795–1910* (London 1918)

Eyre, C. J. *Dick King* (Durban 1932)

Fehr, William *Treasures at the Castle of Good Hope* (Cape Town 1969)

Fisher, John *The Afrikaners* (London 1969)

Forbes, P. W. *Report on the Campaign in Matabeleland* (London 1894)

Fortescue, J. *History of the British Army*, 13 vols (London 1899–1930)

Freeman, J. J. *A Tour in South Africa* (London 1852)

French, G. *Chelmsford and the Zulu War* (London 1939)

Fuller, C. *Louis Trichardt's Trek Across the Drakensberg 1837–1838* (Cape Town 1932)

Fynn, H. F. *The Diary of Henry Francis Fynn*, eds J. Stuart and D. McK. Malcolm (Pietermaritzburg 1950)

Galbraith, J. S. *Reluctant Empire* (Berkley 1963)

Gann, L. H. A. *A History of Southern Rhodesia to 1934* (London 1965)

Gardiner, A. F. *Narrative of a Journey in the Zoolu Country in South Africa* (London 1836)

Gibson, J. Y. *Story of the Zulus* (Pietermaritzburg 1903)

Glass, S. *The Matabele War* (London 1968)

Gluckman, H. *Order and Rebellion in Tribal Africa* (Stellenbosch 1928)

Godee Molsbergen, E. C. *De stichter van Hollands Zuid Afrika: Jan van Riebeeck 1618–1677* (Amsterdam 1912)

Grout, L. *Zululand or Life Among the Zulu-Kaffirs of Natal and Zululand, South Africa* (Philadelphia 1864)

Haggard, H. R. *Cetshwayo and His White Neighbours* (London 1891) *The Days of My Life* (London 1926)

Hancock, W. K. *Smuts, I. The Sanguine Years 1870–1919* (Cambridge 1962); *The Fields of Force* (Cambridge 1968)

Hancock, W. K. and Van der Poel, J. (eds) *Selections from the Smuts Papers*, 4 vols (Cambridge 1966)

Harlow, V. and Maddon, F. (eds) *British Colonial Developments, Select Documents* (Oxford 1953)

Headlam, C. (ed) *The Milner Papers*, 2 vols (London 1931, 1933)

Hepple, A. *South Africa* (London 1966)

Herrman, L. (ed.) *Travels and Adventures in East Africa, Nathaniel Isaacs*, 2 vols (Cape Town 1937)

Hinchcliffe, P. B. *John William Colenso* (London 1964)

Hodgson, T. *Memoirs of the Rev. T. L. Hodgson*, ed. T. Smith (London 1854)

Hockly, H. E. *The Story of the British Settlers of 1820 in South Africa* (Cape Town 1957)

Hofmeyr, J. H. and Reitz, F. W. *The Life of Jan Hendrik Hofmeyr (Onze Jan)* (Cape Town 1913)

Holden, W. C. *History of the Colony of Natal* (London 1855); *Past and Future of the Kaffir Races* (London 1866)

Hole, H. M. *The Jameson Raid* (London 1930); *Lobengula* (London 1929); *The Making of Rhodesia* (London 1926); *The Passing of the Black Kings* (London 1932)

Holt, E. *The Boer War* (London 1958)

Hughes, A. J. B. van Velsen, J. and Kuper, H. *The Shona and Ndbele of Southern Rhodesia* (London 1954)

Kirby, P. R. (ed.) *Andrew Smith and Natal: Documents Relating to the Early History of the Province* (Cape Town 1955)

Kolb, P. *The Present State of the Cape of Good Hope* 2 vols (London 1731)

Kotze, D. J. (ed.) *Letters of the American Missionaries 1835–1838* (Cape Town 1950)

Krige, E. J. *The Social System of the Zulus* (London 1936)

Kruger, D. W. *The Age of the Generals* (Johannesburg 1958); *Paul Kruger*, 2 vols (Johannesburg 1961, 1963); (ed.) *South African Parties and Policies 1910–1960* (Cape Town 1960)

Kruger, R. *Good-Bye Dolly Gray* (London 1959)

Kruger, S. J. P. *The Memoirs of Paul Kruger* (London 1902)

Legum, C. and M. *South Africa – Crisis for the West* (London 1964)

Le May, G. H. L. *British Supremacy in South Africa 1895–1907* (Oxford 1965)

Leonard, A. G. *How We Made Rhodesia* (London 1896)

Lichtenstein, H. *Travels in South Africa 1803–6*, 6 vols (Cape Town 1928–30)

Livingstone, D. *Family Letters* (ed.) I. Schapera, 2 vols (London 1959); *Missionary Correspondence 1841–56* (London 1961); *Private Journals* (Berkeley 1960)

Lockhart, J. G. and Woodhouse, C. M. *Rhodes* (London 1963)

Maccrone, I. D. *Race Attitudes in South Africa* (London 1937)

Mackeurtan, G. *The Cradle Days of Natal 1497–1845* (London 1930)
Macmillan, W. M. *Africa Beyond the Union* (Johannesburg 1949);
   Bantu, Boer and Briton (Oxford 1963); *Cape Colour Question* (London
   1927); *Complex, South Africa* (London 1930)
Magnus, P. *Kitchener* (London 1958)
Malan, M. P. A. *Die Nasionale Party van Suid Afrika 1914–64* (Cape
   Town 1964)
Marais, J. S. *Maynier and the First Boer Republics* (Cape Town 1944);
   The Cape Coloured People (Johannesburg 1957); *The Fall of Kruger's
   Republic* (Oxford 1961)
Maurice, F. M. and Grant, H. M. *History of the War in South Africa
   1899–1902*, 4 vols (London 1906–10)
Merriman, J. X. *Correspondence* (ed. Lewson), 3 vols (Cape Town
   1960, 63, 66)
Millais, J. G. *Life of F. C. Selous* (London 1919)
Milner, Lord *Speeches and Addresses* (London 1913)
Moffat, J. S. *The Lives of Robert and Mary Moffat* (London 1885)
Moffat, R. U. *J. S. Moffat, C.M.G., Missionary, a Memoir* (London
   1921)
Mofolo, T. *Chaka* (London 1931)
Molema, S. M. *Chief Moroka* (Cape Town 1951)
Moodie, D. F. C. *The History of the Battles and Adventures of the British,
   the Boers and the Zulus in South Africa*, 2 vols (Cape Town 1888)
Morris, D. R. *The Washing of the Spears* (New York 1965)
Muller, C. F. J. (*et al.*) *Five Hundred Years: A History of South Africa*
   (Pretoria and Cape Town 1969)
Nathan, M. *The Huguenots in South Africa* (London 1939); *The Voor-
   trekkers of South Africa* (London 1937); *Paul Kruger* (Durban 1944)
Newman, C. L. N. *In Zululand with the British throughout the War of
   1879* (London 1880); *Matabeleland and How We Got It* (London 1895)
Orpen, N. *East African and Abyssinian Campaigns* (Cape Town–
   Johannesburg 1968); *War in the Desert* (Cape Town–Johannesburg
   1971)
Owen, F. *The Diary of the Rev. Francis Owen, M.A.*; *Missionary with
   Dingaan in 1837–38*, ed. G. E. Cory (Cape Town 1926)
Pirow, O. *J. B. M. Hertzog* (Cape Town 1958)
Ploeger, Jan and Smith, A. H. *Pictorial History* (Pretoria 1949)
Potgieter, C. and Theunissen, N. H. *Kommandant-Generaal Hendrik
   Potgieter* (Johannesburg 1938)
Preller, G. S. *Andries Pretorius* (Johannesburg 1938)
Pringle, T. *Narrative of a Residence in South Africa* (London 1835)
Ransford, O. *The Battle of Majuba Hill* (London 1967); *The Rulers of
   Rhodesia* (London 1968); *The Great Trek* (London 1972)
Ritter, E. A. *Shaka Zulu* (London 1955)
Reitz, P. *Commando* (London 1931)
Rhoodie, N. J. and Venter, H. J. *Die Apartheidsgedagte* (Cape Town
   1960)

Rowell, T.   *Natal and the Boers* (London 1900)
Samuelson, R. C.   *Long, Long Ago* (Durban 1929)
Selby, J.   *The Boer War* (London 1969)
Selby, J.   *Shaka's Heirs* (London 1972)
Shooter, J.   *The Kaffirs of Natal and the Zulu Country* (London 1857)
Smith, E. W.   *The Life and Times of Daniel Lindley 1801–1880: Mission-ary to the Zulus* (London 1949)
Smith, G. C. M. (ed)   *The Autobiography of Sir Harry Smith*, 2 vols (London 1903)
Stow, G. W.   *The Native Races of South Africa* (Cape Town 1930)
Theal, G. M. (ed.)   *History of South Africa from 1795–1872*, 5 vols (London 1919)
Tylden, G.   *The Rise of the Basuto* (Cape Town 1950); *A History of Thaba Bosiu* (Maseru 1945)
Uys, C. J.   *In the Era of Shepstone* (London 1933)
Van der Poel, J.   *The Jameson Raid* (Cape Town 1951); *Railways and Customs Policies in South Africa 1885–1910* (London 1933)
Van Jaarsveld, F. A.   *The Afrikaner's Interpretation of South African History* (Cape Town 1964); *The Awakening of Afrikaner Nationalism* (Cape Town 1961)
Van Riebeeck, J.   *Journal of Jan van Riebeeck*, ed. H. B. Thom, 3 vols (Cape Town 1958)
Van Winter, P. J.   *Onder Krugers Hollanders*, 2 vols (Amsterdam 1937, 1938)
Vijn, C.   *Cetshwayo's Dutchman* (London 1949)
Walker, E. A.   *A History of Southern Africa* (London 1959); *The Great Trek* (London 1960)
Wallis, J. P. R. (ed.)   *Matabele Journals of Robert Moffat*, 2 vols (London 1945); *Matabele Mission of J. S. and E. Moffat* (London 1945); *South African Diaries of Thomas Leask* (London 1954)
Whiteside, J.   *History of the Wesleyan Methodist Church of South Africa* (London 1906)
Willcox, A. R.   *The Rock Art of South Africa* (London 1963)
Williams, B.   *Cecil Rhodes* (London 1921)
Willoughby, J.   *Report on the Campaign in Matabeleland* (London 1894)
Wills, W. A. and Collingridge, L. T.   *The Downfall of Lobengula* (London 1894)
Wilmot, A.   *History of the Zulu War* (London 1880)
Wilson, M. and Thompson, L. (eds)   *Oxford History of South Africa*, 2 vols (Oxford 1969–70)
Wood, W.   *Dingaan, King of the Zoolahs* (Cape Town 1840)
Wrench, J. E.   *Alfred Lord Milner* (London 1958)
Year Book   *State of South Africa* (Johannesburg 1972)

Articles, Guides, etc.
Capstickdale, L.   *Blood River* South African Panorama (March 1972); *Spion Kop* South African Panorama (September 1964)

Dart, R. A.   *Man's Evolution* I.S.H.A. (1964)

Durban Local History Guide

Duxbury, G. R. and More, C., Boshoff, D. and 'Commando'   *For Freedom and Justice* (*Magersfontein*) South African Panorama (December 1969)

Hudson-Reed, S.   *Settlers Saga* South African Panorama (November 1963)

Huguenot Memorial Museum Guide, Franschhoek

Jack Hindon Officers Club, Kimberley Brochure

Lantern XX No. 1   *The 1820 Settlers* Articles by Professor Winifred Maxwell and others (September 1970)

Macnab, R.   *The Emergence of Afrikaans as a Literary Language.* Lecture R. Socy. of Arts (March 1957)

Maxwell, W.   Henry Hare Dugmore Lecture (1970)

Miester, J.   *Evolution To-day* I.S.M.A. (1964)

Oberholster, J. J. and Hefer, F. C.   Guide to Fourth Raadsal, Bloemfontein

Ploeger, J.   *Uit die blou van onse hemel* – 1652–1971 (Outline History, Illustrated) (Johannesburg 1972); the Fortification of Pretoria, Fort Klapperkop Yesterday and To-day (Pretoria 1968)

Ploeger, J. *et al.*   Conservation of Our Heritage (Cape Town 1966)

Ploeger, J. and Botha, H. J.   Brochure of the Military Museum at Fort Klapperkop (Pretoria 1966)

Report from South Africa (monthly)

Sentker, H. F.   *Archaelogy and South Africa* (Pretoria 1967)

Schultz, A. H.   *Social Life of Early Man*, ed. S. L. Washburn (Chicago 1961)

South Africa Digest (weekly)

Terry, R. W.   *Man in Africa* (Johannesburg 1963)

Voortrekker Monument, Pretoria   Official Guide